Stereotypes of Women in Power

**Recent Titles in
Contributions in Women's Studies**

Women Changing Work
Patricia W. Lunneborg

From the Hearth to the Open Road: A Feminist Study of Aging in Contemporary
Literature
Barbara Frey Waxman

Women, Equality, and the French Revolution
Candice E. Proctor

Serious Daring from Within: Female Narrative Strategies in Eudora Welty's Novels
Franziska Gygax

Verging on the Abyss: The Social Fiction of Kate Chopin and Edith Wharton
Mary E. Papke

The Feminization of Poverty: Only in America?
Gertrude Schaffner Goldberg and Eleanor Kremen, editors

The Dominion of Women: The Personal and the Political in Canadian Women's
Literature
Wayne Fraser

Successful Career Women: Their Professional and Personal Characteristics
Cecilia Ann Northcutt

The Life of Margaret Fuller: A Revised, Second Edition
Madeleine Stern

The Sea of Becoming: Approaches to the Fiction of Esther Tusquets
Mary S. Vásquez, editor

Gender Differences: Their Impact on Public Policy
Mary Lou Kendrigan, editor

The World of George Sand
Natalie Datlof, Jeanne Fuchs, and David A. Powell, editors

Women of the Grange: Mutuality and Sisterhood in Rural America, 1866–1922
Donald Marti

STEREOTYPES OF WOMEN IN POWER

Historical Perspectives and Revisionist Views

Edited by *Barbara* BARBARA GARLICK,
SUZANNE DIXON,
and PAULINE ALLEN

Contributions in Women's Studies, Number 125

GREENWOOD PRESS

New York • Westport, Connecticut • London

Library of Congress Cataloging-in-Publication Data

Stereotypes of women in power : historical perspectives and
   revisionist views / edited by Barbara Garlick, Suzanne Dixon, and
   Pauline Allen.
       p.   cm.—(Contributions in women's studies, ISSN 0147–104X ;
   no. 125)
     Includes bibliographical references and index.
     ISBN 0–313–27731–1 (alk. paper)
     1. Women in politics—History.   2. Power (Social sciences)
   I. Garlick, Barbara.   II. Dixon, Suzanne.   III. Allen, Pauline.
   IV. Series.
   HQ1236.S735   1992
   305.42—dc20   91–20042

British Library Cataloguing in Publication Data is available.

Library of Congress Catalog Card Number: 91–20042
ISBN: 0–313–27731–1
ISSN: 0147–104X

First published in 1992

Greenwood Press, 88 Post Road West, Westport, CT 06881
An imprint of Greenwood Publishing Group, Inc.

Printed in the United States of America

The paper used in this book complies with the
Permanent Paper Standard issued by the National
Information Standards Organization (Z39.48–1984).

10 9 8 7 6 5 4 3 2 1

Contents

Stereotypes of
Women in Power

Introduction—Public and Private: The Paradigm's Power

Arlene W. Saxonhouse ───────────────────────

'[T]he chief glory of a woman is not to be talked of,' said Pericles, himself a much-talked-of man[.]'
—Virginia Woolf

The scene is the outskirts of Athens in the year 430 B.C., a scene described by the Greek historian Thucydides. It is the end of the first year of the Peloponnesian War, which pitted Athens against Sparta. Pericles, the leader of the Athenians, is following ancestral custom; after the bones of the Athenian warriors killed in battle are placed in a public tomb near the walls of the city, he offers a funeral oration.[2] First he praises Athens. In this city where the citizens live more freely than others, they show greatest regard for the law. In Athens "the beautiful is loved without refinement and wisdom is loved without softness."[3] Then Pericles praises the men who have died, caring more for vengeance on the enemy than for their own safety, men who risked their lives rather than submit to the foreign oppressor. The undying fame of their great deeds will not depend on words inscribed in stone but, fueled by the speech of Pericles, will remain in the memory of all men across the earth. Pericles speaks to the survivors: Those young enough must emulate their dead brothers and fathers; those too old to fight must beget more young. Finally, after his praise of Athens, of the dead, of those about to fight, he turns to offer "brief advice" on "womanly excellence" to the wives who have become widows: "There will be great respect for you who do not fall beneath your proper nature and for whom there is the least renown (*kleos*) among men, whether for virtue or for blame" (II.45).

The speech of Pericles ensures fame (*kleos*) for the warriors. No one will forget what they have done for the greatest of cities. For the women, though, there will be no fame, no deeds to recall. They are removed from the world of male immortality. Life in the realm of the family, or at most in the religious festivals of the city, offers no opportunity for memorable deeds or for great service to the polity at large. Men can become the object of song and speech when they serve the political community either on the battlefield, slaughtering the enemy host (as does the hero Achilles in Homer's epic poem, *The Iliad*), or in the assemblies of men, speaking well and offering good counsel (as does Odysseus). Women neither perform great deeds on the battlefield nor give great speeches in the assemblies of men; they cannot become the objects of song and story.

In the great Homeric epics the reward for great deeds and great speech is the immortality acquired by the retelling of one's feats. It is the poet, though, who through his words distributes immortality. We would not know of the greatness of Achilles were there no Homer, nor would we know of the constancy of Penelope or the virtue of Andromache. Pericles, several centuries later, takes on himself the role of Homer, memorializing the actions of the men who have died for the city, thereby granting them an immortality that they would not otherwise have. In contrast to the Homeric epics, though, Pericles's speech includes women only to exclude them. The political climate has changed. For Homer there is the concern with the suffering of the women and a profound sense of the tragic interaction between the men's wars and the women's households. All are part of the human experience that Homer captures in his poems. As scenes of peaceful natural settings interrupt the brutal battle scenes, he sees that war and its warriors cannot be understood without pictures of women and the family. Women become part of men's stories because, for Homer, men do not exist as heroes without women.

With the rise of the *polis* in seventh-century Greece, devotion to the city comes to dominate the devotion to the personal world that the women inhabit. In Athens, the *polis* became a democracy by undermining the political power of the traditional aristocratic families, setting the individual in direct relation to the city and breaking the bonds to the particular private unit. Arbitrarily defined political units based on geography rather than on familial connections diminished the importance of the ancestral family. Identification with the city became strong while the particularistic family faded into the background, to the degree that Pericles could crassly dismiss the family at the end of his grand speech, seeing it as nothing more than a baby-producing institution. As the importance of particularistic families faded, so too did the individual heroes. The Athenian warriors whom Pericles praises acquire a corporate fame that comes from being members and defenders of a city such as Athens. Thus Pericles can praise the warriors by praising the city for which they fought; they have truly become one with the city and her renown becomes theirs.

For the women of Athens, there is no fame (*kleos*) either individual, as in the Homeric poems, or corporate, as in Pericles's speech. They quietly disappear into the background, allowing the men to defend the city that they have come to love more than their individual selves. The women are to be silent, and there is to be no speech about them. As a consequence, they, as representatives of the private realm, cannot make demands on the city. They are not to complain about the men—brothers, husbands, sons—lost in a war. Silence is necessary lest the glory of the warriors' deeds and the beauty of the city be diminished by the remembrance that there are those whose suffering goes unacknowledged. Should those sufferers emerge from the shadows, the city might need to question the unmitigated devotion it demands of its citizens and its warriors. Pericles says: "For it is just to set manly virtues in war on behalf of one's fatherland before evil in other affairs; for they hid the bad with the good and gave more service publicly than they did harm as individuals" (II.42.3).

Such a conception requires the dismissal of private affairs entirely; deeds in that arena are worthless when contrasted with what one can do for one's city. The Athenian citizen is free, but his freedom entails participation in the life of the city. "We alone think the man who takes no part in affairs not as uninvolved, but as useless" (II.40.2). The final expression of a citizen's participation is his willingness to die for the city. Such participation, though, is denied the women of the city, as is the fame that goes along with it. They are not only uninvolved; they are, in the sterile vision of Pericles, useless.[4]

Again the scene is Athens, this time within the city, on the comic stage. In Aristophanes's play *Lysistrata*, men dressed as women and playing the roles of women express a weariness with the war that has killed so many young men and has kept the warriors away from the beds of their wives. These "women" go on a sex strike and occupy the acropolis of Athens. There they limit access to the public treasury, demanding that the war cease and that their men return home to their beds. In the world of Aristophanic comedy, the sex strike succeeds and the war is over. Twenty or so years later, on the same stage, "women" plan to take over the machinery of the public life of the city (*Ekklesiazousae* or *Women of the Assembly*). The men dressed as women now dress as men, attend an imaginary assembly, and vote to turn over political power in the city to women. Aristophanes's Praxagora, the leader of this group of usurping women, then builds a world of equality and communism where the marketplace becomes the dining room and the port the wine cellar for everyone in the city. The proposals of both comedies are absurd, the language bawdy, and the plots outrageous, and the audience laughs. Women influencing the political decisions of Athens or women taking over political power: this is the stuff of comedy—as funny as a citizen traveling to the heavens on a dung beetle to bring Peace incarnate down to earth (*Peace*). Aristophanes could amuse his audience, win prizes from the judges, and express outrage at the way in which Athenians handled their public life—all by offering portraits of political women, as much an oxymoron then as it is now.

Aristophanes and the Pericles of Thucydides's *Histories* illustrate the opposition between women and politics. Only in comedy can women and political power merge; those attending to the serious stuff of war and battles must send women away, unseen and unheard. Why? Aristophanes's comedies were funny for the Greeks because he juxtaposed what had to be kept separate: women who lived in the private world of the family and the public world of political power. The realm of action and great deeds belonged to the public world of the city. Women inhabited the private realm of the family, about which we hear nothing from Pericles, and which evoked laughter when put upon the stage by Aristophanes.

The separation of the two spheres is, for these two Athenian authors, stark. Along with that separation, however, goes the all-important gender dimension: Male is public, female is private. Beyond the clear division between the two is the evaluative stance; priority goes to the public arena of war and speech where one tends to the community as a whole. Care about the welfare of the whole confers *kleos*. The private world of the family, attending to the particular, separates off a part from the whole and has an identity distinct from the community of the city. It thus has the potential to draw energies away from the community. The egalitarian, democratic society of ancient Athens (at least among its male citizens) depended on the subordination of the family to the needs of the city. Tragedies such as Sophocles's *Antigone* and Aeschylus's *The Seven against Thebes* and *Oresteia* illustrate that this subordination is not easily accomplished. The process of subordinating the family to the values of the city, though, caused women who resided within the household to retreat further and further into silence, while the male self-identification focused more and more on the welfare of the city. In Homer's epics Andromache could stand on the battlements, the proud mother and the frightened wife, reminding Hector of the attachments he had to the private world of family and of love. In the democratic city of Pericles's Athens there is no Andromache to remind the warriors of what they must leave behind as they march into battle. As Pericles stirs his Athenians to an almost erotic love of the city (II.43.1), he cannot allow the women, even the good ones, to remind men of the call of the particular, of the family. Should they remember the women, they might hesitate before merging themselves completely into the corporate person of the city whereby they receive fame.

The chapters in this volume are not concerned primarily with what women actually did or whether women had power, political and public or sexual and private, but rather with how women's actions, when they do cross over into the public realm, have been interpreted and presented by historians, by literary artists, and even by scholars of our own age. The chapters show us what happens to the women who did not follow Pericles's "brief advice." These are the women who did not honor the sharp boundary between the public and the private realms, who crossed over into a realm where it was thought they did not belong. For the most part, these chapters reveal the discomfort with the fame that such women earn when they leave the private world of silence to enter the public world of speech. The picture is not pretty; the women who stride across those established borders appear as perversions of good women, as either domineering dowagers or scheming concubines. Freedom of movement from one sphere to the other was the male's prerogative, he who fathered children within the family and participated in the political sphere outside.

The words of Pericles resound whether one considers ancient Egypt, medieval China, or nineteenth-century England—and societies temporally and spatially in between. V. G. Callender in her chapter on the rulers of ancient Egypt quotes advice from Egypt of 2300 B.C.: A man must treat his wife well but must "not contend with her in court . . . keep her from power . . . make her stay in your house."[5] Moving to scholars of our own age, Callender illustrates how they may have tried to explain away those few cases where the evidence suggests women did possess political power in ancient Egypt. Margaret Clunies Ross gives us examples from the Icelandic sagas where a female's good advice about public affairs is summarily dismissed: "It hasn't been your lot to have the name of earl in the Orkneys."[6] Both Pauline Allen, writing on Procopius's attacks on Empress Theodora, and Lenore Coltheart, writing on the Renaissance world of Machiavelli, offer examples of how women who may have achieved independent political power call forth the most vitriolic condemnations from the men who record their activities.

Pericles, as he spoke to his fellow Athenians, was working within a powerful paradigm that is repeated consistently in the tales told in these chapters. It is a paradigm that preserves the Athenian demarcation between the public world of political life and the private world of the family. The values and the structures of each realm differ fundamentally. The public world is one of universality rather than particularity; it incorporates the whole community, not just a small portion of it. The community itself as the creation of the mind is an abstraction that has no existence in nature; rather, it must be created by men's choices, their minds. The private realm is one of necessity that emerges not from the creative human mind at work. In the private sphere, according to this paradigm, we are driven by the natural instincts that make us eat, seek shelter, and procreate.

The paradigm, though, also establishes a hierarchy of value. The public world is superior; it draws on man's higher capabilities, his mind, his courage, his ability to make choices concerning good and bad and to sacrifice himself for an abstract whole. It separates him from the animals who may live in groups but never in public communities that arise as the result of choice or value decisions. The inferior private realm attends to that aspect of our being that situates us in the world of body and need rather than choice. It caters to that which we share with the beasts and not with the gods.

For whatever reason—and many are the speculative theories on this point—woman has been confined to the world of the body rather than of choice, of necessity rather than freedom. This book is concerned with some of the few women who in the past have been able to escape from the focus on body to cross into the world of reason and of choice. They have done so by acquiring political power themselves as attendants of public figures, or by doing particular deeds that have drawn them out of the household into the arena of public scrutiny. In these chapters we see the power of the public/private dichotomy that in various times and in various places leads to revulsion of public women, those for whom there is *kleos* "whether for blame or for praise." By crossing the threshold out of the darkness of silence into the light of speech, these women have shattered a simple world view of clear dichotomies, sharp boundaries, and established expectations. For this they are execrated not by sermons or "brief advice," but by an interpretive mode that continues to present the perversity of their positions.

All description of human action by artists, scholars, news media, or the gossip over the back fence entails interpretation. In order to interpret we employ paradigms, models of how the world functions so that we can organize the vast variety of human experience. We try with our language to impose meaning on those varied experiences, and the models with which we work help us to communicate our experiences to one another. The artist, the scholar, and the media all take human experience and re-present that experience to us—organize it so that we may "understand" it. The process of organizing the experiences so as to be able to re-present them, though, entails working with particular perceptual frameworks on the part of both the re-presenter and the one to whom the events are re-presented. The chapters in this volume illustrate the ubiquity of the public/private paradigm and its all-important gender component; this paradigm then controls the re-presentation of women who have crossed the boundary and have become public figures.

The paradigm prevents the actions of women from being considered according to the same criteria as those of males. Their deeds may be identical, but the interpretive act takes those identical endeavors and assesses them according to the public/private paradigm. When the women do enter the world of public action, their stature in the public world of political power cannot match that of the males because, according to the paradigm, they do not belong there, striding elegantly in the world of the mind and masculine creativity. They fit awkwardly into the paradigm; as women they ought to remain in the household. The paradigm cannot incorporate their public presence. Should that presence be acknowledged and accepted, the paradigm's capacity to help us impose meaning on their experiences would be undermined. Rather than alter the paradigm and thus the interpretation, the transgression is explained away: a unique occurrence, a misinterpretation of materials, a sign of the deterioration of a community or of the men who are supposed to lead it, an event to be treated as humorous or, more seriously, as dangerous. All of these explanations belittle the political or public woman for she disturbs the model, just as Pericles belittled the Athenian women for disturbing his model of a beautiful, unified city of men who loved only the city itself.

Interpretation also plays a normative and prescriptive role re-enforcing the values of the paradigms we may employ in our attempts to give meaning to our existence. The public/private paradigm with its gender component sets values on our experiences. The paradigm does not simply articulate a boundary between the two spheres; it places a positive normative value on that division. By helping us to comprehend our experiences it has value. Those who ignore the established boundaries endanger a stable world. Preservation of the accepted paradigm becomes critical to social stability.

Those women who do undermine the model, either by possessing power themselves or by influencing those with power, are castigated by unflattering descriptions of their actions as mere continuations of behavior appropriate to the private realm of bodily creativity (i.e., sexuality) or personal rather than corporate benefit. According to Pauline Allen, Procopius, writing about the Empress Theodora of Byzantium in the sixth century, emphasized her promiscuity before her marriage to Justinian and her continued sexual manipulations after she became empress. Margaret Clunies Ross concludes that whatever power women may have held in the public realm according to Icelandic myths was exercised through "dangerous sexuality."[7] In China, as Ellen Soullière points out, women who may have sought political power were portrayed as doing so for the sake of their natal family (the particular realm) and not for the welfare of the whole (the universal). According to Barbara Garlick, nineteenth-century English authors, cartoonists, and journalists portrayed political women not as sexually manipulative but as asexual; the flat-chested, unattractive female could serve as the brunt of political humor, the domineering dowagers could be dismissed with laughter. When they stepped into the public world they became desexualized and thus a negative model for other women. In contrast are the harrowing stories told by Jocelynne A. Scutt about women who have been accused of murdering their husbands and children in recent years in Australia. Scutt argues that, although these were not political crimes, they nevertheless evoked fears of women's devious powers. That power was undermined by suggesting illicit origins: witchcraft and poisoning. In other words, the criminal justice system injected into the private realm the suggestion that female power is illegitimate there as well because it is exercised by women acting as schemers and dragons.

While women with political power could be seen as sexually dangerous, men who had political power could find themselves threatened by insinuations that they were being influenced by women who had become powerful through their sexual favors. These "scheming concubines" inhabited, as Tom Hillard illustrates, the Rome of the late Republic. Whether the women Hillard discusses, in fact, had the influence suggested was less important than the rhetoric that implied the subjection of political leaders to sexually manipulative women. Similarly, as Ellen Soullière reports, the "bad emperors" in China are explained away as those who let themselves be distracted by women's sexuality. Or we find Julia, the daughter of the Roman emperor Augustus, the object of jokes that emphasize her licentiousness. Julia's sexual behavior becomes a tool with which to attack her father, but, as Amy Richlin suggests, the jokes that sexualize Julia may also have emerged from the fear that women in Rome were becoming too strong.

The focus on women's sexuality implies that they belong back in the bedroom, not in public influencing political life; if they do have any influence, it should be as models of domestic purity.

The public/private paradigm that informed so much of Pericles's funeral oration and made Aristophanes's comedies funny 2,500 years ago has not disappeared despite the massive changes in our political, social, economic, and religious lives. With the rise of liberalism in the seventeenth century, the paradigm has taken on some different nuances, but it has not disappeared. When Pericles spoke in the world of the city-state of ancient Athens, he was eager to praise the life devoted to the universal community of the city and to urge men on in their devotion to it. By the time Thomas Hobbes and John Locke were writing in seventeenth-century England, the public world of politics was not so much a realm where one achieved glory for service but rather a realm driven by conflict, intrigue, and the selfish pursuit of power. The goal of Hobbes and Locke became, in part, to remove men from a devotion to political life. Thus we find in their writings the denigration of political power. It is no more than a holding company entrusted with the public welfare; it is not sanctified by God. In Hobbes's version, it only has to be; it does not have to be "good." Men are urged to devote themselves to private life rather than to public conflict; thus they are sent back across the boundary to labor and create wealth or to philosophize and write books like *Leviathan*. The conflicts of political life, in the liberal world, lead to no more fame than the accomplishments in private life.

As citizens in the liberal state spend more time in the private world earning money and creating physical and artistic objects, they bring with them the potential for fame that previously characterized the life of political men. While the paradigm has softened the boundaries by allowing men to gain fame for deeds done away from the universal realm of the city, however, the boundaries, as the following chapters illustrate, are not much more permeable from below than they were when Pericles spoke to the Athenians. Into the paradigm of the public and private, the social may have intruded.[8] It is a space that incorporates neither the universality of the city nor the individualism of the family. It is a space in which men and some women can acquire fame previously accorded only to those who served the political world. But while the new world of the social has found it somewhat easier to accommodate the female in its midst, the ancient paradigm with its gender demarcation between public and private still provides powerful interpretive and evaluative controls on our experience and representation of public women. By ascending to the public realm of political renown, women contaminate the pristine conceptual model of public and private. The dismissive and denigrating language often used today in the representations of women in the male world of politics becomes a mechanism for preserving the boundaries of the past and the normative flavor of those divisions. This volume records for us the power of the paradigm, revealing for us the difficulties we face should we attempt to replace it with an interpretive model that opens those boundaries, that removes the gender associations with each realm, and that accords both the universal and the particular equal value.

NOTES

1. Virginia Woolf, *A Room of One's Own* (New York: Harcourt Brace Jovanovich, 1929), 52.

2. Whether Pericles gave such an oration is, of course, highly speculative. I rely here on Thucydides's report, fully recognizing that the Pericles I describe here may be largely the product of the creative genius of the historian.

3. Thucydides, *Histories*. II. 40.1. Future references to Thucydides appear in parentheses in the text.

4. Elsewhere I raise the possibility that Thucydides may be offering a critique of the self-denying male citizen in the words about women that he attributes to Pericles. See Arlene W. Saxonhouse, "Eros and the Female in Greek Political Thought: An Interpretation of Plato's *Symposium*," *Political Theory* 12, no. 1 (February 1984): 6–8 and *passim*.

5. V. G. Callender, in this volume, 11.

6. Margaret Clunies Ross, in this volume, 111.

7. Ibid., 114–17.

8. Hannah Arendt's work, especially *The Human Condition* (Chicago: University of Chicago Press, 1958), discusses, at the same time that she laments, the emergence of the "social" in modern society.

2

Female Officials in Ancient Egypt and Egyptian Historians

V. G. Callender

INTRODUCTION

It is generally thought that ancient Egyptian men had a most egalitarian attitude toward women during the pharaonic period of history, and indeed there are a number of texts that stress that women should be treated well and mothers should be honored. A closer scrutiny of the evidence, however, suggests that when it came to evaluating women who entered official life the Egyptians had a rather antagonistic attitude. This is evident in the literature and the archeological records from different epochs of Egyptian history, whether it be from Old, Middle, or New Kingdom times.

Our oldest reference, *The Instruction of Ptahhotep*, gives an old man's advice to his son. It was one of the most popular texts in all Egyptian wisdom literature. The sage advises the ambitious man to

> ... love your wife with ardor,
> Fill her belly, clothe her back,
> Ointment soothes her body.
> Gladden her heart as long as you live,
> She is a fertile field for her husband.
> Do not contend with her in court,
> Keep her from power; restrain her.
> Her eye is her storm when she gazes.
> Thus will you make her stay in your house.
> (Lichtheim 1974, 69)

But if this were the accepted male attitude toward upper-class women, some women do not seem to have been content to accept it. As the long history of

Egypt unrolls one can see the desire for social and political recognition among the more privileged Egyptian women. Presumably the women themselves were instrumental in the struggle to gain political recognition, but even about this aspect we cannot be sure. Given the dominant role taken by men in Egyptian society, one would assume that some men could have been involved in promoting the standing of the individual women with whom they were concerned, but if men did seek to advance these women, then it was only on an ad hoc basis, and any privilege they were given did not necessarily transmit to the next generation. In general, there was no overt increase in the number of women holding bureaucratic posts from one epoch to another. Rather, if any generalization were to be made, the reverse was the case.

Egyptian literature reveals that a women's rank in society was a reflection of her husband's position. A later piece of instruction poetry states that:

> Rank creates its rules:
> A woman is asked about her husband,
> A man is asked about his rank.
> (Lichtheim 1976, 140)

For women rank was not an indication of ability or worth, but merely a consequence of marriage. Even a princess who married an official had the social rank of that official, and administrative and social recognition (as expressed in the titles held by women) was regulated by the rank of the woman's husband (Ward 1986, 27).

A Note on Chronology

Egypt's pharaonic history is divided into three major epochs: the Old Kingdom, when solid stone pyramids were built; the Middle Kingdom, when mud-brick pyramids were built and great engineering works were initiated; and the New Kingdom, when kings dug horizontal tombs in the Valley of the Kings and when Egypt's rulers conducted regular, foreign campaigns. This chapter concentrates on the first two epochs.

In each epoch a succession of families, or dynasties, ruled the country. To refer to dynasties, rather than dates, is the usual chronological reference for Egyptian historians. Altogether there were thirty-one dynasties; the Hellenistic monarchies are not included. These dynasties cover a period of roughly 3,000 years, of which this chapter covers approximately one-half.

A HISTORY OF ADMINISTRATIVE TITLES FOR WOMEN IN OLD KINGDOM EGYPT

The Earliest Period

Egypt had once been two kingdoms: Upper Egypt in the south and Lower Egypt in the northern, or Delta, region. These two lands were unified by King

Narmer of Upper Egypt some time close to 3100 B.C. That date marks the commencement of the First Dynasty.

Prior to unification we are unsure about political offices for either men or women. Archeological investigation of cemeteries in Upper Egypt have revealed that, in the preunification days, there was little differentiation between the graves of men and women with regard to the size and shape of the grave and to the tomb equipment. As far as Egyptian burial customs are concerned, these factors are indicative of the standing of the deceased within his or her community. In some cemeteries several men had the larger graves; in other cemeteries some women had the more prestigious graves. This pattern has led one historian to ask whether some of these early rulers of local communities might have been women (Baumgartel 1960, 123f, 143).

Non-Royal Women

After unification the numbers of administrative offices increased dramatically. Basically, this was the period when the Egyptians organized their bureaucracy on lines that underpinned the remainder of their history. A great many posts were devised, but none of these positions was held by a woman.

By the Fourth Dynasty the situation had altered. Now among the wealthier classes appeared women who held minor religious offices. The most common title was that of *hmt-k3*, or mortuary priestess, whose duty was to see that offerings—which were made to enable the deceased to live in the afterlife—were made at the tomb of the deceased. Men also held a similar post. To enable the *hmt-k3* to carry out those duties a plot of land was given to her so that the offerings could be made from the produce of that land.

Other women—mainly the relations of the king—served as *hmt ntr*, or female priests, in the temple of female gods. The Egyptians had numerous gods, some more important than others. Re and Horus were the most important male gods in this period; Hathor, Neith, and Wadjet were the major female gods. Males and females served as priests of female gods, but only queens could be female priests of male gods. Princesses could be priests of a king's cult if they were related to him. All kings were considered to be gods after their demise.

The most common office held by non-royal women of the higher social classes was priest, either of Hathor, the female god of love and beauty, or of Neith, a female warrior-god of the Delta region. Although the titles of *hmt k3* and *hmt ntr* sound important, these religious offices were very minor, and the duties of female priests consisted of singing, dancing, and shaking the sistrum (Blackman 1921, 22f). Nonpriestly women also could sing and dance at ceremonies. Male priests, however, had many more hierarchic posts open to them. Women were excluded from these.

Apart from the priesthoods, some minor bureaucratic posts were filled by women in the Old Kingdom period. By the Fifth Dynasty there were several female overseers of the king's *hnr*, a word of doubtful meaning, but probably a collection of musical performers who danced and sang (Nord 1981). One of these female overseers has a substantial tomb at Giza (Hassan 1944, 204–8), and another overseer's tomb is located at Saqqara (Mariette 1885, tomb no. C.15). Other overseers of religious *ḥnr* for the gods Horus (CG 28006) and Bat (Stewart 1979, UC Collection no. 14312) are known for the First Intermediate Period. One office, whose precise duties are uncertain, was that of *jmjj-r st̲3*, the Master of Secrets, a counsellor's office. One woman holding this post is known from Saqqara (Mariette 1885, D.47). Also recorded for this time is a female overseer of the royal *jpt*, or women's quarters (Hassan 1944, 204). Several male officials also held this post (Ward 1986: 81–94).

In the Sixth Dynasty the situation had further altered: Nonreligious positions for women were more common. Most of these separate instances have already been tabulated by H. G. Fischer (1976, 69–79). One woman was a steward (Junker 1937, 185, fig. 57); another was an overseer of stores (CG 1513); and a third was an inspector of the king's repast. Others included a director of the dining hall, several treasurers from Aswan, an inspector of treasure, and supervisors of cloth (Macramallah 1935, plate 17) as well as funerary overseers (Murray 1905, plate 7; Fraser 1902, plate 3). There is an overseer of the Wearers of the Kilt (Fischer 1960, 188–90), another religious institution, but this time a very significant post since it involved control over higher officials. In addition to these posts there are female overseers of doctors, weavers, and wigmakers and the chancellor of the King's House (Fischer 1976, 71f.). Many of these tasks, however, were performed by women for other women of royal rank.

From the provincial town of Qasr es-sayyed in the same period there is one tomb that records two more female officials. One was overseer of women associated with funeral rites, the other was a seal bearer (Edel 1981, 48f).

There were also a number of women who were inspectors and overseers of dancing and entertainment in the First Intermediate period (Petrie 1908, plate 8). Both men and women held such posts; however, after the Eleventh Dynasty, only men held these administrative posts.

Altogether, an interesting variety of administrative occupations was open to women in Old Kingdom times, but, significantly, there were no female scribes. (The absence of scribal titles does not necessarily mean that those official women already mentioned could not read or write; this is one of those areas where we lack information.) Given the prestige attached to being a scribe in ancient Egypt, however, the absence of women from such a significant administrative activity highlights the difference between the social status of male and female bureaucrats—even when both of them held the same type of office. Even though the god of writing, Seshat, was female, no woman ever appears in this guise in the whole corpus of Egyptian art, although men frequently had themselves portrayed as scribes.

Amidst the holders of those administrative positions already mentioned, one woman stands aloof from her colleagues. Like many of them, she flourished during the mid-Sixth Dynasty. She was the vizier (or chief minister) for Upper

Egypt during the reign of Pepy I (c. 2300 B.C.). Next to the king himself, this was the most important political office in the land. The Vizier Nebet was made an official Hereditary Princess, She of the Curtain, Judge and Vizier, Daughter of Thoth, Companion of the King of Lower Egypt, Daughter of Geb, and Daughter of Horus (CG 1431, 1575). Three of these titles name Nebet as the daughter of gods, an unprecedented honor, indicating that her titles were superior to those of any other official in Old Kingdom times; no other official had ever been recorded as the son of a god. Nebet stood alone on this administrative pinnacle until the Twenty-sixth Dynasty, when she was joined by another female vizier (CG 42205), Amenirdis, chief priestess of the god Amen (*ḥmt nṯr n Jmn*) and the daughter of the king. In spite of this almost unique occurrence, Nebet is seldom discussed in modern histories dealing with Old Kingdom administration.

H. Kees includes a discussion on Nebet's titles in his study (1940, 42, n.3) but does not go into detail about her role as vizier. Wolfgang Helck in his standard text on administrative offices in pharaonic Egypt does not mention Nebet at all, even though his examination of the office purports to include all known viziers (Helck 1954, 134–42).

Fischer mentions her titles (1976, 74f.) and suggests that she was given the position of vizier because she was the king's mother-in-law. (Evidence for the claim that it was she who was Pepy I's mother-in-law is ambiguous.) Fischer suggests that her husband lacked the vizier's titles because his wife already possessed them, that the titles were given to her in an effort to increase the prestige of the king's mother-in-law, and that her husband, Khwi, was the one who performed the duties of the vizier. Fischer feels that Nebet's title of vizier was merely honorific, entailing no practical exercise of power at all. N. Kanawati, however, stresses that the vizierate in this instance was not a titular post (1981, 210–11).

In an earlier work Kanawati (1980, 31–33, 62–64) had expressed the opinion that Nebet's titles were not merely honorific ones, although he suggested that "her husband (Khwi) . . . might have assisted her in some of her duties" (1980, 31). Due to our lack of sources here we cannot ascertain whether Khwi helped his wife at all, although, as Khwi's offices were not ones associated with the vizierate (Kanawati 1980, 31), there is no certainty that Khwi did the work.

In a more recent study of Egyptian administration, Nigel Strudwick provides a meticulous prosopography of each of the higher ranking Egyptian officials during the Old Kingdom period. Nebet's entry, however, is relegated to an aside: "It appears from the stele of Khwi and Nebet from Abydos that Nebet, the mother-in-law of Pepy I, also held this title [of vizier], although it is likely that it was not in a full administrative capacity" (Strudwick 1985, 303). He cites, as support for his claim, Kanawati's opinion. Strudwick does not include Nebet within his list of viziers.

One would think that Nebet's unique position in the Old Kingdom would merit at least a reference among the standard texts, but this is not the case. The general public is unaware of Nebet's historical significance as the world's earliest known female prime minister. Nebet has no entry in *Lexikon der Aegyptologie*, either, yet lesser lights among male officials receive good coverage.

Thus we can sum up the situation regarding women who held public posts in the Old Kingdom: Although there were no openings available for them at the beginning of Egypt's dynastic history, by the end of the Sixth Dynasty some women held posts among lower officialdom. One woman achieved the highest office in the land, but her prominence has, on the whole, received very little positive comment from modern historians. Although one scholar is prepared to credit her with the actual management of some of the duties associated with this office, most scholars ignore her presence among the viziers of the Old Kingdom.

ADMINISTRATIVE OFFICES DURING THE MIDDLE KINGDOM

Although the historical development of religious and administrative offices shows a distinct growth during Old Kingdom times, the situation is different for the next epoch. The Middle Kingdom reveals a severe retraction in the number of posts for women and the frequency with which these posts were held (Guest 1926, 46–50; Fischer 1976, 79f.; Ward 1986).

E. M. Guest noticed that not only secular but also religious titles were less frequent for women in the Middle Kingdom. Only the title "Priestess of Hathor" occurs with any frequency.

Among the secular titles the most common one is *nbt-pr*, or "mistress of the house," a title implying that the woman was in control of the household. This title was introduced in the time of Amenemhat III, in the Middle Kingdom period (Malaise 1977, 183–93).

The most frequent title, apart from that of housewife, is *mn^{c}t*, a word whose uncertain meaning is usually translated as "nurse," although it is closer to our use of the words "governess" or "tutor," for it conveys more prestige than the functions of a nurse. Both men and women held this title.

Other common female occupations from this period were those of singers, dancers, and musicians, although these were not, strictly speaking, administrative positions. There were, however, a number of official posts, among which were one female overseer of the storehouse (Ward 1982, no. 423), a female hall keeper (no. 499), a keeper of the queen's signet ring (no. 556), a confidante (*^{c}kjjt*) (no. 635), two female butlers (nos. 706, 772), a female member of the council (*st nt knbt*) (no. 1242), and a countess (*h3tjjt-^{c}*) (no. 890). Two female overseers of the butchers of the Acacia House were recorded on ostraca found at Helwan and El Kab (Fischer 1960, 187ff.). A similar title also appeared for several queens from the Old Kingdom.

Apart from these positions, Middle Kingdom offices for women were few. One woman, wife of a most powerful provincial nomarch called Khnumhotep, was the "seal bearer," or chancellor of her husband's administration (Guest 1926, 49). Other seal bearers are known from other locations (Petrie 1908, plate

8; Firth and Gunn 1926, 204 and plate 21b). One woman had the enviable job of being overseer of the kitchens; several others were keepers of the chamber (Fischer 1976, 77). A few other women held the office of hairdresser. Another post was that of *h3jjt-pr*, "one who was the foremost person in the house," a post also held by a male official (Fischer 1976, 79). Three other women were "directors of works" for the High Priest of Ptah during this period (Fischer 1976, 79). They received their posts from their brother, Sehetepibre-ankh, who was the High Priest.

A Twelfth Dynasty woman called Idwy deserves special mention. She is the earliest recorded female scribe yet known (Fischer 1976, 76). Several other records are known from this period, but the title has been questioned. It is claimed that these women were "painters of the lips," or cosmeticians, not scribes. One of the reasons for this suggestion is that those women were not shown with scribal equipment (Posener 1969). But no woman, even those who did own pens and palette, appears in Egyptian art holding writing implements, although Princess Idut (late Fifth Dynasty) is thought to have taken her scribal equipment with her during a ride in a boat (Schultze 1987, 109). These items appear, discreetly tucked under their chairs, with the women of the New Kingdom (Bryan 1984, 19). Favorite animals were similarly shown. That women did own scribal equipment in New Kingdom times, at least, is attested by the writing palette owned by Akhenaten's daughter, which was found in the tomb of Tutankhamen (Carter 1933, plate 22A). These scattered instances do suggest that some of the wealthier women had been taught to read and write.

Although Fischer accepts that those alleged female scribes probably had a lowly status, he insists that Idwy, at least, cannot be assigned to their category, since she owned a scarab, and only higher officials were permitted to use a title and name on a seal of this nature (Fischer 1976, 78). Thus, while the evidence appears to indicate that women might have been taught to write by Middle Kingdom times at least, it is clear that few of them had employment as scribes. Since there was a marked broadening of the classes who were literate after the collapse of the Old Kingdom (Baines and Eyre 1983, 68), the inclusion of some women among the group could be expected, particularly as the New Kingdom evidence provides a larger number of examples of female literacy (Baines and Eyre 1983, 68; Bryan 1984).

The administrative posts available to women in the Middle Kingdom were fewer in variety and of less importance than they had been in Old Kingdom times. According to Fischer,

Even if one makes due allowance for the fact that the repertory of titles held by men is also less abundant, less varied, and generally more modest, than that of the Old Kingdom, it is difficult to avoid the impression that women of the Middle Kingdom were less frequently and significantly engaged in administering people and property than previously was the case—not that the role was ever of great importance except, of course, in the case of the mother, wife or daughter of kings. (Fischer 1976, 79)

With the exception of the seal bearers and those sisters of Sehetepibre-ankh, few of these posts held by Middle Kingdom women had much substance, and it would seem that women's efforts at establishing themselves in administrative or religious posts had suffered something of a setback at this time.

Neither Guest nor Fischer can suggest an explanation for this sudden contraction of official posts for the women of the Middle Kingdom, and perhaps we will never know the reason for it. It is clear from the literature and archeological records, however, that Egyptian officials resisted the idea of women having any authority—especially over men. Perhaps the decrease in the number of administrative posts for women in Middle Kingdom times merely reflects this attitude or, perhaps, it reflects the current social milieu: Men, too, suffered a decrease in the number of bureaucratic posts open to them after the end of the Old Kingdom although a wide range of positions was still available to men. As working women have always been the earliest targets in times of diminished prosperity, this phenomenon may have contributed to the decline in female positions during the Middle Kingdom period. In the case of *jmjjt-r ḥnr*, this has been documented. At first male overseers held the post alongside female overseers, but then the post was held by men only after the Eleventh Dynasty (Nord 1981, 144). Apart from female positions relating to the dining hall, men can be seen in the Middle Kingdom occupying the administrative posts that some women had held during Old Kingdom times.

There is little to offer in the way of detail concerning the nature of the authority exercised by these non-royal women. Other than their names and their titles, which appear in their husbands' tombs, nothing is known either about the women or about the positions they held. Only among the royal women is it possible to gauge something about the power exercised by women from these times. Although information about them is also depressingly scant, a clearer picture can be seen in the palace.

THE DEVELOPMENT OF THE TITULATURE OF QUEENS
FROM THE FIRST THROUGH THE FIFTH DYNASTIES

Earlier in this chapter I referred to E. J. Baumgartel's analysis of ancient Egyptian cemeteries before the period of unification. Baumgartel's survey concluded that, among those cemeteries, the tombs of some women were a little larger than those of the males (Baumgartel 1970, 6). She also suggested that, as the largest graves in Egyptian cemeteries are traditionally reserved for the rulers, in some centers women might have been community leaders (Baumgartel 1960, 122, 142).

More recently, Juan Castillos, who reexamined the findings of those earlier archeologists, has questioned Baumgartel's conclusions, showing that she had miscalculated in some instances and that the evidence showed that the larger graves in some cemeteries really belonged to men (Castillos 1982, 43). But when some of Castillos's own tables are scrutinized carefully, one can see instances where, as in Tables 2.1 and 2.2, Baumgartel has read the data correctly, and that the richest and largest graves in some cemeteries do actually belong to women. Whether this fact makes them rulers of their communities is another question altogether, but certainly the graves of known rulers from all epochs in Egyptian history are larger than those of their subjects. It would appear, therefore, that not all of the evidence is as Castillos would suggest.

Archeological evidence reveals the existence of an interesting social pattern during the unification of Egypt. In the graves at Abydos, in Upper Egypt, a very large number of women from the Delta region were buried. We can tell that they originated from this region because their theophoric names are compounded with those of the Delta gods, Neith (the warrior goddess) and Ptah (patron god of Memphis). The names of the first three queens from this period are compounded with Neith. This phenomenon has led scholars to suggest that Narmer and his successors consolidated their conquest of northern Egypt by wedding prestigious women from among the conquered people (Emery 1965, 46f.; Gardiner 1961, 142).

What is of greater interest to us is that two queens from the early part of the First Dynasty have special significance: Their names have been found written in special boxes called *serekhs*. Throughout the whole course of Egyptian iconographical history there is no instance of a serekh being used for anyone other than a monarch. The consorts of kings in any period of Egyptian history never possessed serekhs, no matter how high their status was among their contemporaries.

All serekhs have the same shape: a representation of the palace occupying the lower half and, above this, a rectangular space in which the name of the ruler is written in hieroglyphs. A patron god surmounts the serekh itself. (In some early serekhs the god is omitted.) There are several known types of serekhs (Figure 2.1). The only way in which the serekhs of these early queens differ from those of the kings is that their female patron, the goddess Neith, is represented above their serekhs—an appropriate symbol, given the political climate of those unsettled times. The use of the serekh suggests that Baumgartel's hypothesis concerning regnant female chieftains or queens, for some areas of predynastic Egypt, might indeed have some substance.

But what powers did these queens hold? Did they have political control over Egypt's population, as Helck, Petrie, and Emery (Helck 1968, 30; Petrie 1900, passim and 1904, 19; Emery 1954, 140) have suggested? Or were their names put in serekhs merely to persuade a subject Lower Egypt that there was joint rule in these turbulent times? So much material from that period has been destroyed that it is difficult to assert just what powers any ruler had. What we can point to with Queen Neithotep and Queen Merneit is that their names appeared in serekhs and that Merneit at least had the double tomb of a full ruler, one tomb at Saqqara and the other at Abydos. Like the tombs of the kings, her monuments at both sites are located within the groups that hold the tombs of other kings.

Table 2.1
Men vs. Size, Shape, Wealth, Coffins, and Orientation

		A	B	C	Rect.	>10	Coffins	Fac. E	Fac. W
EARLY PREDYNASTIC	Q.H.B. (Badarian)	45%	45%	10%	1%	5%	-	10%	90%
	Deir Tasa (Tasian)	0%	44%	56%	11%	-	-	0%	100%
	Most./DT (Badarian)	27%	65%	8%	10%	3%	-	21%	79%
	Matmar (Badarian)	21%	47%	32%	5%	-	-	-	-
MIDDLE AND LATE PREDYNASTIC	Naga-ed-Dêr	60%	39%	1%	8%	4%	1%	4%	96%
	Q.H.B. (SD 30-80)	58%	38%	4%	-	15%	7%	4%	96%
	Most./DT (SD 30-80)	61%	36%	3%	-	5%	8%	0%	100%
	Matmar (SD 30-80)	58%	34%	8%	21%	20%	9%	3%	97%
	Armant (SD 30-80)	31%	69%	0%	-	14%	-	18%	82%
	Naqada	47%	44%	9%	85%	12%	-	-	-
	Abydos	14%	76%	10%	-	10%	-	20%	80%
	Harageh	-	-	-	-	25%	-	0%	100%
EARLY DYNASTIC	Q.H.B. (SD 76-84)	72%	22%	6%	-	14%	14%	69%	31%
	Ab. Meleq (SD 60-80)	57%	43%	0%	88%	31%	3%	0%	100%
	Tarkhan	78%	21%	1%	94%	10%	13%	38%	62%
	Sakkara	68%	22%	10%	-	12%	42%	85%	15%

AVERAGES FOR THE ABOVE THREE PERIODS

	A	B	C	Rect.	>10	Coffins	Fac. E	Fac. W
EARLY PREDYNASTIC	33% (60	53% 96 in 181)	14% 25	6% (10in 181)	4% (6in 160)	0% (0in 245)	13% (17 in 129)	87% 112
MIDDLE AND LATE PREDYN.	54% (198	42% 156 in 367)	4% 13	21% (54in 253)	11% (48in 437)	4% (13in 302)	4% (11 in 278)	96% 267
EARLY DYNASTIC	74% (329	22% 97 in 443)	4% 17	94% (289in 308)	12% (53in 436)	17% (76in 436)	47% (171 in 365)	53% 194

A: largest graves; B: medium-sized graves; C: smallest graves.

Source: J.J. Castillos, *A Reappraisal of the Published Evidence on Egyptian Predynastic and Early Dynastic Cemeteries* (Toronto: Benben, 1982), 28.

Table 2.2
Women vs. Size, Shape, Wealth, Coffins, and Orientation

		A	B	C	Rect.	>10	Coffins	Fac. E	Fac. W
EARLY PREDYNASTIC	Q.H.B. (Badarian)	59%	33%	8%	2%	6%	-	21%	79%
	Deir Tasa (Tasian)	0%	50%	50%	0%	-	-	11%	89%
	Most./DT (Badarian)	30%	61%	9%	7%	6%	-	6%	94%
	Matmar (Badarian)	20%	73%	7%	7%	-	-	-	-
MIDDLE AND LATE PREDYNASTIC	Naga-ed-Dêr	68%	30%	2%	5%	6%	2%	1%	99%
	Q.H.B. (SD 30-80)	53%	44%	3%	-	25%	11%	3%	97%
	Most./DT (SD 30-80)	62%	36%	2%	-	20%	4%	6%	94%
	Matmar (SD 30-80)	67%	32%	1%	10%	20%	11%	2%	98%
	Armant (SD 30-80)	41%	59%	0%	-	17%	-	14%	86%
	Naqada	79%	21%	0%	70%	13%	-	-	-
	Abydos	0%	62%	38%	-	50%	-	7%	93%
	Harageh	-	-	-	-	67%	-	50%	50%
EARLY DYNASTIC	Q.H.B. (SD 76-84)	75%	25%	0%	-	18%	12%	50%	50%
	Ab. Meleq (SD 60-80)	33%	67%	0%	90%	35%	0%	0%	100%
	Tarkhan	87%	13%	0%	93%	8%	9%	39%	61%
	Sakkara	90%	10%	0%	-	22%	50%	80%	20%

AVERAGES FOR THE ABOVE THREE PERIODS

	A	B	C	Rect.	>10	Coffins	Fac. E	Fac. W
EARLY PREDYNASTIC	37% (48	51% 65 in 128)	12% 15	5% (6in 126)	6% (6in 103)	0% (0in 186)	14% (12 in 88)	86% 76
MIDDLE AND LATE PREDYN.	63% (264	34% 142 in 417)	3% 11	15% (47in 307)	16% (77in 496)	5% (19in 352)	3% (9 in 335)	97% 326
EARLY DYNASTIC	87% (332	13% 51 in 383)	0% 0	93% (324in 350)	11% (43in 408)	10% (42in 408)	40% (122 in 302)	60% 180

A: largest graves; B: medium-sized graves; C: smallest graves.

Source: Castillos, 30.

Figure 2.1
A Selection of Serekhs Used by Monarchs during Dynasties I and II.

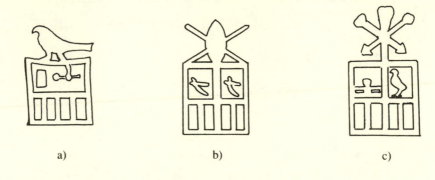

a)   b)   c)

d)   e)   f)

a)   Serekh of King Aha

b)   Serekh of Queen Merneit

c)   Serekh of Queen Neithotep

d)   Serekh of King Djer

e)   Serekh of King Peribsen

f)   Serekh of King Khasekhemwy

Unlike vizier Nebet, queens Neithotep and Merneit appear in history textbooks, although they usually receive their mention as the wives of kings and not as full monarchs. Gardiner expresses the opinion that these two queens were royal women from the Delta who made diplomatic marriages with the conquerors of Upper Egypt. Although Gardiner draws attention to the serekhs, he does not explore their full significance, merely mentioning that their names were "written in a most interesting way" (1961, 411f.). Most other texts adopt the position of Gardiner, if they mention these queens at all. Considering the importance of the information available, it is very disappointing that more prominence and discussion are not given to these early queens in Egyptian histories.

One other woman from the First Dynasty might be a queen (Emery 1965, 60 and passim). Unlike the previously mentioned queens, however, Herneit's name is not written in a serekh although, like them, she has a most elaborate tomb at Saqqara. Her status is shown by two titles: *hntjj*, "one who is in charge of the cellar," and *sm3 nbwjj*, "one who unites the Two Lords." The former title, which is associated with all rulers of the First Dynasty, refers to the provisioning of the royal palace[1] (Kaplony 1963/4, 442); the latter title, "one who unites the Two Lords," referring to the gods of Upper and Lower Egypt, a title possessed only by queens from the First to Sixth Dynasties, stresses the role played by the queens in the active unification of Egypt.[2]

In the time of King Djer—at least seventy years after the death of King Narmer—the practice of sacrificing large numbers of royal retainers was introduced. The few queens whose tombs have been identified were buried among these sacrificed retainers. They had been sacrificed too. Their tombs are no more distinguished than those of the artisans, female servants, and officials who went to their deaths when the king was buried. The only title these women carry on the stelae of their graves is the simple *m33t Ḥr St*, "she who sees Horus and Seth," i.e., the two lords of Upper and Lower Egypt, a title denoting their positions as queens. It is the most common title carried by queens between the First and Sixth Dynasties. Although women with the titles of a queen have been found within the cemeteries of kings Djer and Den, no other female royal burials have been identified for the remaining rulers of the First and Second Dynasties. The wives of Djer and Den were buried in small tombs. They lacked the large monuments provided for Neithotep, Herneit, and Merneit. This difference is at present difficult to explain, but it might be due to a difference in status since two of these queens also used the serekh symbolic of a ruler. No other female ruler is known for another 800 years.

Although virtually nothing is known about any of these First Dynasty queens, we know most about Queen Merneit. She was the mother of a king—perhaps the later King Den—as is evident from a recently published mud seal impression (Dreyer 1986). Here her name appears among a list of early First Dynasty kings, probably for the purposes of a collective royal mortuary cult (Dreyer 1986, 37).

Merneit's use of the serekh, the location of her tombs in the royal cemeteries, and her inclusion in the royal mortuary cult indicate clearly that she had, at one

time, exercised some political power. The nature of this in the third millenium
B.C. is very difficult to determine.

It is possible that Merneit may have attained this position via a regency held
on behalf of her son. In later times queens Hatshepsut and Twosret are known
to have gained access to the crown via regencies. Like them, she may have been
a coregent. Perhaps this assumption of power led to a later resentment—as theirs
did. Certainly, it is clear that the ancient Egyptians believed females had the
right to rule, for the historian Manetho of the Ptolemaic period records that,
during the reign of King Nynetjer (Second Dynasty), "it was decided that women
might hold the kingly office" (*Manetho* 1971, fragments 8, 9, 10).

Thus, during the First Dynasty, the status of queens appears to be more elevated
in the earlier years than it was during the remainder of the dynasty. After the
deaths of Herneit and Merneit, queens lost the prestige of a grave approaching
the sophistication of the king's monument, and they lost the privilege of having
a *ḥntjj* official.

In the succeeding centuries it becomes obvious that Egyptian queens attempted
to increase their status. This is evident in their gradual acquisition of titles and
epithets. The story of this accretion is too long to tell here (Callender 1987),
but, by the Fourth Dynasty, the queens possessed a small group of traditional
titles—such as "King's Wife," "She who unites the Two Ladies" (a variation
on "Uniter of the Two Lords"), "She who sees Horus and Seth," and "Great
one of the *Ḥts* Sceptre"—and a number of epithets—such as "Great of praise"
and "One who is honored by the king." This was a typical practice among
those who wished to elevate their rank in Egyptian society. A gradual accumulation of titles is also apparent among the officials who served the king as
they, too, increased their social prestige.

In the Fourth Dynasty the first of the administrative offices for queens appeared:
Queen Hetepheres I was a "Controller of the Butchers of the Acacia House"
and Queen Hetepheres II was a "Controller of the affairs of the Kilt-wearers,"
the higher ranking male officials of the government. Strudwick says that the
latter title, a prestigious one, first appears for male officials in the Fifth Dynasty
and is common in the Sixth (Strudwick 1985, 316). Hetepheres II, however,
held this title in the mid-Fourth Dynasty.

Concurrent with the increase in titles came an increase in the size of the
queens' tombs. Although the sites for the tombs of the queens prior to the Fourth
Dynasty are not known, by the time of Khufu (Cheops, mid-Fourth Dynasty)
the queens' tombs were quite large and well decorated. Most of them seem to
have been the house-like mastabas, which consisted of several rooms with decorated walls, but many historians consider that the satellite pyramids in front of
the kings' tombs at Giza were also tombs of queens; however, the ownership
of none of these pyramids has been established (but see Lehner 1985).

At the end of the Fourth Dynasty Queen Khentkawes I built her tomb at Giza.
Sometimes referred to as the "Fourth Pyramid," it is not a pyramid at all (Figure
2.2). This queen has the distinction of having a special priest to serve her mortuary

Figure 2.2
Tomb of Queen Khentkawes at Giza

The tomb of Queen Khentkawes is very similar to that of King Shepseskaf at Saqqara, leading historians to think that the two might have been husband and wife. Both tombs are alternative structures to pyramids.

cult. Up to this time no person other than the king had a *ḥm ntr*, or "Priest of the God," for only the king was considered a god after his demise. Khentkawes may have been given this status either because she herself was a monarch, or because she had produced two sons who became kings in her lifetime—the evidence is ambiguous.[3] The very size and position of her monument indicate the prestige of this queen. Moreover, in recent times, it has been established that a large complex at Abusir had also been devoted to a temple for the cult of this queen (Verner 1980).

In the Fifth Dynasty the wives of kings were given pyramids located close to those of their husbands and, as time went on, their tomb complexes became larger and more elaborate; however, there is no other indication of any development in the role of the queen in this dynasty. For an appreciation of the greatest strides made toward women's political involvement, it is necessary to look at the next dynasty.

SCHEMING WIVES

In this discussion of the development of non-royal and royal female administrative and political achievement in ancient Egypt, there has been little indication of the political power such women possessed. In the Sixth Dynasty, however, the situation clarifies somewhat, and the queens show themselves briefly as women of some substance.

The first episode concerns an unnamed queen who was the wife of Pepy I (c. 2318–2292 B.C.). Reference to her accusation is inscribed on a poorly preserved limestone block that forms part of the biography of an assiduous official named Weni. Weni boasts how he was asked to be the sole judge in a trial of a queen from the royal harim[4] evidently on charges of treason:

When there was a secret charge in the royal harim against the king's wife and great ornament, [name is missing] his majesty caused me go down to hear it, I alone. There was no judge or vizier, no official was there, except I alone; because I was trustworthy, and firmly established in the heart of his majesty. . . . I myself put it in writing, together with one other senior warden of Nekhen, while my rank was only that of Overseer of Royal Tenants [ḥntjjw-s]. Never before had someone like me heard a secret of the King's Harim; but his majesty caused me to hear it, because I was worthy in his majesty's heart beyond any official of his, beyond any noble of his, beyond any servant of his. (Sethe 1933, 100f.)

This is the only direct information we have about this interesting affair, but other material provides us with the sequel to this extract. The queen was certain to have been found guilty; otherwise, Weni would not have boasted of the trial. The issue was a delicate one, and the vizier who would normally adjudicate harim matters was not present. It seems most odd that neither the vizier nor any other senior judges were brought in. It has been suggested, therefore, that those senior officials might also have been involved in the conspiracy (Kanawati 1980, 31f.). It would appear that Pepy could not trust anyone else to investigate the case. The extent of at least that queen's political influence must have been considerable.

This is not the only case we have of a harim intrigue. Another, better documented, account, which comes from the Twentieth Dynasty in the late New Kingdom, helps us understand more clearly the enigmatic remarks made by Weni in the Sixth Dynasty. Pepy's queen was almost certainly acting in the interests of her son, as is indicated by the investigation into the harim intrigue conducted during the reign of Rameses III, in the Twentieth Dynasty, almost 1,100 years after Weni's case. In the conspiracy trial of the Ramesside period, the queen, six other wives from the harim, a large number of officials, and several army officers were found guilty of stirring up rebellion among the population. Their aim was to murder Rameses and to put the queen's son on the throne. A total of twenty-eight men and more than eight women were found guilty of being involved in the plot. During the trial five of the judges showed that they lacked the probity of Weni, for they were caught drinking with some of the accused women in a local beer house. One judge received the death penalty, one was reprimanded, and three were mutilated, their noses and ears being lopped off

(Le Page Renouf 1876, 57–65). *Mutatis mutandis,* the extent of the Ramesside queen's political influence might approximate that of Pepy's unnamed queen.

In neither instance was the punishment accorded the queen hinted at; but as a consequence of the Sixth Dynasty conspiracy, King Pepy married a commoner called Meryreankhenes. Some time later he married her sister, who was also called Meryreankhenes. Both sisters gave birth to sons who became king after the death of Pepy I, first Merenre, then Pepy II.

Merenre's reign was short and, because he had no heir, his half brother, Pepy, succeeded him as ruler when he was only six years of age. A regent governed for him who was, as in every case known to me for ancient Egypt, the senior wife of the deceased king. Queen Meryreankhenes II became regent for her son, Pepy II. For the first time in the records of Egypt a known commoner queen took control of the state.

We do not know how long the regency of the queen lasted, but it probably continued quite a few years, due to the extreme youth of her son at the time of his succession. Meryreankhenes II certainly was an active political figure in the government of the country during this time; several records state her position. There is a statue of the queen on the throne of Egypt, with her son seated upon her knee; more instructive is the record of an expedition she sent to Sinai to quarry stone (Figure 2.3). On the rock inscription the names and titles of the queen and her son are shown, but the scribe has also sketched a picture of the queen, not the king, which is very interesting. This queen, together with her sister and their brother Djau, was further honored by a *ḥwt ntr*, or gods' temple, in Abydos.

It was Pepy II who honored his queens still further, with the ultimate religious privilege accorded to royal women. He built a pyramid for each of them, and in each burial chamber he had inscribed on the walls copies of the Pyramid Texts, which contained spells and prayers designed to guarantee each queen immortality in the afterlife. Like the king himself, these women were destined to be gods in the afterlife. No other royal wives had been honored in this fashion. The Pyramid Texts referred to each queen as if she, too, had become a god in the afterlife—a privilege previously given only to kings. It appears that these queens had at last achieved the status that had been lost since the time of Queen Merneit in the First Dynasty, nearly 1,000 years earlier.

One of the last rulers of the Sixth Dynasty was a woman, Queen Neitkrety, or ''Nitokris,'' as the Greeks called her. Neitkrety almost certainly would have been a member of Pepy II's family—possibly his granddaughter. Her name appears in Herodotus's *Histories* II, 100, in the Turin list of Egyptian kings, and in the epitome Fragment 22 of Syncellus, from the work of Manetho. According to Manetho, she reigned for twelve years; however, so far, no archeological remains associated with this queen have been found.

Manetho says that she was the most beautiful woman of her day, a sentiment that can also be found in Herodotus, who adds at some length a fascinating tale. He says that her brother was murdered after a brief reign and that she was put

Figure 2.3
Record of an Expedition to Sinai in the Time of Pepy II

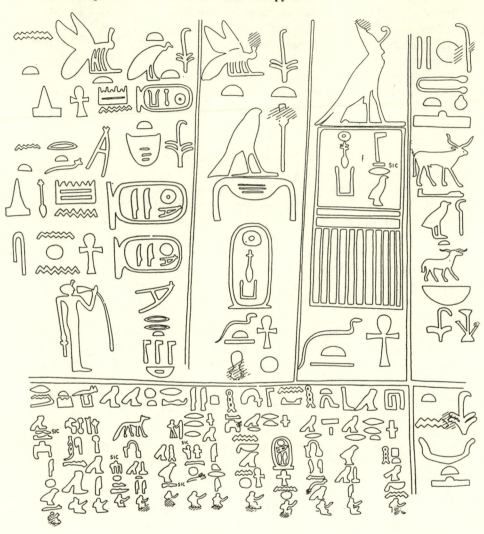

An inscription of Meryreankhenes II and her son, King Pepy II, from Wadi Maghara, in the Sinai, recording an excursion made by their Egyptian officials to cut stone. Note the unusual way in which the queen's relationship to the king is shown: The vulture (meaning "mother of") comes between the two signs for King of Upper and Lower Egypt. All of this queen's inscriptions feature this writing.
—Gardiner and Peet 1952, *Sinai* I, Plate IX.

on the throne. The queen then took revenge on her brother's murderers. She built a large, underground banqueting hall and invited those implicated in her brother's murder to attend the inaugural feast in the building. At the height of the festivities the queen opened the sluice gate of a concealed pipe and drowned all of those who were there. Then, unable to face the consequences, she committed suicide.

It is a colorful tale for which there is no evidence. The story is just another diverting anecdote about Egypt that Herodotus delights in telling. Similar stories can be found in many ancient Egyptian papyri. But although Herodotus may have repeated a folktale about the queen, the milieu he describes is pretty close to the reality of those times. The Turin Canon shows that Neitkrety did follow a ruler who had held the throne for only just over a year; her own reign was followed by that of Neferka-the-child. There is every likelihood that Neitkrety was both the sister and the wife of her predecessor. Unlike Queen Meryrean-khenes II, however, whose name does not appear on the Turin Canon, Neitkrety was a monarch. The times in which she lived were turbulent; several monarchs later, the Old Kingdom came to an end. According to one epitomator of Manetho, the next dynasty "consisted of 70 kings from Memphis who reigned for 70 days" (*Manetho* 1971, 56f.). This unsettled period saw the complete breakdown of centralized government in what is known as the First Intermediate period. After an uncertain length of time, the Egyptians saw the inception of the Middle Kingdom period, when social order was again restored.

THE MIDDLE KINGDOM QUEENS

There is no stirring tale of political women in the following centuries of Middle Kingdom government. Earlier it was emphasized how few were the administrative posts for non-royal women during Middle Kingdom times. This situation is reflected by our lack of interesting material concerning the queens.

Until the Eleventh Dynasty only one of the wives of a ruler is known, and not until the Twelfth Dynasty do we notice any significant increase in the titulary of these women. Absolutely no historical details of any of them exist, other than their often most complex genealogies. The majority of them have fewer titles than their Old Kingdom sisters, although one title, *nbt t3wjj*, "Mistress of the Two Lands," a most important-sounding one, is the female equivalent of the king's title, "Lord of the Two Lands." Whether the title involved any real power is just not known.

Only at the end of the Twelfth Dynasty did a royal woman exercise the duties of a king. She was Queen Sebekneferu, the daughter of King Amenemhat III, and she was as instrumental as her father in the construction of the famous Labyrinth (Petrie 1912, 50–53). Herodotus (Book II, 148f.) says that it was the most amazing building that he had ever seen—a structure, in his opinion, that surpassed the grandeur of the pyramids. Yet, no historian other than Petrie mentions the queen's contribution to this grand temple.

Although the queen's reign was brief, she managed to set her stamp on a number of monuments: many statues in the east Delta, a temple in Herakleopolis, the Labyrinth, and the Nile register at Semnah in Nubia (see also Vallogia 1964, 45–53). She was a fitting predecessor to the famous Queen Hatshepsut of New Kingdom times. (Rameses II left the names of both queens out of his list of rulers at Abydos.)

HISTORIANS OF EGYPT

As the story of Queen Sebekneferu indicates, neither ancient Egyptian nor modern historians have always given female Egyptian rulers their due place in the history of Egypt. A brief account of these prominent women is given in this chapter because so little is known about them. The remainder of this chapter considers the attitudes of modern historians toward women who exercise political power. Gardiner's opinion about Sebekneferu is a convenient point to start.

Gardiner's remarks on Queen Sebekneferu are prefaced by a confusion over the nature of the reign of her father and brother; he thinks that she might have shared a coregency with her father. That matter was cleared up by others after Gardiner's book appeared. However, Gardiner goes on to construct history in these words:

On such observations [as a coregency between Amenemhat III and both Sebekneferu and Amenemhat IV] it is dangerous to base any positive conclusions, but there seems considerable likelihood of a family feud out of which Sebeknofru [sic] emerged the victor. It would be the second time in Egyptian history that a woman succeeded in establishing herself as "King of Upper and Lower Egypt," but so abnormal a situation contained the seed of disaster. After Sebeknofru, as after Nitocris [i.e., Queen Neitkrety], there followed a succession of kings none of whose reigns, so far as can be seen, exceeded three years. From whatever cause, the glorious Middle Kingdom had finally broken down. (Gardiner 1961, 141)

Now, although, in Gardiner's defense, there are very few details of Sebekneferu's reign, there is not a single piece of evidence to support the family feud he puts forward. Neither was the Thirteenth Dynasty a disaster: The government continued in an orderly way for decades after Queen Sebekneferu's time despite Gardiner's phrase "for whatever cause," which implies that the queen was responsible for the chaos he envisages.

Gardiner's greatest literary skills, however, are saved for Queen Hatshepsut of the Eighteenth Dynasty. No other ruler suffers the semantic obloquy that she receives at his hands: "Twice before in Egypt's history a queen had usurped the kingship" (1961, 183). In this statement, he refers to Queen Neitkrety and Queen Sebekneferu (he does not consider the First Dynasty queens to have been rulers), yet neither of those queens has ever been suspected of usurpation; indeed, Neitkrety is alleged to have exercised a terrible revenge on those who murdered her brother. Both these queens apparently became rulers because their husbands died without male issue. It was stated that, in the Second Dynasty, women had the right to become rulers (*Manetho* 1971, 36–39); it is therefore difficult to know on what grounds they can be said to have usurped the throne. That Hatshepsut might be considered a usurper is a moot point, but, as her circumstances differ from theirs, the three queens should not be lumped together in this way.

Gardiner's later remarks do not dispel this impression that he objects to women rulers. On page 184, he writes, "It is not to be imagined, however, that even a woman of the most virile character could have attained such a pinnacle of power without masculine support. The Theban capital still displays many splendid tombs of her officials, all speaking of her in terms of cringing deference." It is self-evident, of course, that no king could have avoided using male officials to carry out his or her orders, for nearly all the court officials were men, and they were no more cringing toward Hatshepsut than they were to any other king they served.

If other historians also portray her reign as tyrannical, it is because the official, Ineni, in his tomb biography says of her:

[T]he Divine Consort, Hatshepsut, settled the affairs of the Two Lands by reason of her plans. Egypt was made to labor with bowed head for her, the excellent seed of the god, which came forth from him. The bow-rope of the South, the mooring-stake of the Southerners; the excellent stern-rope of the Northland is she; the mistress of command, whose plans are excellent, who satisfies the Two Regions, when she speaks. (Breasted 1906, II, 341)

This passage has been taken to mean that the queen treated her people as slaves. Other biographies from this period do not convey this impression, although the numbers of her monuments were certainly extensive, giving the impression of a vigorous ruler.

It is regrettable that Gardiner does not apply such remarks to the succession of Thutmose III, whose position also depended on assistance from the priesthood of Amen in Thebes. The priesthood would have given approval to the story that the god Amen had chosen Thutmose to be king when he was only a child. Hatshepsut may well have had that sort of assistance herself, and the legend of the queen's birth as a bodily daughter of Amen is perhaps an expression of her dependence upon the cult officials. Both rulers needed such support, and both rulers rewarded the priesthood by generous donations to the cult of Amen, especially the one at Thebes.

One of the lesser-known monuments of Hatshepsut's reign is a smallish, out-of-the-way temple, known as the Speos Artemidos, near Beni Hassan, in central Egypt. This monument has great importance for historians because above its portico Hatshepsut left a long inscription recording the achievements of her reign, which Gardiner has translated and published (Gardiner 1946).

The inscription begins with a list of the queen's monuments at Karnak, after which she mentions that foreign lands respect her and that she exploited the turquoise mines in the Sinai. She mentions the Speos Artemidos and she reports that she repaired other temples and restored their religious rites and festivals. Then she explains why she did this: "I have never slumbered as one forgetful, but have made strong what was decayed. I have raised up what was dismembered, even from the first time when the Asiatics [she refers to the so-called Hyksos invaders] were in Avaris of the North Land, roving hordes in the midst of them overturning what had been made" (lines 47f.).

Since Gardiner himself made that translation, it seems inexplicable that he should say in his history, "her special pride lay in having restored the sanctuaries of Middle Egypt which had remained neglected ever since the Asiatics were in Avaris. . . . Doubtless the claim is exaggerated and does scant justice to the merits of her predecessors" (Gardiner 1961, 188). There is no evidence to support Gardiner's opinion here, whereas the queen's claims are amply endorsed by archeological remains. No previous king ever did make the same claim as Hatshepsut, so Gardiner's opinion remains unsubstantiated.

Gardiner is not the only contemporary historian (see Steindorff and Seele 1957, 40–46) to consider Hatshepsut a rather ineffectual figurehead for the Egyptian state; nevertheless, he is the most important. He was in a position to know that she conducted wars, but these are not mentioned in his history. Instead he confines himself to this offhand remark, "The reign of Hashepsowe had been barren of any military enterprise except an unimportant raid into Nubia" (Gardiner 1961, 189). He omits the important detail that the queen herself led her troops into battle (Habachi 1957, 99f.; Sethe 1933, 4:438).[5] Conversely, he makes much of the wars of Thutmose III, the successor to Hatshepsut. These are not the only examples of the belittling remarks Gardiner makes in his history, but they are sufficient to illustrate that this historian has not presented unbiased accounts of the reigns of either Sebekneferu or Hatshepsut.

Gardiner's work is a classic and, as such, will exert its influence over historical thinking for generations to come. The bias noticed here is not a novelty, however. Both Manetho and Herodotus reported on Queen Neitkrety as a woman, not as a ruler, and no doubt other sources in the past omitted discussion of women for whom no interesting story was known. Regnant queens were left off some of the official king lists, too, as if the Egyptians did not wish to acknowledge them, and their monuments were neglected—some were even deliberately destroyed. Indeed, the achievements of any of Egypt's female political figures in the period discussed here are not well known. Only the patient work of archeologists has made any attempt to redress this paucity of source material. When we become aware that even this modest amount is passed over by the more influential scholars, then it behooves us to point out the bias of established historians and to publicize the meagre inroads made by the women who wanted to participate in the political arenas of their times.

NOTES

1. It is thought to have been at this time a taxation title, in all likelihood, associated with the palace. Its first appearance is in Merneit's grave, and her name is linked on the potsherd concerned. It would belong to the cellarer who had been appointed to her.

2. Later queens had titles that were important variants of this. See Fischer 1974, 94–99.

3. For an understanding of the problems involved, see Hassan 1943, 1–35; Altenmüller 1970; Verner 1980; Verner 1990.

4. The word "harim" comes from the Turkish. The Egyptian harim does not correlate with the Turkish word except that it is also a domain of women. Primarily, it was a place where royal women were domiciled when not in company with the king. Weaving, singing, and dancing were the main occupations of the lesser women there. It was also the place where royal princes and sons of favorite officials were educated.

5. She was not the only queen to do so, apparently. A Ramesside ostracon (CG25125) shows a queen in a chariot, firing arrows at a king coming from the opposite direction. This may be an allegorical sketch, but a more sober historical stele (Sethe 1933, 4:21) reports that Queen Ahhotep II put down a rebellion in southern Egypt when the king was absent.

REFERENCES

Altenmüller, H. 1970. "Die Stellung der Königsmutter Chentkaus beim Übergang von der 4. zur 5. Dynastie." *Chronique d'Égypte* 45: 223–35.

Baines, J., and C. J. Eyre. 1983. "Four Notes on Literacy." *Göttinger Miszellen* 6:65–96.

Baumgartel, E. J. 1960. *The Cultures of Prehistoric Egypt.* Vol. 2. Oxford: Griffith Institute, Oxford University Press.

———. 1970. *Petrie's Naqada Excavation: A Supplement.* London: Bernard Quaritch.

Blackman, A. M. 1921. "On the Position of Women in the Ancient Egyptian Hierarchy." *Journal of Egyptian Archaeology* 7: 8–30.

Breasted, J. H. 1906. *Ancient Records of Egypt.* Chicago: University of Chicago Press.

Bryan, B. M. 1984. "Evidence for Female Literacy from Theban Tombs." *Bulletin of the Egyptological Seminar* 6:17–32.

Callender, G. 1987. *Portraits of Queens from Oldest Egypt.* Sydney: History Teacher's Association.

———. 1988. "A Critical Examination of the Reign of Hatshepsut." *Ancient History* 18, no. 2:86–102.

Carter, H. 1933. *The Tomb of Tut-Ankh-Amen.* Vol. 3. London: Cassell.

Castillos, J. 1982. *A Reappraisal of the Published Evidence on Egyptian Predynastic and Early Dynastic Cemeteries.* Toronto: Benben.

CG = *Catalogue Général.* Cairo Museum. The numbers refer to items in the Cairo Catalogue. The catalogue itself is contained in scores of volumes published under different authors, but the volumes run in sequences.

Dreyer, G. 1986. "Ein Siegel der frühzeitlichen Königsnekropole von Abydos." *Mitteilungen des deutschen Instituts für ägyptische Altertumskunde, Kairo* 43:33–43.

Edel, E. 1981. *Hieroglyphische Inschriften des Alten Reiches*. Munich: Westdeutscher Verlag.

Edwards, I.E.S. 1971. *Cambridge Ancient History*. Vol. I, Part 2A. Cambridge: Cambridge University Press.

Emery, W. B. 1954. *Great Tombs of the First Dynasty*. Vol. 2. Oxford: Egypt Exploration Society. Oxford University Press.

———. 1965. *Archaic Egypt*. Harmondsworth, England: Penguin.

Firth, C. M., and B. Gunn. 1926. *Teti Pyramid Cemeteries*. Vol. 1. Cairo: Service des Antiquités de l'Égypte.

Fischer, H. G. 1960. "The Butcher Pḥ-r-nfr." *Orientalia* 29:180–90.

———. 1974. "NBTY in Old Kingdom Titles and Names." *Journal of Egyptian Archaeology* 60:94–99.

———. 1976. "Administrative Titles of Women in the Old and Middle Kingdom." *Varia* 69–79. New York: Metropolitan Museum of Art.

Fraser, G. 1902. *Annales du Service*. Vol. 3. Plate 3 following p. 192.

Gardiner, A. H. 1946. "Davies' Copy of the Great Speos Artemidos Inscription." *Journal of Egyptian Archeology* 32:43–56.

———. 1961. *Egypt of the Pharaohs*. Oxford: Oxford University Press.

Gardiner, A. H. and T. E. Peet. 1952. *Inscriptions of Sinai*. Part I. London: Egypt Exploration Fund.

Guest, E. M. 1926. "Women's Titles in the Middle Kingdom." *Ancient Egypt* 46–50.

Habachi, L. 1957. "Two Grafitti at Sehel, from the Reign of Queen Hatshepsut." *Journal of Near Eastern Studies* 16:88–104.

Hassam, S. 1943. *Excavations at Giza*. Vol. 4 Cairo: Government Press.

———. 1944. *Excavations at Giza*. Vol. 2. Cairo: Government Press.

Helck, W. 1954. *Untersuchungen zu den Beamtentiteln*. Glückstadt, Germany: Augustin.

———. 1968. *Geschichte des alten Ägyptes*. Leiden, Netherlands: E.J. Brill.

Junker, H. 1937. *Giza: Bericht Grabungen auf dem Friedhof des Alten Reiches bei den Pyramiden von Giza*. Vol. 5. Vienna and Leipzig: Hölder-Pichler-Tempsky A.G.

Kanawati, N. 1980. *Governmental Reforms in Old Kingdom Egypt*. Warminster, England: Aris and Phillips.

———. 1981. "Deux conspirations contre Pepy Ier." *Chronique d'Égypte* 56, 112:210–11.

Kaplony. P. 1963/4. *Die Inschriften der ägyptischen Frühzeit*. Vol. 1. Ägyptologische Abhandlungen 8 and 9. Wiesbaden, Germany: Otto Harrassowitz.

Kees, H. 1940. *Beiträge zur Geschichte des Vezirats im Alten Reich*. Nachrichten von der Kgl. Göttingen, Germany: Gesellschaft der Wissenschaften zu Göttingen.

Lehner, M. 1985. *The Pyramid Tomb of Hetep-heres and the Satellite Pyramid of Khufu*. Mainz, Germany: Philipp von Zabern.

Le Page Renouf, P. 1876. "A Case of Conspiracy." *Records of the Past*. First Series. Vol. 8:53–65. London: Bagster & Sons.

Lichtheim, M. 1974. *Ancient Egyptian Literature: A Book of Readings*. Vol. 1, *The Old and Middle Kingdoms*. Berkeley: University of California Press.

———. 1976. *Ancient Egyptian Literature: A Book of Readings*. Vol. 2, *The New Kingdom*. Berkeley: University of California Press.

Macramallah, R. 1935. *Le Mastaba d'Idout*. Cairo: Imprimerie de L'Institut Français.

Malaise, M. 1977. "La Position de la femme sur les stèles du Moyen Empire." *Studien zur altägyptischen Kultur* 5:183–93.

Manetho. 1971. Translated by W. G. Waddell. Loeb Library. London: Wm. Heinemann.

Mariette, A. 1885. *Les mastabas de l'ancien empire.* Paris: F. Vieweg.

Murray, M. A. 1905. *Saqqarah Mastabas.* London: Egyptological Research Association.

Nord, D. 1981. "The term *'ḥnr':* 'Harim' or 'Musical Performers'?" In *Studies in Ancient Egypt, the Aegean and the Sudan,* edited by W. K. Simpson, 137–46. Boston: Museum of Fine Arts.

Petrie, W.M.F. 1900. *Royal Tombs of the First Dynasty.* Part I. London: Egypt Exploration Fund.

———. 1904. *A History of Egypt.* 4th ed. London: Methuen.

———. 1908. *Athribis.* London: Egypt Exploration Fund.

———. 1912. *The Labyrinth, Gerzeh and Mazghuneh.* London: Bernard Quaritch.

Posener, G. 1969. " 'Maquilleuse' en Égyptien." *Revue d'Égyptologie* 21:150f.

Schultze, P. 1987. *Frauen im Alten Ägypten.* Bergisch Gladbach, Germany: Gustav Lübbe Verlag.

Sethe, K. 1933. *Urkunden des Alten Reiches.* Vol. 1. Leipzig, Germany: J. C. Hinrichsische Buchhandlung.

Steindorff, G., and K. Seele. 1957. *When Egypt Ruled the East.* 2d ed. Chicago: University of Chicago Press.

Stewart, H. M. 1979. *Egyptian Stelae, Reliefs and Painting from the Petrie Collection.* Part 2. Warminster, U.K.: Aris and Phillips.

Strudwick, N. 1985. *The Administration of Egypt in the Old Kingdom.* London: K.P.I.

Vallogia, M. 1964. "Remarques sur les noms de la reine Sebek-ka-re Neferu-Sobek." *Revue d'Égyptologie* 16:45–53.

Verner, M. 1980. "Die Königsmutter Chentkaus von Abusir und einige Bemerkungen zur Geschicht der 5. Dynastie." *Studien zur altägyptischen Kultur* 8:243–68.

———. 1990. "Das 'Chent-kaus-Problem.' " *Festschrift Korostovtzev,* Moscow. Forthcoming.

Ward, W. A. 1982. *Index of Egyptian Administrative and Religious Titles of the Middle Kingdom.* Beirut: American University of Beirut.

———. 1986. *Essays on Feminine Titles of the Middle Kingdom and Related Subjects.* Beirut: American University of Beirut.

3

On the Stage, Behind the Curtain: Images of Politically Active Women in the Late Roman Republic

Tom Hillard

No Roman mother who aspired to respectability needed to be told not to put her daughter on the stage. The standard of performance was not the issue. It was understood that the stage was not a respectable place for her. The advice would be pressed home: Even an accidental role might be castigated if one was caught lurking in the wings. Very little publicity was good publicity.

This early advice would be remembered by any woman who later found herself with the opportunity, talent, or temptation to become involved in backstage management. The high price to be paid in reputation was all too well known. This chapter explores the ubiquity of the metaphor.

Other chapters in this volume provide examples of women who exercised regal authority in antiquity: Egyptian queens and Byzantine empresses stand at opposite ends of the chronological spectrum. Between times, the ancient world witnessed numerous examples of women who were no mere titular heads of state, even if they labored under traditional concepts of a woman's place. Artemisia, queen of Halicarnassus in the early fifth century B.C., for example, was a leading counsellor of Xerxes, king of Persia, during his invasion of mainland Greece in 480 and 479, yet we may well believe, as the historian of the period Herodotus imagined, that her counsels were prefaced with the accepted clichés of gender deference and that, at the sea battle of Salamis, having witnessed a display of her daring, Xerxes exclaimed, "My men are behaving like women, my women like men," making it clear that he chose to regard her superior talents as freakish, even while appreciating them.

At that battle of Salamis the first Artemisia was a marked woman because the Athenians, enraged that they should be reduced to fighting a woman, set a reward for her capture; in the following century, the republic of Rhodes rebelled against a second Artemisia because the citizens could not abide, it was said, to be ruled by a woman. A woman, it seems, might attain the heights in a monarchy, but that was something not to be tolerated in a democracy or republic.[1]

The Roman Republic was just such a society. The exemplar tradition, to which Romans were taught to look for models of behavior, elevated one woman of daring initiative. In the Forum, the public center of Rome, stood an equestrian statue commemorating the celebrated escapee from enemy custody, Cloelia, a heroine of the sixth century B.C.: "an unprecedented honor for an unprecedented act," wrote the historian Livy five centuries later. From the same legendary period, however, the acceptable female models were examples of restraint, propriety, and fortitude; that such standards persisted into the first century B.C. is witnessed by the retention of these *exempla* and by the addition of similar ones. The other side of the coin was represented by female traitors or the wives of the tyrants. While kingship itself was an institution damned in Roman memory, a woman like Tullia, wife of the last Tarquin, was depicted as the epitome of savagery, unbridled by any feelings of decency or by public responsibilities.[2]

Nor did Rome's expansion beyond the Italian peninsula and its much touted cultural submission to older civilizations do much to broaden the collective mind in this particular regard. In 230 B.C., Rome found itself in violent confrontation with the Illyrian queen, Teuta, who followed the aggressive foreign policy of her deceased husband. She was the first queen with whom the Roman Republic had to contend, and the standard accounts leave no room for doubt as to the prevalent Roman attitude. A woman in authority was something repugnant. A near contemporary source asserts that she "suffered from a typically feminine weakness, that of taking only the short view of everything; she could see not further than her people's recent successes, and thus had no eyes for events elsewhere." Her policy-making is depicted as erratic—dominated by fits of passion and lack of judgment—fickle, and petulant, alternately overly bold and cowardly, and always the result of gender weaknesses.[3] Two hundred years later, at the end of the republican era (to illustrate the persistence of a theme), a propaganda war was waged against Cleopatra, queen of Egypt, along similar lines, and the portrait was subsequently canonized.[4]

The term *Republic* covers that period of Roman history stretching from the fifth century to the second part of the first century B.C.; the late Republic refers to that period of upheaval from the last part of the second century to the political disintegration of the Roman government in the middle of the first century, a time when traditional ideas and traditional behavior were under challenge. The term *res publica* was understood by Romans to mean the state or public affairs; the nearest literal translation in English is commonwealth. If it implied to them a political system at all, it was (as the term literally advertised) *open* government, characterized by collegiality in office (to limit the tenure of such authority) and, nominally at least, popular sovereignty through popular assemblies. In this system of government, women played no part. They could hold no office (except for some religious posts), exercise no vote, and on *dies comitiales* (that is, days on which an assembly might be conducted) were debarred even from the Forum

(Aulus Gellius *Attic Nights* 5.19.10). Although Roman women had always enjoyed freer movement than, say, the women of classical Athens, the presence of women was considered incompatible with this ideal of the public conduct of state affairs, and it was but a short step to the intuition that there was something intrinsically unsavory about a woman having strayed from her ideally secluded domain too close to the public stage.

Of course, this adumbration of the system does not tell the full story by any means. In a society which lacked, to list only three crucial items, a police force, a fire brigade, and (until very late) any form of centralized welfare agency, power lay in wealth and patronage, and, in effect, by the late Republic was in the hands of the great patrons, a hierarchy of families which had the wherewithal to see done what they thought ought to be done, to "vindicate their rights" and the rights of their "friends."

Clients were inherited or acquired through reputation and current political success, and since patronage was a family affair no one ought to be surprised to find *patronae* as well as *patroni*. Many a client would press his or her suit with a *patrona* who would take action according to her own will and using her own slaves, freedmen or women, or financial resources. Only in a matter of major importance might a woman be obliged to press that suit in turn with her husband. This power in the social sphere shaded into the political, and women's voices were heard in family councils when political issues were discussed. In 44 B.C., for instance, after the assassination of Julius Caesar, the assassins sat down to a family conference with senior well-wishers. Women of the family, who were there as a matter of course, gave voice. Such an occurrence would pass almost without comment.[5]

The important decision making frequently occurred in these private councils (often set in a family context), and the execution of those decisions was effected through the workings of patronage and obligation. Political action, therefore, was pursued through social channels and institutions to an extraordinary degree, a degree that practically demands the recognition of these channels as part of the formal political structure. The social and the political (to use the latter term in its narrower sense to mean competition for power in the public arena) were blurred, not just apparently but in very real ways, hence the exercise of political influence, by women as well as by men, through respected social roles. The most satisfying exercise of such influence came from bringing *auctoritas* to bear. *Auctoritas* offered the ability to exert one's will through an inherent authority. It was to be regarded as a personal quality, rather than something awarded or delegated. By the late Republic, many aristocratic women enjoyed such a quality by virtue of their considerable wealth as patrons of individuals and communities (municipal and provincial, both inside the Italian peninsula and beyond), as mothers (as mothers *over* influential sons and as mothers *of* influential sons), and through valuable personal contacts and a profound knowledge of the political networks. They were indeed individuals of recognized substance.[6] Attempting, however, to track down actual instances of such influence—that is to say, substantive evidence that is not anecdotal in character—is, of course, a vain quest. Both the concealment for political purposes and the ubiquity of personalized relationships and procedures, even within the elites of societies where government is institutionalized to a far greater degree than it was in the Roman Republic (and societies for which far more information is available on political processes), make a satisfactory academic exposé unlikely.

The majority of women within the aristocracy must have been, in the cultural sphere, as highly educated as their brothers, and they were an integral part of the social life of their class. Their role, even in conservative families, was surely enhanced by the fact that the elite of which they were members was social as much as political; since eminence was not as hereditary as is often assumed, the quest for elegance would have assumed major importance. Families achieving political prominence would have found it necessary to establish and maintain their social prestige. In this it might be assumed that the accomplished women of the great families played a leading role. Great emphasis was placed on what was, or was not, accepted behavior; and even though the ground rules were rapidly changing, novelty was never prized at Rome. Propriety lay with custom. For the same reason that *novitas* could raise a sneer, or worse, the women of the family, precisely because of their supposedly limited social intercourse, could be relied upon to maintain the values of old and to set a tone which their male kinsfolk, busy grasping or retaining power, had not been able to cultivate to the same degree. Authors concerned with such matters observed the satisfyingly antique diction of Roman *matronae*, a trait which was said to assist greatly the oratorical training of their sons.[7]

A paradox will be readily apparent. In the late Republic, women had access to power, and their social role was an important one, demanding (in one sense) a high profile. Yet that role recognizably belonged to the private rather than the public sphere in which women were officially denied the right of participation. Whatever the reality, the ideal of constricted social roles for women was maintained. Epitaphs bear witness to women supervising the household and spinning the wool (or, at least, overseeing such activity). Lip service only may have been paid to these values, but it was paid. It is worth noting that when a rioting crowd broke into the house of the leading magistrate, toward the end of the Republican era, they gave vent to their anger by smashing his wife's loom, which apparently they found in or near the entrance hall. Given the nature of the aristocratic house and the public access to its major rooms, it is unlikely that this loom was left unattended by the women all day and, even when it was, it stood as a public symbol of the matron's place.[8]

The traditional conception of public and private spheres and of the distinction between them is, and has been, a popular one, even though the most recent analyses have stressed that it is not realistic and even obscures useful analysis and debate. In Rome that traditional conception was strong. The distinction has been rendered all the more visible in the contemporary industrialized world by the spatial division that exists in the wake of the suburban spread of modern cities. In Rome, at first sight, the physical distinction may not have been as apparent: The public and private worlds shared space. The *atrium*, or reception hall, wherein stood the matron's loom, abutted the *tablinum*, or the master's study, which saw a political life of its own. Both worlds met regularly in the *triclinium*, or dining room. This may obscure an essential point for many modern analysts of Roman aristocratic society, that is, the abiding distinction in the Roman mind.[9]

A stock anecdote that glorified the hoodwinking and public humiliation of an inquisitive woman by her canny son indicates the firm boundary in the Roman male mind of what was and was not a woman's business. Public affairs were not. By way of noting the tale's durability, it might be said that it is dated to the third century B.C. and is retailed as a morally edifying item in a collection of the second century A.D. that cites as its source (in this instance) an oration of the second century B.C. (It is also included in a similar collection of intellectual trivia from the fifth century.) It involved a youth in his early teens, admitted— as custom allowed—to a senatorial session with his father in order that he might thereby gain experience. Pressured by his mother to reveal the matter of the day's discussion—a pressure that grew all the more intense when the boy reiterated that he was bound to secrecy because an item of importance had been adjourned until the morrow—the youth fabricated the story that the Senate was debating whether it was expedient to allow men two wives, or vice versa. When the Senate was confronted on the following day with a near riot of demonstrating women, the boy told all. Thus alerted to this danger to confidentiality, the Senate resolved that henceforward no youths would be admitted to the House, with the exception of this particular individual who was honored in a variety of ways for his precocious sense of decency.[10]

Given the endurance of this orthodoxy, it is clear that there was a tension in Roman society between reality and potential on the one hand, and ideals of propriety on the other. Any woman's exercise of influence in the public domain would have needed to be discreet. Moreover, even an interest in the public domain might need to be "decently" shrouded. One of the clearest illustrations is given in a letter of the senator Pliny to the aunt of his third wife, Calpurnia. The evidence belongs to a later period—it is written about A.D. 100—but its sentiments are surely applicable to the Republic. Pliny praises his wife's intelligence, diligence, and informed interest in his doings.

She is so anxious when she knows that I am going to plead in court, and so happy when all is over! She arranges to be kept informed of the sort of reception and applause I receive, and what verdict I win in the case. [Note, in passing, the assumption of separation as the husband takes up public business—even though that business is of interest to the woman and even though no business of her own distracts her.] If I am giving a reading she sits behind a curtain nearby and greedily drinks in every word of appreciation.[11]

After the collapse of the Republic, the warlord Octavian, known to history as the emperor Augustus, established an autocratic regime; his successors administered the empire through agents. Open government gave way to in-house management, and politics became equated with intrigue within the ruling house. Although the important debates now took place *in camera* and were therefore the subject of guesswork only, the role of the women in the imperial family seemed more apparent. They did not have to abandon the home to be effective in government. Yet, almost a century after the effective death of the Republic, the formidable Agrippina, wife of the emperor Claudius and mother of the emperor Nero—a woman who, according to the historian Tacitus, had boasted during the reign of her husband that she was a partner in empire; had set a precedent by being present on the public podium before Rome's military standards while Claudius had received the surrender of a foreign king; had entered the religious center of Rome, the Capitol hill, in a chariot (a practice previously reserved for priests and sacred objects); and was said to dominate the young Nero—found it expedient not to be *seen* when policy was being discussed. Again according to Tacitus, senators were summoned to the palace for important meetings so that Agrippina "could station herself at a newly-added door in their rear, shut off by a curtain thick enough to conceal her from view but not to debar her from hearing."[12]

Two generations before that, Livia, the wife of Augustus, had been asked how she had obtained such a commanding influence over Augustus. She replied that she had been scrupulously chaste herself, did gladly whatever pleased him, and did not meddle in any of his affairs (Dio 57.2.5). One of the arts of influence has always been not to claim it.

That women from a wider range of families influenced the course of politics during the period of the late Republic may be assumed and, indeed, *was* assumed and alleged in various source material for the period. The enforced clandestine nature of such interventions, however, easily gave rise to sinister imagery. (Successful instances of such influence will not be known.) Those who recorded history despised scheming concubines and looked askance at domineering dowagers. I would argue that an intrinsic part of the image was the notion of something lacking in the men on whom they exercised their wiles or exerted their influence. It will be convenient to begin with the archetypal image of a domineering concubine to demonstrate the ways in which the imagery could be easily but devastatingly transferred.

In 70 B.C. Cicero produced his Verrine orations, an expanded literary version of his case for the prosecution in the trial of Caius Verres for corruption as the governor of Sicily from 73–71. Whatever the professed altruism of the cause, these speeches established Cicero as Rome's leading orator and represented the state of the art in character assassination, the traduction of an enemy, and the demolition of a reputation. In these documents, the woman Chelidon makes several appearances. (They are the only sources that record her existence.) She was an associate of Verres during his praetorship in 74, that is, when he was one of the eight men holding the second highest executive office in the empire. She was, by Cicero's definition, a *meretrix*, or prostitute, though by no means a streetwalker. Her name, which is Greek for swallow, may have been her exotic professional title. It may even have been a titillating advertisement of her profession since *chelidon* was a euphemism for vagina. (Cicero seems to make a play on this potential meaning of the word in any case.)[13]

All of the previous offices that Verres is known to have held kept him out of Rome. The year 74 offered him the opportunity for coveted and necessary public exposure, and it will be useful to digress for a moment with a brief look at contemporary *male* needs. The antithetic relevance to the female experience will become apparent. One of the essential features of an aristocrat's life was the need to be ever before the people, explaining in part the open nature of their houses. There was an equation between the words *nobilis*, the primary meaning of which was "notable," and *clarus*, meaning "bright," "clear," or "luminous." To be the most noble of all, by Roman terminology, was to be *clarissimus*, the "most conspicuous." To cease to be visible (for one's ongoing achievement or past glories to cease to be conspicuous) was to see one's *nobilitas* tarnished, if not lapse. A nobleman's character was to be a *lumen*, a shining beacon. Cicero observed that when a man had the good fortune to become a celebrity all eyes were upon him. No word of his, no action could remain in darkness. It was as if the man were standing in a bright light. Sallust, a contemporary historian, took up the theme: "[T]he glory of ancestors is, as it were, a light shining upon their posterity, suffering neither their virtues nor their faults to be hidden." The metaphor of light and dark was developed by the contemporary poet Lucretius: Ambitious men strive for the light, those left in the dark bitterly complain. It was easy for a Roman noble to see himself as strutting the stage: The crucial common denominator between nobility and the actor's profession was the very public nature of both callings. A statesman's public life, as opposed to his private conduct, was said by Cicero to have been played *in scaena* (i.e., "on stage").[14]

Thus Verres was to tread the boards. The lot had awarded him the urban praetorship, the most prestigious praetorian office, in which he would administer justice in Rome. His theater was the praetor's tribunal. His stage was the podium, a one-meter-high wooden platform exposed to the bustle of the Forum. On the days set for hearings, a crowd would be drawn to the Forum's southeast corner to be entertained by the drama of people engaged in litigation and the oratorical artistry of the various speakers.[15] Verres's error, by conservative tenets, was to allow Chelidon into the spotlight. It was a "mistake" of which Cicero made effective use. (The theatrical metaphor could in no way be applied harmlessly to a woman, but that is a theme to be explored further below. Cicero does not pursue such a metaphor in this instance because it was altogether unnecessary. The fact of a woman's presence in so public a place was enough.)

Need I give you any proof of the criminal way in which this man administers the law as he chooses? Did you not all see how he administered it in Rome? Was the proper legal procedure available at any time for anyone during his term of office if Chelidon willed otherwise? . . . One is a fact so notorious, so well known to everyone, that during the consulship of Lucullus and Cotta [74 B.C.] not even the simplest rustic from the remotest provincial town came to Rome, in connection with any case heard in the law courts, without learning that all the decisions pronounced by the city praetor were controlled by the good will and pleasure of that *meretrix* Chelidon.[16]

Clearly the point Cicero intended to make was heightened by what he would have chosen to assume were the character failings of Chelidon, specifically, her calling. Yet little is made of the latter. At one point, Cicero even deigns to acknowledge a certain graciousness in the woman (*Verrines* 2.1.136). But she is very much a secondary target. Her calling is not the point, although it provides a useful garnishing. It is the sexual politics that are tacitly to the fore. And it is the weakness of Verres with which Cicero is concerned: The presence of a woman serves as a disgraceful explanation of an erratic public conduct:

Pray recall to your memories, gentlemen, the wanton character of Verres' administration of the law, the lack of uniformity in his decision, the trafficking that went on; how empty were the houses of all the experts in civil law whom it is the practice to consult, how densely crowded was the house of Chelidon. As often as that woman came up to him and whispered in his ear, he would call back the parties to a case that he had already judged, and alter his judgment: at other times he would, without the least scruple, deliver in one case a judgment directly opposed to that which he had delivered in the previous case a few minutes before. (*Verrines* 2.1.120)

The image is self-evidently absurd, although it is not clear whether Cicero intends to convey a picture of Chelidon's intervention while Verres actually sat atop the podium or quieter interference in a more private venue subsequently. The latter is of course more likely, but the former was not impossible. Though the tribunal was meant to convey the impression of standing apart, it was not so elevated as to deny access to friends or, even, according to a much later poet, admirers. It is possible that Cicero was conjuring, four years after the event, with the more disgraceful image, the physical demeaning of the podium's majesty.[17]

Chelidon's station outside respectable society made her conspicuous and that fact served Cicero's purpose. The *stola*, or concealing long gown worn by matrons, marked them out for the respect considered their due. Those abandoning such modesty were not accorded such respect (or protection under law).[18] The more exposed, the less respected.[19] There is no suggestion that Chelidon worked the streets. She had her own establishment, which, from Cicero's description, was substantial. Cicero paints a picture of three victims of Verres (or, more precisely, three representatives of an underaged victim) who were visiting Chelidon to plead their suit. The house, he says, was full.

Decisions, judgments, methods of procedure—none ever heard of before—were being applied for: "make him give me possession," "don't let him pronounce against me," "get him to award me the property." Some were paying her cash, others were signing promissory notes; the house was filled, not with the visitors of a *meretrix*, but with the crowd that attends a praetor's court. *As soon as they were allowed*, the gentlemen I have named approached the woman. (*Verrines* 2.1.136f. See note 16 above.)

That last statement suggests a sizable antechamber with traffic regulated by a steward.

Chelidon and numerous multitalented women like her lived in a *demimonde* through which the male members of the aristocracy moved easily. These were women celebrated for their wit, beauty, and intelligence, whose portraits appeared in prominent places (in one case, in the decoration of a temple). Their attention could be won or bought with substantial gifts. Some enjoyed considerable wealth, enough to support an impecunious favorite of their own. Within such a world criticism was visited upon the male gentry who enjoyed their company only when an individual appeared to go beyond his financial resources or damaged his reputation by too fond an attachment.[20]

Yet conservative social morality remained the dominant ideology.[21] For all the celebration of Chelidon and those like her within their *milieu*, they had to formally register with the aediles (the magistrates who, in the absence of a police force, were—among many other duties—responsible for public order). More to the point, it is noteworthy that although Latin has over fifty words which might denote a prostitute, it has no quasi-technical terms to distinguish, as Greek does with *hetaira* and *porne*, between courtesans and prostitutes without drifting into euphemisms such as *puella* (girl) or *delicata* (dainty one). A *meretrix* was a *meretrix*. When a synopsist of the comic playwright Terence found himself in need of a gentler word to translate the spirit of the Greek, he retreated into the diminutive *meretricula*. (Terence himself never bothers with such a nicety.) Even in polite language, these women might be labelled by those who did not approve of their behavior as *famosae* (those who are much talked of). While *famosus* might be an epithet coveted by a man, it would not be enjoyed by a woman. The ubiquitous double standards are obvious even in this euphemism. The historian Livy refers to a woman called Hispala Faecenia as a *scortum nobile libertina*, a celebrated whore and freedwoman. The juxtaposition of the first two words is at first sight jarring: *Scortum* is the more abrasive word for prostitute, and *nobilis* is a word readily associated with the aristocracy. But that latter usage (though the more prominent) is of course a secondary one (and in *that* sense women are rarely elevated to association with it). Its primary meaning was simply "notable" or "prominent." No Roman reader would have read that phrase as "noble whore."[22]

Indeed it was the very celebration of Chelidon and her more successful sisters that made them vulnerable. It was scarcely possible for a woman to be both talked of (for any but the most conservative and restrictive virtues) and respected. Even women involved in public commerce could be associated with prostitution or fall under snide suspicion, especially those who worked in taverns even if they managed the inns. They were all overexposed. The term for wine shop-keeper, *copa*, came to connote prostitute.[23]

It was more than a question of name-calling, of course. According to Cicero, to enter Chelidon's establishment sullied men of moral quality:

Yes, they went to see Chelidon: Caius Mustius, knight and collector of revenue, as honorable a man as lives; . . . the honest and upright Marcus Iunius; and . . . Publius Titius, respectable and conscientious, than whom no man of his rank is esteemed more highly. Ah, Verres, how many there are to whom your praetorship has brought pain and misery and shame! To speak of nothing else, I bid you think simply of the feelings of disgust and shame with which such men must have entered the dwelling of a *meretrix*. For no consideration would they have brought themselves to stoop so low, had not regard for duty and friendship compelled them. They went, as I have said, to see Chelidon.

To Cicero, Chelidon was a *meretrix*, pure and simple. It made her someone who might be expected to have been involved in untoward schemes and clandestine activity: the antithesis of the republican ideal. It made her someone not to be trusted. *Meretrices*—whether streetwalkers or courtesans—suffered *infamia*, a civil degradation that meant, among other things, that their witness was not to be accepted in court.[24]

The status of Chelidon simply made the issue clear cut. The undeniable fact was Chelidon's visibility: a certain kind of prominence indivisible from her lack of respectability. The very word *infamia* encapsulated this concept. This must have been what made her presence so valuable to those who would blacken the character of Verres. He was guilty by association, and, in this case, it was only *his* reputation that mattered to those who fixed the record.

Secondary vilifications—vilifications of the women involved—were surely part of the same image making, especially when it concerned women whose "moral turpitude" was not self-evident in terms of their profession or social status. Probably any woman who chose to thus enter the male domain was seen to have (or could be argued to have) transgressed propriety by the established standards. Hence if any successful allegation of a woman's (improper) participation in the political process was to be made, with the object of damaging the credibility of the men to whom she was giving support, then it followed that the woman was not of good character and ought to be exposed as such. The elaboration was not strictly necessary since the impropriety was understood and the woman's reputation was not the prime target, but, in the rhetorical contexts in which such allegations were usually made, it could only strengthen the case.

It is time to examine the ways in which women who would have regarded themselves very differently, but who could be charged with having in some way "gone public," were vulnerable. It can be argued that, whatever the reality in the late Republic, any "evidence" of politically active or politically motivated women originates in political polemic. It consists of allegation rather than observation; it alleges nonobservable activities; it is aimed at reducing the credibility of politically powerful men with whom the women are legitimately or illegitimately associated; and any such literature, even if only coincidentally, dissuaded women of talent from being seen to exercise it. Over time, such a rhetorical motif may have served as a conditioning agent fostering something analogous to the now familiar "motive to avoid success." It is just possible, however, that the imagery that was applied to politically active aristocratic women represents a conscious discouragement, and that it was being aimed at them in an era when changing mores threatened to challenge the male monopoly of the public arena.[25]

The portrait of Sempronia, who appears fleetingly in one source only, is classic. She was an associate of Lucius Catilina, a three-time loser in his bid for the consulship, who was accused in 63 B.C. of plotting a bloody overthrow of the establishment and of the elected government. The rights and wrongs of Catilina's suppression and the justice of Catilina's cause remained a much debated issue until the end of the Republic. In an account of the aborted coup, which was published two decades after the event, the discredited politician-turned-historian Sallust introduces Sempronia as a sympathizer to the conspiracy who lent her house, in the absence of her husband, for a clandestine meeting. (One may wonder just how germane Sallust's lengthy digression on the woman was to his professed theme. No formal charges are known to have been made against Sempronia and no punishment, state or domestic, is known to have been meted out to her. Sallust offers nothing of her subsequent history. Hence she disappears from view. On one score at least, then, the relevance of this memorable projection to reality is open to question.) For those unfamiliar with the portrait, it is worth quoting in full. Modern scholars often seem at a loss to discern which elements represent criticism and which praise. There is so much that strikes one as admirable that the grudging admiration of the historian, or even a more complex involvement, has been asserted, and much lively speculation has been exercised on the psychology of Sallust's motivation for this elaborate but digressive profile.

At that time Catiline is said to have gained the support of many men of all conditions and even of some women; the latter at first had met their enormous expenses by prostitution, but later, when their time of life had set a limit to their traffic but not to their extravagance, had contracted a huge debt. Through their help Catiline believed that he could tempt the city slaves to his side and set fire to Rome; and then either attach the women's husbands to his cause or make away with them.

Now among these women was Sempronia, who had often committed many crimes of masculine daring. In birth and beauty; in her husband also and children, she was abundantly favored by fortune; well read in the literature of Greece and Rome, able to play the lyre and dance more skilfully than an honest woman need, and having many other accomplishments which minister to voluptuousness. But there was nothing which she held so cheap as modesty and chastity; you could not easily say whether she was less sparing of her money or her honor; her desires were so ardent that she sought men more often than she was sought by them. Even before the time of the conspiracy she had often broken her word, repudiated her debts, been privy to murder; poverty and extravagance combined had driven her headlong. Nevertheless, she was a woman of no mean endowments; she could write verses, bandy jests, and use language which was modest, or tender, or wanton; in fine, she possessed a high degree of wit and of charm. (*The Conspiracy of Catiline* 24.3–25.5)

Such is Sallust's account of Sempronia.

[O]ne ought not to forget the notorious Sempronia, a woman of noble birth, cultured tastes and considerable charm. Wife of an ex-consul and daughter of a distinguished house, she has now passed her prime and exhausted her resources. Indebtedness and appetite for pleasure led her to indulge in intrigue. Sempronia combined feminine wiles with masculine audacity—a valuable contribution to conspiratorial designs. (Gruen 1974, 422. See also Cadoux 1980, 93–122)

This verdict *cum* gloss by one modern scholar illustrates the tireless efforts to find implicit (if backhanded) panegyric in the passage. (The last sentence, one would like to think, is tongue-in-cheek.) But any attempt to distinguish praise from blame is misguided. The portrait comes as a package and it is hostile. Her attainments were regarded as improperly developed, her profile too high. Her conspicuous skills put her beyond respectable society.

Clodia Metelli provides another outstanding example of male denigration of a prominent aristocratic woman. Clodia was indeed a noblewoman. In fact, to her alone among womankind did Cicero apply the term *nobilis*. It will be clear from what has been already said about the word that this is an ambivalent application, and there is no doubt that Cicero intended it to be undercutting. He also accorded her the label, unique in extant Latin literature, *illa consularis* (the consular woman). In view of the denial of women's access to magisterial power and the consequent *auctoritas* which flowed from past tenure of office, the tag was strictly inappropriate. Cicero meant this too to be pejorative. It signified her inappropriate pretensions. When we meet her in the historical records ca. 60 B.C., she is the daughter of a household that traced its consulships back six generations and its history back farther than the Republic. She is the wife of an ex-consul; she is the sister of three brothers who can all reasonably expect to win the consulship at the appropriate time; and she has been the sister-in-law of Pompey "the Great" and of two other ex-consuls. She was regarded by Cicero as a loud woman and an opinionated one. According to one late source—on the strength of what evidence we cannot know—Cicero toyed with the idea of a union with her and, through her, with her family. If so, a break occurred in 61 B.C. In Cicero's first extant reference to her, a letter to her husband in 62, his neutral statement accords her the respect due to a woman of her station. According to my reading of his correspondence in the following years, he was usually hostile to her, though he could express an eagerness to hear what she had to say. She received some unwelcome publicity in 61 at the trial of her youngest brother, of whom she was very fond and who became Cicero's bête noire, when an accusation of adulterous incest was leveled. Her most spectacular publicity was received when she appeared in April, in 56 B.C., as a witness for the prosecution at the trial of the twenty-five-year-old Marcus Caelius Rufus, who was said to have been a former lover. Clodia must have been about thirty. She was, at the time, a widow.[26]

Clodia was not concerned with the bulk of, or indeed the most serious, charges against Caelius; but Cicero, appearing for the young man, turned her into the be-all and the end-all of his speech for the defense, effecting to discern her shadowy figure behind the whole prosecution: Her motive was the ruination of a fickle paramour; the means was her alleged influence over the formal prosecutors who are depicted as mere ciphers, whose own motives for attacking Caelius are dismissed, and whose case against Caelius is thus discredited. Again we see the allegation of a clandestine presence. At the same time, Cicero bases his moral case against Clodia (into which he has turned his defense of Caelius) on the woman's conspicuousness. A recent essay has nicely explored the manner in which Cicero manipulated the motif of concealment and visibility at several levels. The orator plays cat and mouse with Clodia as a witness, with Clodia's reputation, and with the jury all at the same time. He introduces her, then drops the subject, leaving the jurors on the edges of their seats awaiting the next installment. Then, just after the middle point of speech, the curtain is dropped (the metaphor needs to be reversed for Rome—the curtain was lowered to reveal the stage), and Clodia stands revealed in the glaring light of day (Ramage 1984, 1985):

Now there are two charges, one about some gold, one about some poison, in which one and the same person is involved. It is alleged that the gold was taken from Clodia, the poison procured to be given to Clodia. All the other matters complained of are not accusations, but slanders; they smack rather of vulgar vituperation than of a court of justice. (*Cael.* 30)

As serious as this charge of fraud and allegation of attempted murder may have been, Cicero conveniently overlooks the fact that the other charges include one of responsibility for the murder of an Egyptian ambassador. The obfuscation continues in a similar vein:

To call Caelius an adulterer, a lewd fellow, a dealer in bribes, is abuse, not accusation; there is no foundation for these charges, no ground; they are insulting taunts hurled at random by an accuser who is in a rage and who speaks without any authority. But as for the two charges I have mentioned, I can see that there is someone in the background, I can see that they have a source, I can see a definite individual as their fountain-head. "Caelius wanted gold, he took it from Clodia, took it without witnesses, and kept it as long as he wanted." I see in this strong evidence of a quite remarkable intimacy. "He wanted to put her to death; he procured poison, prepared it, incited whom he could, fixed on a time and place, brought it." Here, again, I see violent hatred had taken shape with a most distressing rupture. In this case, gentlemen, we are concerned entirely with Clodia, a woman not only of noble birth, but also of notoriety, of whom I will say no more than what is necessary to repel the charge. But you, with your great wisdom, Gnaeus Domitius

[Cicero here addresses the judge], understand that it is with this woman alone that we have to deal. (*In Defence of Caelius* 30–32)

Personal vilification of opponents is routine in Roman forensic practice, but the point is that Clodia has been effectively cast as Caelius's main enemy, thus excusing Cicero's concentration upon her for the remaining portion of the speech. I say "effectively" because very few commentators, ancient or modern, have seen her as anything but that. She is not the prosecutor of course, but the real prosecutors have been portrayed as being *without authority*. Her posited role in the prosecution, then, is a concealed one and therefore untoward. On the other hand, Cicero's concentration on the woman in the oration plays upon her general visibility and therefore suggests (even without the elaboration he affords the theme) that her actions are likely to be improper ones. She was not only of repute by respect of her birth but "known": *non solum nobilis sed nota*. The two words are juxtaposed in such a way as to allow the first an element of respectability, but Cicero's audience would not have missed the intended ambivalence. She was altogether "notorious."[27]

Appearing publicly as a witness, Clodia was in a no-win situation. "If she denies that she lent Caelius gold, if she does not allege that he tried to poison her, we are behaving disgracefully in using a matron's name otherwise than as a matron's virtue demands" (*Cael* 32). (Cicero intends to illustrate later in the speech that Clodia does not conduct herself as a *materfamilias* should.) Either things are as Clodia claims, Cicero is saying, and Clodia is, ergo, the type of woman being portrayed, or the prosecution has no case. If Clodia *is* this type of woman, however, her testimony is not to be accepted. "But with this woman removed from the case, our enemies have no accusation left nor means to attack Caelius, what other course is open to us who are his counsel than to refute those who attack him?" (*Cael*. 32; *Cael*. 57).

Again, it is Clodia's public image (rather than her case against Caelius) that Cicero brings to center stage. He rounds off this particular passage with an affected sigh: "For indeed I never thought that I should have to engage in quarrels with women, still less with a woman whom everyone has always thought to be everyone's friend rather than anyone's enemy." An ancient commentator on the speech, a teacher of rhetorical style, draws attention to the intended play on words here: a double entendre that hardly needs to be pointed out in the twentieth century either (Quintilian *Institutes of Oratory* 9.2.99). In Latin, the female form of "friend" might serve as another euphemism for a kept woman. Such is the price Clodia paid for her foray into the public domain.

Several passages farther on, Cicero elaborates on the image with regard to Clodia's behavior at the beachside resort of Baiae, just to the north of the bay of Naples:

Does not then that notorious neighborhood put us on the scent: Does public rumor, does Baiae itself say nothing? Yes, Baiae does not merely talk, but even cries aloud that there is no woman whose amorous passions are so degraded that, far from seeking privacy and darkness and the usual screens for vice, she revels in her degraded lusts amid the most open publicity and in the broadest daylight (*sed in turpissimis rebus frequentissima celebritate et clarissima luce laetetur*).

Apart from the crescendo of superlatives, note the allegation of unashamed display. She chooses the clearest light (*clarissima lux*): the very limelight that the Roman nobleman sought and would be acclaimed for winning. Cicero regarded himself as a *vir clarissimus* and wished others so to regard him.[28]

   With feigned propriety Cicero elects not to connect Clodia's name directly to this portrait of infamy:

If a woman without a husband opens her house to all men's desires, and publicly leads the life of a *meretrix*; if she is in the habit of attending dinner-parties with men who are perfect strangers; if she does this in the city, in her park, amid all those crowds at Baiae; if, in fact, she so behaves that not only the ardor of her looks and the licentiousness of her gossip but also her embraces and caresses, her beach-parties, her water-parties, her dinner-parties, proclaim her to be not only a *meretrix*, but also a shameless and wanton *meretrix*; if a young man should happen to be found with this woman, would you, Lucius Herennius, consider him to be an adulterer or a lover? Would you think that he desired to ravage her chastity, or only to satisfy his passion?. . . . I am now forgetting, Clodia, the wrongs you have done me: I am putting aside the memory of what I have suffered; I pass over your cruel actions towards my family during my absence; pray do not imagine that what I have said was meant against you. But I ask you yourself, since the accusers assert that you are the source of this charge and that they have you yourself as a witness to this charge, I ask you, if there existed a woman such as I painted a short while ago, one quite unlike you, with the life and manners of a *meretrix*—would you think it very shameful or disgraceful that a young man should have had some dealings with such a woman? If you are not this woman, as I prefer to think, for what have the accusers to reproach Caelius? But if they will have it that *you* are such a person, why should we be afraid of this accusation, if you despise it? Then it is for you to show us our way and method of defense; for either your sense of propriety will disapprove any vicious behavior by Caelius, or your utter impropriety will afford both him and the rest a fine opportunity for self-defense. (*Cael.* 69)

   If Clodia is to be seen as a *meretrix*—and this is made to follow the very fact that she conducts so public a life—she then suffers *infamia*. Her testimony is invalid. Cicero returns to the theme later: "You have now seen what I would rather not say. It may not even be true. But, alas, even if it is not . . . , it is *seen* to square with that lady's reputation and style" (*Cael.* 69). There is no assertion in all this that Clodia is literally a prostitute, but the metaphor has been allowed to impinge on reality.
   Cicero then turns to the substance of Clodia's testimony, her version of Caelius's plot against her own life, and he plays it for all the comic potential he can find in it, "the whole of this little play, by a poetess of experience who had already composed many others—how devoid it is of plot, how utterly it fails to

find an ending!'' (See *Cael.* 64–69 for Clodia as playwright.) Clodia has been brought out into the world of the theater and is thus to be submitted to further degradation. Roman attitudes to the theater were ambivalent. As noted earlier, a nobleman might regard his public life as conducted on stage.[29] The parallels were many. Aspiring orators were advised to learn from the gestures of actors while actors frequented the Forum to watch great orators in action.[30] On the other hand, the theater world and the acting profession in particular were regarded as sordid. The reputations of those nobles who enjoyed too genuine a familiarity with actors and actresses suffered.[31] The stigma attaching to the profession went beyond social restraints.

Legislation kept the acting profession in its place. An ancient law gave magistrates *coercitio* (the right of summary punishment, i.e., physical chastisement) over actors. It seems that the praetors, at least, had the ''use of the lash'' in this regard. Actors, who were not uncommonly slaves, were, even if free, burdened with the same *infamia* as prostitutes. They were not qualified to stand for any office, and, at law, they were treated as slaves for the purpose of marriage and so on.[32] Cicero had already toyed with this theme during another trial a month earlier when he had taken the opportunity to attack Clodia's brother, whom he called ''the arch-buffoon—not just a spectator but a performer and an entertainer—who knows all his sister's interludes.'' The word used is *embolia*, balletic interludes danced between acts. An ancient scholiast, commenting on that very passage, explained that Clodia was an accomplished dancer, more accomplished (like Sempronia) than a respectable woman needed to be.[33]

Women on the stage were held in even lower esteem. For a woman (more commonly, a girl) to step onto the boards was to take an irreversible step. Insofar as the profession had respectability, it was represented by its guild. (It is uncertain when this college reached Rome.) This guild formally *excluded* all mime artists, women, and slaves. Women seem to have entered the theater as performers with the introduction of mimes, when masks were discarded—along with much else— and female roles could be played by women. Cicero explicitly identifies Clodia with this world. Having delivered his own slapstick version of her evidence in court, he offers the criticism that its ''resolution'' is ''not the sort of finale for a real play. It is more the ending of a song-and-dance show [*mimus*]—the type of production where no-one has been able to think of an ending, and so someone escapes from someone else, and the clappers sound, and it's the curtain.'' As T. P. Wiseman rightly points out, mention of the mime reduces the ''librettist's'' dignity even further than the earlier slurs on her character had done. ''Moreover a moment later [anticipating evidence to be given by friends of Clodia], Cicero drops a malicious allusion to the most popular of all mime plots, the concealed adulterer. . . . His brilliant and shameless innuendo leads his audience to think of her not just as a writer of mimes but as a character in one.''[34]

Some individual *mimae* became celebrated successes but that did not raise the stock of the profession. Conservative society shunned their company.[35] Mimes very often were obscene; mime artists very often were prostitutes; and mimes could be performed nude. The assumption that actresses were prostitutes was automatically made. Their honor was held to be of no account. Although elsewhere in his writings Cicero calumniates against rape, when he defended Cnaeus Plancius and had to deflect attacks on his client's character, he cheerily dismissed the charge that Plancius had assaulted an actress:

You say that he raped a ballet-girl; we hear that this crime was once committed at Atina by a band of youths who took advantage of an old privilege allowed at the scenic games, especially in country towns. What a tribute to the propriety of my client's youthful days. He is reproached with an act which he was permitted by privilege to commit, and yet even that reproach is found to be baseless.[36]

Any too open association with the theater put a woman's respectability at risk. An affair with an actor was heinous. Even entering the theater as a spectator could compromise any but the most careful. In an erotic manual from the next generation, the poet Ovid recommends the theater as *the* place above all others to find "girls." The immorality of the environs was presumably thought to be infectious.[37]

This was the world into which the theatrical metaphor cast Clodia. This and the image of the prostitute (Cicero further developed the image of the prostitute insinuating, along with Caelius himself, that Clodia accepted payment for sexual favors) constituted the high price paid for a public profile. The literature concerning the political influence of women in the late Republic is such that modern discussions can lump together (even if not disregarding the differences among) Clodia, Sempronia, and other aristocratic women on the one hand and Chelidon and Praecia on the other. The former would have been scandalized—as was, indeed, the intention.[38]

This selective survey might conclude with a look at the image of Servilia. This woman was twice married, first to a noble executed during the civil war in 77 B.C. and second to a man who reached the consulship in 62 B.C. and died shortly afterward. She remained particularly close to, and was reputed to carry great influence with, her half brother Cato, the conservative gadfly of Republican politics during the final turmoil. Marriage connections linked her to a great many other noble houses. A personal friendship linked her with Julius Caesar; her son Brutus was one of the chief assassins of Caesar in 44 B.C. These connections ensured that Servilia was center stage during much of her widowhood.

Apparently her relationship with Cato could not be impugned on moral grounds, the propinquity of children raised together otherwise being a favorite target of political polemicists. Instead she was said to exercise "an almost maternal authority" over her brother. In itself this hardly discredited Servilia. The influence of mothers, even their advice on political matters, was respected in Roman society, as was the role of the widow. Of course, the suggestion did not say much for the credibility of the forty-year-old Cato, who was *not* her son. That was the intention of the remark: to damage Cato's credibility. In this instance, Servilia has been cast as the domineering dowager though the characterization is no more friendly than the casting of the scheming concubines. At the time when the "allegation" was made (for such it was), Cato was a praetor, and it was suggested that Servilia was in a position to make personal overtures that could affect the outcome of cases over which Cato presided and in which she chose to take an interest. She is cast in a stereotypical female role, a role that might be respected outside the political world, but one that was automatically untoward because of its inroads into the public domain.

Elsewhere Servilia is cast as the scheming concubine through her familiarity with Caesar, whose easygoing behavior in his private life made gossip an easy matter. In 59 B.C., during Caesar's first consulship, a curious overnight alteration in public disclosures over which Caesar was thought to have clandestine control and which affected the fortunes of Brutus led Cicero to the snide "observation" that "nocturnal interventions" had taken place. If Servilia were to influence public affairs, it would be insinuated that such influence had occurred in the bedroom, that the business necessarily was sordid. Middle age brought a new charge. She was cast as a procuress: It was claimed that she had introduced her daughter Tertia to Caesar's affections. (Tertia was married at the time to Cassius who would later be another of Caesar's murderers.)

But beyond all others Caesar loved Servilia, the mother of Marcus Brutus, for whom in his first consulship he bought a pearl costing 60,000 sesterces. During the civil war, too, besides other presents, he knocked down some fine estates to her in public auction at a nominal price, and when some expressed their surprise at the low figure, Cicero wittily remarked: "It's a better bargain than you think, for there is a third off (*tertia deducta*)." And in fact it was thought that Servilia was prostituting her own daughter Tertia to Caesar.

Suetonius's language leaves little doubt as to Servilia's role: She was now a *lena*. With prostitution and acting, procuring completes a triad of disreputable female pursuits, images of which Ciceronian "wit" could apply to politically active women.[39]

The *lena* was a ubiquitous figure in Latin literature, less vicious than the *leno* (male pimp) and perhaps less degraded, but extremely unattractive nonetheless. *Lenones*, whether male or female, were not persecuted by the law during the Republican period except that, like prostitutes, they suffered *infamia* and paid a special tax (and presumably had to declare themselves to the aediles). The fullest elaborations of the literary stereotype are found in the poet Propertius's vilification of the woman Acanthis and in Ovid's depiction of a bibulous aged madam whom he calls Dipsa. Propertius opens with a curse: "May the earth cover your tomb with thorns, bawd, and may your shade be parched with thirst, since you hate thirst. May your ghost find no rest among your ashes, and may vengeful Cerberus frighten your dishonored bones with hungry howl." Both women are portrayed as advising beautiful young protégées on the ways in which to milk lovesick admirers. Acanthis's advice includes the exhortation, "Spurn your oath, and down with the gods! Break all the laws of chastity; they bring but loss!'' The themes are traditional ones running back through old Roman comedy to Greek motifs. It ought to cause no surprise that the women are also thought to be exponents of magic, thus linking them to the more sinister arts in a peculiarly female way. They then become not simply objects of loathing but of fear. Nor was the theme of the mother as procuress uncommon in plays or in poetry.

Given that the *topos* is hackneyed, what is still remarkable is the vehemence (rather, violence) of the poets' antagonism toward these women who stand between them and the easy gratification of their social and physical desires. Ovid fantasizes about physical assault: "But my hands could scarce restrain themselves from tearing her sparse white hair, and her eyes, all lachrymose from wine, and her wrinkled cheeks. May the gods give you no abode and helpless age, and long winters and everlasting thirst!'' Likewise Propertius closes, as he opens, with a hateful curse. After a blood-curdling catalogue of repulsive physical features, he prays, "Let the bawd's tomb be an old wine-jar with broken neck, and over it, wild fig-tree, put forth your might. [Fig trees were thought to destroy funerary monuments.] Whoever loves, batter this grave with jagged stones, and mingled with the stones add words of cursing!'' Cicero's offhand characterization of Servilia's influence as that of *lena* was not a light jibe.[40] A woman who "went public'' risked being branded a "public woman'' and the forfeit of her respectability. Her role (alleged or real) would automatically be categorized as sordid or improper.[41]

Roman Republican women (with the opportunity and inclination to do so) necessarily wielded power *outside* office, and that was bound to lead to legitimate concerns with nonaccountable presences in any community committed to open government, however nominally. This problem was exacerbated by traditional attitudes as to what constituted appropriate exposure for women. Male associates of a Roman woman, mindful of *her* reputation and *their* dignity, would urge her to stay behind the curtain, if not out of the wings altogether. Their enemies would be quick to observe or to allege any rustlings in that curtain and to draw the woman into undesirable publicity. Even a woman conspicuous in the audience might suffer for her notability. So might her associates. Sexual allusions were common.

The Roman Republic knew women of influence. It respected many and admired a number. Yet even in the late Republic, when constraints were relaxed, antique standards of propriety prevailed, and active roles in public (outside the ceremonial) were rarely endorsed. If their role was to become celebrated, their reputations might suffer reproachful and vindictive redefinition.

NOTES

I gratefully acknowledge the benefits received from the various discussions during the conference at which this chapter was first delivered and from the comments of anonymous readers. I have gained much in understanding from discussing the topic with friends Margaret Beattie, Lea Beness, Sandra Bushell, and Shirley Fitzgerald and from many friendly arguments with Suzanne Dixon. They are not to be held accountable for my views.

1. For the first Artemisia, Herodotus, 7.99, 8.68, 87ff., 93, 101f.; Polyaenus, 8.53; Pausanias, 3.11.3. For the second, Cicero, *Tusculan Disputations* 3.31.75; Strabo, 14.2.17; Diodorus Siculus, 16.36, 45; Valerius Maximus, 4.6 ext. 1; Vitruvius, 2.8; Aulus Gellius, 10.18.

2. On Cloelia, Livy, 2.13; [anon.] *de viris illustribus* 13. Acceptable models: (Lucretia) Livy, 1.55f.; Dionysius of Halicarnassus, 4.64f.; (Volumnia) Livy, 2.40; Plutarch, *Coriolanus* 33–37; (Cornelia, a later *exemplum*) Plutarch, *T. Gracchus* 1; *C. Gracchus* 19. Unacceptable models: (Tarpia) Livy, 1.11; (Horatia) Livy, 1.26; Dionysius, 3.21; (Tullia) Livy, 1.46–48; Ovid, *Fasti* 6.585ff. The readiness of later Roman writers to cast all women of energy in the same mold has led even careful scholars astray. M. I. Finley (1968) accepts the picture and attempts a sympathetic explanation. J.P.V.D. Balsdon (1960) offers an even more naive defense of the silent majority.

3. On Teuta, Polybius, 2.4ff.; paraphrased by Dio Cassius, 12, frag. 49 (and Zonaras 8.19). The translations are from the Loeb editions. Polybius, a contemporary source, was not a Roman but a Greek hostage, yet it is clear that he reproduces the Roman version of events (Harris 1979, 171).

4. As regards contemporary propaganda, only one fragment of her enemy Octavian's own memoirs is preserved (fragment 14, Servius, *Commentary on Virgil's Aeneid* 8.696), but the gist of that propaganda clearly survives in the contemporary poets, Virgil, Horace, and Propertius. A lengthy speech of Octavian on the subject is retailed by Dio Cassius, who elsewhere cites the memoirs as a source. They were probably the source at this point also.

5. Livia as the patron of Samos: Reynolds 1982, no. 13 (an official imperial response on stone formally acknowledging Livia's championing of the island—unsuccessfully, as it turned out). Family conference in 44 B.C.: Cicero, *Letters to Atticus* 15.11.

6. On the considerable resources available to some women, see, for example, Dixon 1983, 1984, 1985; cf. Gardner 1986, 233–40. On the strong role of the Roman mother, see Dixon 1988; although see my caveat, Hillard 1983. Dixon's rather quick (and totally speculative) psychoanalysis of my "position" (1988, 9 and 188, n. 51) avoids the point. Judith Hallett (1984) has argued for the central role of daughters in the Roman aristocratic family.

7. Fewer families than imagined maintained their position within the nobility (Burton and Hopkins 1983, 31–119. Leading social roles: There are parallels (although the situations are not strictly analogous) with the social *cum* fashionable elite (and its leading hostesses) of New York in the later part of the nineteenth century. On Roman urbanity and its changing rules, see Ramage 1973, 52–76. Diction of *matronae*: Cicero, *On Oratory* 3.45; cf. *Brutus* 211; Quintilian, *Institutes of Oratory* 1.1.6.

8. See the very useful remarks on the important symbolism of wool making and its typification of *pudicitia* by R. M. Ogilvie 1965, 222. *Pudicitia*, a virtue personified as a goddess in Rome, embodied chastity and modesty. The modern survival of such a notion is demonstrated by the "advisability" of a British prime minister, if a woman, being photographed with a shopping cart as proof that she has not abandoned traditional

roles. On the riot in 52 B.C.: Asconius, *Commentarii*, p. 38, ed. Stangl. On the aristocratic house: Vitruvius, *On Architecture* 6.5.2.

9. For an elaboration of the distinction, see Elshtain 1981 *passim*. See, however, the exhortations of Siltanen and Stanworth (1984); and the argument of Saxonhouse (1985), reading a more balanced view in the mainsprings of Western political thought. With regard to Rome, Saxonhouse (1985, 95) usefully points out that "public affairs" were not seen as the preserve of men in general, but only of certain men. This status consciousness *might* have facilitated the entry of privileged women into that world. Instead, the attitudes that are illustrated below and were effective on women coming from the upper echelons of society (see notes 10 and 11) meant that conceived levels of legitimate involvement in the public political processes placed those women allegedly making inroads doubly out of line. Saxonhouse (1985, 99) indicates where Cicero, in a unique philosophical reference to women, explicitly departs from his Platonic model, consigning women to subjection in the private realm. On the other hand, she argues that the Roman historical tradition recognized women as individual participants in the political processes, "[becoming] important when they emerge from the limits of the household and influence political activity directly" (123–24). She demonstrates quite clearly (107–24) the extent to which the Romans did not distinguish between public and private morality, but the evidence supporting her concluding assertion could as easily be read to indicate that women were elevated as models to be emulated precisely when the public world cruelly invaded their private realms (Livy); and vice versa when they, in turn, invaded the public (Tacitus). In Greece, the distinction was architecturally reinforced with women's quarters upstairs to restrict social commerce of a public nature (Pomeroy 1976, 79–84). Archaeological confirmation: Walker 1983, 81–91. For a full discussion of the distinction between *oikos* and *polis*, see Humphries 1983, 1–21.

10. Aulus Gellius, *Attic Nights* 1.23. Repeated: Macrobius, *Saturnalia* 1.6.19–25. It is almost certainly unhistorical but that matters little. The historical accuracy of the tale was of no great concern to its purveyors (Balsdon 1962, 318, n. 15). A similar anecdote is told by the moral philosopher Plutarch (de *garrulitate* 11 = *Moralia* 507B-F).

11. Pliny, *Letters* 4.19. Cf. *Letters* 6.4 and 7; 7.5 (all written to Calpurnia herself) where business keeps Pliny from her.

12. On the change in style of government, the new secrecy, and consequent historiographical problems, see the apposite remarks of the historian Dio Cassius, 53.19. On Agrippina, Tacitus, *Annals* 12.37; 12.42; 13.5. It might be noted that Tacitus divulges the last item in the context of reporting that a Senate resolution went through despite the opposition of Agrippina. It should also be noted that the last reference cites an occasion on which Agrippina attempted to trespass the crucial threshold by mounting the emperor's tribunal during the reception of a foreign delegation. She was thwarted by the spontaneous action of Nero's tutor Seneca who, "while others stood aghast, admonished the sovereign to step down and meet his mother: an assumption of filial piety which averted a scandal."

13. Appearances of Chelidon in Cicero's *Verrine Orations*: 2 *Verr.* 1.104; 106; 120; 136ff.; 2.38–39; 5.34. On the meaning of *chelidon*, see Adams 1982, 82n. Cicero's pun: Cic. 2 *Verr.* 1.104. "After Verres became praetor he took the auspices [this is usually the reading of omens by observing the flight of birds] while in the embrace of Chelidon."

14. On the importance of exposure in Rome, Cicero, *In defence of Plancius* 13; 63–66; Plutarch, *Cicero* 6. For the definition of *nobilitas*, see Gelzer ([1912] 1969: esp. 27–40 and 52), which has withstood recent attempts at its modification. *Lumen*: Cicero, *De*

re publica 6.12; Cicero, *On Duties* 2.44; Sallust, *The Jugurthine War* 85.23 (Loeb translation); Lucretius, *On Nature* 3.75–8. *In scaena*: Cicero, *In defence of Plancius* 29.

15. Crowding and expectations of entertainment: Valerius Maximus, 8.10.2; Cicero, *In defense of Caelius* I; Catullus, *Poems* 53; cf. Geffcken 1973, 11ff.

16. The translations of Cicero's *Verrines* 2.2.39 and 34 are from the Loeb edition except that the Latin *meretrix* is left where the translator has unnecessarily softened the translation with the word courtesan. Latin did not so finely distinguish, as will be discussed below.

17. On the sense of "apartness," see Frier 1985, 57–63. The poet Martial (11.98.14–19) cites a "mad kisser" who would not be deterred even by the dignity of the place. Dio Cassius (55.7.2) refers to a friend of Augustus who was unable to push through the crowds of bystanders while Augustus was conducting hearings. Yet he was able to press close enough to toss a tablet into Augustus's lap.

18. On prostitution, see Schneider 1931; Navarre 1900; Gardner 1986, 132–34, 250–53. (It used to be considered that the dress was legally prescribed. Gardner properly questions this assumption.) The wearing of "immodest" clothing exposed a woman to less respectful treatment in public. Laws against harassment precluded young girls dressed as slaves or women dressed as prostitutes (Gardner 1986, 118).

19. For example, the *proseda* ("one who sits outside" [a brothel]) and *prostibulum* ("one who is in front of an inn"). The verbs *prostare* ("to stand forward") and *prostituare* ("to be made to stand forward") came to acquire such a connotation; cf. Adams 1983, 329–32.

20. Famous examples: (Flora) Plutarch, *Pompey* 2; (Praecia) Plutarch, *Lucullus* 6. Talents: Balsdon 1962, 226f. Supporting a favorite: Livy, 39.9.2. Suitable expense: *ibid*. Avoiding criticism: Plutarch, *Pompey* 2. On this world, see Griffin 1985, *passim*., but esp. 88–111 and 112–41; cf. Wiseman 1985.

21. In 56 B.C., during his defense of a younger client, Cicero asserted the rights of young men to sow wild oats (Cicero, *In defence of Caelius* 48; cf. 28–30; 37–43; Plautus, *Curculio* 23–38; Horace, *Satires* 1.2.31). Yet Cicero's defense is just that—defensive and apologetic. It is clear that L. Herennius Balbus, Cicero's opponent in that debate, had clearly occupied the moral highground. For a useful survey of the traditionally acclaimed virtues, see Lind (1979). Lind's study, however, is flawed by its readiness to accept the (self-serving) pessimistic protestations of our moralizing sources.

22. Registering with aediles: Tacitus, *Annals* 2.85; Suetonius, *Tiberius* 35; cf. Gardner 1986, 130, 250. On Greek distinctions: Demosthenes, *Against Neaira* 122, distinguishes between wives, *hetairai* (who "give pleasure") and *pallakai*, personal slaves, owned concubines (who give "daily therapy for our bodies"). The *porne* is presumably not thought worthy of mention by the "fastidious" speaker. *Meretricula*: C. Sulpicius Apollinaris, *Summary of Terence's Mother-in-law*. On the (slight) difference between *scortum* and *meretrix*, see Adams 1983, 321f. Faecenia: Livy 39.9. Noble women: Gelzer [1912] 1969, 28–31, in a list of those designated *nobilis* by Cicero, gives only one female example, and that is double-edged (see below). Donatus, an ancient commentator on Terence's *Mother-in-law* (797), offers the information (somewhat gratuitously) that "both gladiators and *meretrices* are customarily called *nobiles*" (cf. Austin 1960, 89). A character in Terence's *Self Tormentor* (227) describes his "wayward" mistress (*meretrix* in the *dramatis personae*) as *inpotens* (in this sense, unbridled, headstrong), *procax* (insolent), *magnifica* (which ought to mean "eminent" but clearly, in context, is meant to imply "pompous" or "full of herself"), *sumptuosa* (extravagant), and *nobilis*. While

this assertion of Latin nuances is, I believe, uncontroversial, the distinction cannot be pushed to extremes. Livy calls Lucretia *nobilis*. There was, on the other hand, a range of qualifiers that could be applied to "respectable" noble women. (They are covered by Hellegouarc'h 1963, 464–66.) One was *lecta*, meaning "select[ed]" (in the sense of possessing desirable qualities): Cicero, *Catilinarian Orations* 4.13 (of the sister of L. Caesar); *The Defence of Fonteius* 46 (the mother of Fonteius); and the *Verrine Orations* 2.2.1.94 (of the wife of a quaestor). In all these cases the women were of senatorial rank (though the word could be used of the equestrian order, the next highest grade in Roman society). Another was *primaria*, meaning "of the first rank." This term could also be used with regard to the equestrian class, but in known instances is only applied to women of the grand families: Cicero, *Verrine Orations* 2.1.153 (Annia, daughter of P. Annius Asellus); 2.2.24 (Servilia, mother-in-law of Hortensius); 3.97 (wife of C. Cassius); and *Letters to his Friends* 5.11.2 (Pompeia, wife of Vatinius). Still another, which perhaps requires explanation, was *spectata*, used of Caecilia, daughter of Q. Caecilius Metellus Balearicus (Cicero, *Defence of Roscius of Ameria* 147). Originally carrying the sense "known," *spectatus/a* came to mean "illustrious," taking on an abstract quality with certain moral overtones (Hellegouarc'h 1963, 465–66; see esp. 465, n. 10). On the image of *meretrices* in Roman comedy, see Gilula 1980. Positive images, if they did appear, are the exception. In outlines of stock characters, Plautus and Terence recognized only "bad" prostitutes (*meretrices malae*): *The Captives* 57–58, and *The Eunuch* 37, respectively. Donatus, on the other hand, asserts that Terence, with some courage and daring, introduced the *bona meretrix* (774). Providing a review of actual characters in the extant plays, Gilula doubts this. All *meretrices* in Roman comedy, she argues, are *malae*, and Donatus is confused by the changed *mores* of his day (148–49).

23. On women in the entertaining and catering industries, see Gardner 1986, 245–50. On hot food outlets as places of ill fame, see *ibid.*, 132, 248–50. On consequent lack of respect and loss of legal protection from harassment, see *ibid.*, 130. The only way in which a proprietress could save her reputation was by proving that she did not herself serve customers (references in *ibid.*, 136, n. 49). The proud registration of a wide range of female occupations on humble tombstones may suggest otherwise (see examples in Lefkowitz and Fant 1982, 168–71); however, the wife of a butcher carefully records in her epitaph that she did not know the crowd (*Corpus Inscriptionum Latinarum* 1^2, 1221).

24. Chelidon: Cicero, *2 Verr.* 1.136. On *infamia* generally, see Greenidge 1894. Incapacity to witness: *ibid.*, 165ff. *Infamia* applied to women: *ibid.*, 171–76. *Infamia* and prostitutes: *ibid.*, 173–74; cf. Gardner 1986, 132–33.

25. For a critique of the available source material on politically active individual women, see Hillard 1989. On the "motive to avoid success," see Horner 1968. For a critique of this and subsequent studies, see Ward 1979; cf. Baxter and Lansing 1983, 48ff. Something of the elements necessary to instill this mentality seems to be present in Sallust's assessment of Sempronia's skills (discussed below) and in Plutarch's endorsement (*Pompey* 55.1–2) of the moderate use of her talents by Cornelia, daughter of Metellus Scipio and Pompey's fifth wife.

26. Clodia *nobilis*: Cicero, *In defence of Caelius* 31. For a discussion of the word's application, see note 22 above and further below. *Illa consularis*: Cicero, *Letters to Atticus* 2.1.5. Discussion: McDermott 1974. On Clodia, Cicero, *Letters to his Friends* 5.2.6; *Letters to Atticus* 2.1.5, 9.1, 12.2, 14.1, 22.5; Plutarch, *Cicero* 29. Cicero's eagerness to hear: Cicero, *Att.* 2.14.1. Charges of incest: Plutarch, *Cicero* 29. For the

fullest critique of the evidence relating to Clodia, see Skinner 1983. For the fullest recent coverage, see Wiseman 1985, esp. 15–53.

27. For the standard appraisal of Clodia's centrality, see Austin 1960, viii. Dorey 1958 (see esp. 175, n. 2 for further references) moves toward a proper exposure of Cicero's obfuscation of the issue, but still does not question sufficiently Clodia's role, the incidental nature of which he senses. Similarly see Ramage, who otherwise untangles Cicero's manipulation of images: 1984, 201, n. 1. Skinner's insightful analysis of the evidence in terms of rhetorical *topoi* (1983) moves in a different direction altogether, attempting to establish Clodia's strengths from the distorted information and believing that it is still possible to espy the real attributes of the historical Clodia that lent veracity to a "recognizable caricature of one particular individual" (285).

28. Baiae: Cicero, *In defence of Caelius* 47–50. Skinner (1983, 285–86) usefully highlights Cicero's opportunity to turn Clodia's visibility, "her recognized affluence and autonomy into a weapon against her."

29. In his dying moments, the emperor Augustus made the equation easily: Suetonius, *Augustus* 99.1. Compare his words with Plautus, *Mostellaria* 1181.

30. Cicero, *On Oratory* 3.83, 220; Quintilian, *Institutes of Oratory* 11.3, 86, 111, 181; Valerius Maximus, 8.10.1. Cicero, Rome's greatest orator, and Roscius, arguably Rome's greatest actor, used to compete in their powers of expression: Macrobius, *Saturnalia* 5.14.11; cf. 3.14.11.

31. A certain moral reserve which always greeted such skilled insincerity (as was called for in acting) persisted throughout the Graeco-Roman period: Plutarch, *Solon* 29.5 (Solon to Thespis, "founder" of the art); Cicero, *On Oratory* 3.214 (on the "imitators of truth"). Loss of reputation: Plutarch, *Sulla* 2, 36.

32. The law: Suetonius, *Augustus* 45.3. Use of the lash: Tacitus, *Annals* 1.77, assuming that the conservative proposals of A.D. 15 harkened back to this "ancient law." *Infamia* and the acting profession: Tertullian, *On the spectacles* 22; Augustine, *City of God* 2.13; Greenidge 1894, 7, 34–35, 67–68, 124, nn. 3 and 4 (for the relevant legislation); cf. 170 and n. 3. For the moral *cum* social disgrace of appearing as a mime, see Macrobius, *Saturnalia* 2.7.3.

33. The attack: Cicero, *In defence of Sestius* 116. Clodia's dancing: Scholia Bobiensia; 135 (ed., Stangl).

34. Guild: Garton 1972, 156, 306, n. 50. Mimes: *ibid.*, 147ff.; Gardner 1986: 246–47; cf. Antipater of Sidon, *Palatine Anthology* 9.567. The saintly Augustine records how the obscene rites performed by mime artists for some of the great Roman festivals were scene stealers. For source material on mimes and *mimica licentia*, see Wiseman 1985, 27 and n. 43, 13–14, nn. 46 and 47. Clodia and mime endings: Cicero, *In defence of Caelius* 64–69. Cicero's innuendo: Wiseman 1985, 28–29.

35. Cicero, *Letters to his Friends* 9.26 (with reference to the celebrated Volumnia Cytheris); cf. *Letters to Atticus* 10.16.5, 15.22; *Second Philippic* 20, 58, 69.

36. For the equation of *meretrices* and *mimae*, see Wiseman 1985, 48, n. 114. For such an equation from the early imperial period, see the melancholy anecdote concerning the admirable Quintilia: Josephus, *Jewish Antiquities* 19.33–36. Cicero against rape: *Catilinarian Orations* 4.12; *On the consular provinces* 6; *3rd Philippic* 31. The rape at Atina: Cicero, *Defence of Plancius* 30–31.

37. At Petronius, *Satyricon* 126, actors are classed with gladiators and dust-covered mule drivers as examples of the dregs of society. Women attending the theater: Ovid,

Art of Love 1.89–90: "Also the theatre's curve is a very good place for your hunting. More opportunity here, maybe, than anywhere else" (trans. Rolfe Humphries).

38. Allegations of Clodia's accepting money: Cicero, *In defence of Caelius* 62; Quintilian, 8.6.53; picked up by Plutarch, *Cicero* 29.

39. Cato *was* attacked for his close relationship with another stepsister: Plutarch, *Cato minor* 54.1–2. *Materna auctoritas*: Asconius, *Commentary on Cicero's defence of Scaurus*: 23 (Stangl). Motherhood and widowhood: Dixon 1988, see esp. 168–203. (On the other hand, I have argued elsewhere (Hillard 1983), in a paper with which Dixon disagrees *op. cit.* 9 and 10, that limits may have been placed on what was considered the proper influence of a mother.) "Nocturnal intervention": Cicero, *Letters to Atticus* 2.24.3. Tertia: Suetonius, *Divine Iulius* 50.

40. On *lenones*, *lenae*, and *lenocinium* (procuring), see Humbert and Lécrivain 1900: 1101; Gardner 1986, 131–32; cf. Balsdon 1962, 224–27; Griffin 1985, 114ff. *Infamia*: *Digest* 23.2.43. A particularly useful discussion of the procuress in Greek and Latin literature will be found in Gutzwiller 1985, 105–15 (even if one does not share the view that there is an element of sympathy in Propertius's treatment). The poems: Propertius, 4.5 (Loeb translation adapted by the omission of archaizing forms once considered suitable for the translation of Latin verse); and Ovid, *Amores* 1.8. The motif: Barsby 1973: 91ff., see 91, nn. 4 and 5 for reference to other poetry on the subject; Camps 1965, 96. Ovid himself (*Amores* 1.15.16–17) registers the "untrustworthy bawd" as one of the four staple characterizations of the Hellenistic playwright Menander. Magic: Tibullus, *Elegies* 1.5.59; Ovid, *Amores* 1.8.5ff; Propertius, 4.5.5–18; cf. Gutzwiller 1985, 113, n. 6 for further references. Mothers as bawds: Syra and Cleareta in Plautus's *Cistellaria* and *Asinaria* respectively (both women had formerly been prostitutes themselves) and Syra in Terence's *Mother-in-Law*. In the comedies, men are depicted as helpless victims of such women (*Asinaria* 178–80 and 215–21; *Mother-in-Law* 64–66, "Plunder, worry, harass every man you come across!"). Tibullus, *Elegies* 1.6.57–66 provides a relatively rare appreciation of a sympathetic mother. Although it should not be forced, I interpret Propertius's reference to Cynthia's mother at 2.15.20 (where he invites Cynthia to contemplate taking bruised limbs home to the old woman) as Camps, 1967, 126, tentatively allows. Certainly Cynthia's mother is spoken of as complicitous.

41. On vocal women, Valerius Maximus, 8.3. *Praefatio*, and 1–3, translated in Lefkowitz and Fant 1982, 206 (Reading no. 205).

REFERENCES

Unless otherwise stated, Loeb Classical Library texts (Heinemann/Harvard University Press) have been used throughout. These editions are always filed under the author's and not the editor's name.

Adams, J. N. 1982. *The Latin Sexual Vocabulary*. London: Duckworth.

———. 1983. "Words for 'Prostitute' in Latin." *Rheinisches Museum für Philologie* 126:321–58.

Austin, R. G. 1960. *M. Tulli Ciceronis Pro M. Caelio Oratio*. Oxford: Clarendon Press.

Balsdon, J.P.V.D. 1960. "Women in Imperial Rome." *History Today* 10:24–31.

———. 1962. *Roman Women: Their History and Habits*. London: Bodley Head.

Barsby, J. 1973. *Ovid: Amores I*. Oxford: Oxford University Press. [1979: Bristol University Press.]

Baxter, S., and M. Lansing. 1983. *Women and Politics*. Ann Arbor: University of Michigan Press.

Cadoux, Theodore. 1980. "Sallust and Sempronia." In *Vindex Humanitatis: Essays in Honour of John Huntly Bishop*, edited by Bruce Marshall, 93–122. Armidale,Australia: University of New England.

Camps, W. A. 1965. *Propertius: Elegies Book IV*. Cambridge: Cambridge University Press.

———. 1967. *Propertius: Elegies Book II*. Cambridge: Cambridge University Press.

Corpus Inscriptionum Latinarum I, 2. 1918, edited by Th. Mommsen. Berlin: Apud Georgium Reimerum.

Dixon, Suzanne. 1983. "A Family Business: Women's Role in Patronage and Politics at Rome, 80–44 B.C." *Classica et Mediaevalia* 34:91–112.

———. 1984. "Family Finances: Tullia and Terentia." *Antichthon* 18:78–101.

———. 1985. "Polybius on Roman Women and Property." *American Journal of Philology* 106:147–70.

———. 1988. *The Roman Mother*. London: Croom Helm.

Dorey, T. A. 1958. "Cicero, Clodia and the Pro Caelio." *Greece and Rome* 27:175–80.

Elshtain, J. B. 1981. *Public Man, Private Woman: Women in Social and Political Thought*. Princeton, N.J.: Princeton University Press.

Finley, M. I. 1968. "The Silent Women of Rome." In *Aspects of Antiquity: Discoveries and Controversies*, 129–42. London: Chatto and Windus.

Frier, B. W. 1985. *The Rise of the Roman Jurists: Studies in Cicero's Pro Caecina*. Princeton, N.J.: Princeton University Press.

Gardner, Jane F. 1986. *Women in Roman Law and Society*. London: Croom Helm.

Garton, Charles. 1972. *Personal Aspects of the Roman Theater*. Toronto: Hakkert.

Geffcken, Katherine A. 1973. *Comedy in the Pro Caelio*. Leiden, Netherlands: Brill.

Gelzer, Matthias. [1912] 1969. *The Roman Nobility*, translated with an introduction by Robin Seager. Oxford: Blackwell.

Gilula, Dwora. 1980. "The Concept of the *Bona Meretrix*. A Study of Terence's Courtesans." *Rivista di fililogica e instruzione classica* 108:142–64.

Greenidge, A.H.J. 1894. *Infamia: Its Place in Roman Public and Private Law*. Oxford: Clarendon Press.

Griffen, Jasper. 1985. *Latin Poets and Roman Life*. London: Duckworth.

Gruen, Erich S. 1974. *The Last Generation of the Roman Republic*. Berkeley: University of California Press.

Gutzwiller, K. J. 1985. "The Lover and the *Lena*: Propertius 4.5." *Ramus* 14:105–15.

Hallett, Judith P. 1984. *Fathers and Daughters in Roman Society*. Princeton, N.J.: Princeton University Press.

Harris, W. V. 1979. *War and Imperialism in Republican Rome 327–70 B.C.* Oxford: Clarendon Press.

Hellegouarc'h, J. 1963. *Le vocabulaire latin des relations et des partis politiques sous la République*. Publications de la Faculté des Lettres et Sciences Humaines de l'Université de Lille. Paris: Les Belles Lettres.

Hillard, T. W. 1983. "*Materna Auctoritas*: The Political Influence of Roman Matronae." *Classicum* 22:10–13 and 28.

———. 1989. "Republican Politics, Women and the Evidence." *Helios* 16:165–82.

Hopkins, Keith, and Graham Burton. 1983. "Political Succession in the Late Republic

(249–50 B.C.).'' In *Death and Renewal*, edited by Keith Hopkins. Sociological Studies in Roman History 2. Cambridge: Cambridge University Press.

Horner, M. S. 1968. *Sex Differences in Achievement Motivation and Performance in Competitive and Non-competitive Situations*. Ann Arbor, Mich.: University Microfilms.

Humbert, G., and C. Lécrivain. 1900. *"Lenocinium."* In *Dictionnaire des Antiquités Grecques et Romaines*, edited by C. Daremberg and E. Saglio, III.2, 1101. Paris: Hachette.

Humphries, Sally C. 1983. *The Family, Women and Death: Comparative Studies*. London: Routledge and Kegan Paul.

Jaher, Frederic C. 1975. "Style and Status: High Society in Late Nineteenth-Century New York." In *The Rich, the Well Born, and the Powerful: Elites and Upper Classes in History*, edited by Frederic Cople Jaher, 258–84. Urbana: University of Illinois Press.

Jory, E. J. 1986. "Continuity and Change in the Roman Theatre." In *Studies in Honour of T.B.L. Webster* I, edited by J. H. Betts et al., 143–52. Bristol, U.K.: Bristol Classical Press.

Lacey, W. K., and B.W.J.G. Wilson. 1970. *"Res Publica": Roman Politics and Society According to Cicero*. Oxford: Oxford University Press.

Lefkowitz, Mary R., and Maureen B. Fant. 1982. *Women's Life in Greece and Rome: A Source Book in Translation*. London: Duckworth.

Lind, L. R. 1979. "The Tradition of Roman Moral Conservatism." In *Studies in Latin Literature and Roman History I*, edited by Carl Deroux, 7–58. Collection Latomus 164. Brussels, Belgium: Latomus.

MacBain, B. 1982. *Prodigy and Expiation: A Study in Religion and Politics in Republican Rome*. Collection Latomus 177. Brussels, Belgium: Latomus.

McDermott, W. C. 1974. "Cic. Att. 2.1.5." *Classical Philology* 67:294–95.

Marshall, Anthony J. 1990. "Roman Ladies on Trial: The Case of Maesia of Sentinum." *Phoenix* 44:46–59.

Millar, Fergus. 1977. *The Emperor in the Roman World*. Ithaca, N.Y.: Cornell University Press.

Navarre, O. 1900. *"Meretrices* II. Rome." In *Dictionnaire des Antiquités Grecques et Romaines* edited by C. Daremberg and E. Saglio, III. 2, 1834–39. Paris: Hachette.

Nowotny, H. 1981. "Women in Public Life in Austria." In *Access to Power: Cross-National Studies of Women and Elites*, edited by C. F. Epstein and R. L. Coser, 147–56. London: Allen and Unwin.

Ogilvie, R. M. 1965. *A Commentary on Livy Books 1–5*. Oxford: Clarendon Press.

Pomeroy, Sarah B. 1976. *Goddesses, Whores, Wives, and Slaves: Women in Classical Antiquity*. New York: Schocken Books.

Ramage, Edwin S. 1973. *Urbanitas: Ancient Sophistication and Refinement*. Norman: University of Oklahoma Press.

———. 1984. "Clodia in Cicero's *Pro Caelio*." In *Classical Texts and Their Traditions: Studies in Honour of C. R. Trahman*, edited by David F. Bright and Edwin S. Ramage, 201–11. Chico, Calif.: Scholars Press.

———. 1985. "Strategy and Methods in Cicero's *Pro Caelio*." *Atene e Roma* 30:1–8.

Reynolds. Joyce. 1982. *Aphrodisias and Rome: Documents from the Excavations of the Theatre of Aphrodisias Conducted by Professor Kenan T. Erim, Together with Some Related Texts*. London: Society for the Promotion of Roman Studies.

Saxonhouse, A. 1985. *Women in the History of Political Thought: Ancient Greece to Machiavelli*. New York: Praeger.

Schneider, K. 1931. "Meretrix." In *Paulys Real encyclopaedie der Classischen Altertumswissenschaft*, edited by Georg Wissowa and Wilhelm Kroll, XV. 1, 1018–27. Stuttgart, Germany: Metzler.

Siltanen, Janet, and Michelle Stanworth. 1984. *Women and the Public Sphere: A Critique of Sociology and Politics*. London: Hutchinson.

Skinner, Marilyn B. 1983. "Clodia Metelli." *Transactions of the American Philological Association* 113:273–87.

Stangl, Thomas, ed. 1912. *Ciceronis Orationum Scholiastae*. Vienna: F. Tempsky.

Walker, Susan. 1983. "Women and Housing in Classical Greece: The Archaeological Evidence." In *Images of Women in Antiquity*, edited by Averil Cameron and Amélie Kuhrt, 81–91. London: Croom Helm.

Ward, C. 1979. "Is There a Motive in Women to Avoid Success?" In *Sex-Role Stereotyping: Collected Papers*, edited by O. Hartnett et al., 140–56. London: Tavistock.

Wiseman, T. P. 1985. *Catullus and His World: A Reappraisal*. Cambridge: Cambridge University Press.

4

Julia's Jokes, Galla Placidia, and the Roman Use of Women as Political Icons

Amy Richlin

Preserved in Macrobius's *Saturnalia* lies a group of jokes attributed to Julia, daughter of Augustus (39 B.C.–ca. A.D. 14). They constitute only the last of many accounts of a remarkably well-attested Roman woman: Her lurid story appears in the most nearly contemporary extant Roman historian, Velleius Paterculus, and it is retailed in turn by Seneca, Pliny, Tacitus, Suetonius, and Dio. We hear of her again from the antiquarian Macrobius in the fifth century. Historians today use these sources to determine what really happened to Julia, but this chapter instead considers how the Romans and others use prominent women as political icons. Texts by Roman women are so rare that the jokes compel attention; their double context—in Augustus's court in 2 B.C. and in the Christian Rome of the fifth century A.D.—lets us align a double set of implications. Overall this text supports several levels of inquiry: into the lives of Julia and her peers, into Roman political ideology, into the reuse of oral material, and finally into patriarchal ideology in general.

INTRODUCTION

Stereotypes of Western royal women are clearly linked to sexuality. At the center lies the normative model of the ruling woman as perfect wife and mother, the "first lady." Modern examples include Queen Victoria and Barbara Bush; ancient ones may begin with the Hellenistic queens, sometimes worshiped along with their consorts, prominent for their public works, and touted as patterns of wifeliness.[1] Augustus's second wife, Livia, cast herself in this mold, in the Roman tradition of female decorum (see esp. Flory 1984); we see few imitations among her successors, but the model returns in the Antonine women and in the much-memorialized Julia Domna, wife of Septimius Severus.[2] Macrobius's contemporary Eudocia, wife of the fifth-century Byzantine emperor Theodosius II, represents a tendency toward this model in the Christian empresses. The typical text that makes a first lady is the eulogy, citing her children, her dutifulness as a wife, and her modest comportment; the result resembles the standard ancient praise of good wives but sets the normal virtues in light of their value to the dynasty. These women produce legitimate heirs.

The advent of Christian asceticism made a new model possible: the celibate. Pulcheria, Eudocia's sister-in-law and rival, at an early age forswore marriage to live a life of exemplary Christian piety—a clear example of a ruling woman using this model to avoid the lessened status entailed by marriage (we may compare Elizabeth I of England). But Pulcheria derived much of her authority from the model of the Virgin Mary as Theotokos, mother of God, and from the doctrine that Mary had redeemed the inherent sinfulness of women by her double status as virgin and mother.[3] The model of the celibate here represents a transformation of the model of wife and mother; thus eulogies preserve this stereotype, too.

At the other extreme, some royal women are labeled promiscuous. This model exceeds the normal stereotype of the adulteress just as the model of first lady exceeds that of wife, by emphasizing the stakes: power and dynastic succession. The stereotype of the *meretrix augusta* seems also to be compelled by the oxymoron, and to be reacting against the first lady model. The typical text for such women is the racy anecdote: Their children are of dubious paternity, or they use birth control; they are adulterous or too often married; their dress and comportment are questionable. Julia's jokes provide a rare example of this stereotype supposedly professed by its objective correlative; more often the stories are hostile, as for the exile of Julia and her daughter Julia the younger, or for the fifth-century pair Galla Placidia, half sister of the emperor Honorius, and her daughter, Justa Grata Honoria. The stories grow with the power involved, culminating in a Cleopatra or a Catherine the Great.[4]

Thus images of ruling women range from the sexless celibate (has no mate) modeled on Mary who attained motherhood without sexuality, to the wife and mother (has one mate) who produces children but maintains perfect fidelity, to the promiscuous one (has many mates) whose maternity is only a byproduct of her sexuality.[5] Only occasionally can we tell how much of an image stems from real behavior, how differently the women involved perceived themselves, and whether the image was deliberately sought by them or was created by their families or enemies. In several cases, including those of Julia, Galla Placidia, and Justa Grata Honoria, conflicting stereotypes are applied to the same woman; in the case of Julia, the relation between the two is particularly clear.

Like ruling men, but unlike other women, women who rule appear in a wide range of especially formal media. Whereas an elite woman like Clodia or Sempronia appears in anecdotes, history, letters, law court speeches, and even poetry (suitably disguised), the odd benefactress or female relative takes her place in inscription or *laudatio*, and the simplest slave girl haunts the epigrams that deny her any individuality, ruling women duly appear in the same histories, eulogistic poems, speeches, coins, and (sometimes) monumental sculpture as do their male kin. Female virtues thus have for them a more specifically political use than for their female coevals, for the sexuality of these women is being consciously used by their male kin—and sometimes by themselves—to represent something else. So the icon covers over the woman inside it; the fascination of commentators at the time, and since, with such women is only the worship the icons elicit.

But why should ruling women's sexuality bear such significance? Why does the icon take this shape, and what is its use? Sherry Ortner links the high valuation of female purity with "states, or at least systems with fairly highly developed stratification." Rejecting functionalist explanations, she argues that female purity is valued where there is hypergamy, or "vertical alliance"—intermarriage between classes:

The assumption of hypergamy would also account for one of the major puzzles of the female purity phenomenon, namely, that the women of a given group are expected to be purer than the men, that upon their higher purity hinges the honor of the group. . . . the women are *not*, contrary to native ideology, representing and maintaining the group's *actual* status, but are oriented upwards and represent the ideal higher status of the group. . . . female purity . . . in fact . . . is oriented toward an ideal and generally unattainable status. The unattainability may in turn account for some of the sadism and anger toward women expressed in these purity patterns, for the women are representing the over-classes themselves. (Ortner 1978, 32)

For Roman women, we do not have to deal with Ortner's examples of sadism: branding the genitals or confinement to the seraglio. Nevertheless, we do have in Rome an actively hypergamous system in which contamination of women's purity leads to punishment. Applying Ortner's theory to Julia's jokes, we will have to ask what "over-classes," or what "unattainable status," may be represented by the purity of Roman imperial women.

JULIA'S HISTORY

The sources cited in the opening paragraph make up a patchwork narrative of Julia's life. Suetonius gives the greatest detail (*Aug*. 65). She was born, in 39 B.C., of Augustus's first marriage, to Scribonia (Suet. *Aug*. 63.1), which ended in divorce on the day Julia was born (Suet. *Aug*. 62.2; Dio 48.34.3). Augustus's second marriage, to Livia, soon followed, and Julia was raised in her father's house, where she was taught to spin and weave and was strictly chaperoned (then and afterward) in quasi-Republican austerity (Suet. *Aug*. 64.2). She would have been eight years old in the year of Actium (the beginning of Augustus's rule) and marriageable in 27, a year after her father first attempted to reform Roman marriage law. Suetonius reports Antony's claim that Augustus intended to betroth Julia to Cotiso, king of the Getae, in exchange for Cotiso's daughter

(*Aug.* 63.2); this claim must be seen in the context of the civil war and Antony's own extra-Roman alliance. Her first marriage, to the adored heir apparent Marcellus (Suet. *Aug.* 63.1), took place when she was fourteen, in 25 B.C., and lasted until Marcellus's death in 23. In 21 she was married to Agrippa (who had to divorce his wife, Marcellus's sister, Suet. *Aug.* 63.1), a marriage which lasted until his death in 12 B.C. In the course of these nine years Augustus's marriage laws were passed, with their strictures against adultery and rewards for production of children. Julia, traveling with Agrippa, bore him five children—three boys, Gaius, Lucius, and Agrippa (born posthumously), and two girls, Julia and Agrippina (Suet. *Aug.* 64.1). She was married off a year after Agrippa's death to her stepbrother Tiberius (Suet. *Aug.* 63.2), to whom she bore one child who died in infancy (Suet. *Tib.* 7.3). Tacitus says that she "scorned him as beneath her" (*Ann.* 1.53)[6]; Suetonius says that Tiberius married her with regret because he was forced to divorce his beloved wife for a woman whom he considered unchaste (*Tib.* 7.2).

Nine years later, with Tiberius in exile, amid great scandal Julia was exiled, charged with multiple adulteries (Vell. Pat. 2.100.3; Pliny *HN* 7.149; Suet. *Aug.* 65.1, 2–4). Velleius comments that the scandal broke in a glorious year that featured Augustus's dedication of a temple to Mars (2.100.2); this year also saw Augustus named *pater patriae*. Later writers add torrid details of Julia's nocturnal debaucheries in the Forum and on the rostra (Sen. *De Ben.* 6.32.1–2; Dio 55.10.12–13), especially near the statue of the satyr Marsyas (Seneca), which Pliny says she garlanded (*HN* 21.9). Seneca quotes Augustus's denunciation of her defilement of the very rostra from which he had put forth the adultery laws. Augustus chose an apparently remarkable manner of accusation of behavior now criminal: He made it public (*in publicum emisit, publicaverat*, Sen. *De Ben.* 6.32.1, 2; cf. Pliny *HN* 21.9 *litterae gemunt*), although Seneca adds he later regretted this. Suetonius says more specifically that Augustus "made it known to the Senate in his absence, a communiqué being read off by a quaestor" (*Aug.* 65.2), which Dio echoes (55.10.14); Tacitus's statement that Augustus exceeded the law "by labeling her crime with the weighty name of wounded piety and violated majesty" (*Ann.* 3.24) perhaps alludes to this communiqué. Augustus also caricatured normal procedure by sending Julia a divorce decree in Tiberius's name, prompting Tiberius to write from exile in his wife's behalf (Suet. *Tib.* 11.4).

Velleius gives a list of five adulterers, all bearing noble Republican names: Iullus Antonius (2.100.4), Quintius Crispinus, Appius Claudius, Sempronius Gracchus, and Scipio (2.100.5). He says there were many others, less illustrious, as well. The sources differ as to these adulterers' fates (Seneca *De Clem.* 1.10.3; Tacitus *Ann.* 1.53, 3.24). Dio (55.10.15) says that Iullus Antonius was executed with some other suspect aristocrats and that the rest were exiled to islands. This execution, Dio says, was on the grounds that Iullus was plotting a coup; Pliny hints this of Julia herself (*HN* 7.149), as does Seneca (*De Brev. Vit.* 4.5): "[O]nce again a woman to be feared with an Antony." The ex-

plicit analogy between Julia and Cleopatra recalls the feverishness of the propaganda against Augustus's old enemy, whose defeat at Actium with Antony
(Iullus's father) enabled Augustus to reign: Cleopatra was not only foreign but
also Egyptian and Eastern; she worshiped strange gods and was drunken and
profligate. Augustus declared war on her in lieu of Antony, and there were rumors that she wanted to take Rome itself (cf. Horace *Odes* 1.37); these are the
resonances of Seneca's jibe.

Suetonius mentions only a later plot involving an attempt to restore Julia (*Aug.*
19.2). Hers was a harsh exile, to the island of Pandateria (Tac. *Ann.* 1.53; Dio
55.10.14), where Augustus prohibited her from drinking wine and limited entrée
to those of whom he had an exact physical description (Suet. *Aug.* 65.3). Her
mother, Scribonia (*gravis femina*, Sen. *Epp.* 70.10), chose to go along (Vell.
Pat. 2.100.5; Dio 55.10.14), and there was a public outcry for Julia's return,
rejected in an assembly (Suet. *Aug.* 65.3; Dio 55.13.1). Eventually Augustus
moved her from Pandateria, Suetonius says, after five years (*Aug.* 65.3), to
Rhegium, according to Tacitus (*Ann.* 1.53). But there were stories of his anger:
When Julia's freedwoman Phoebe hanged herself when the scandal broke, he
said he would rather be Phoebe's father (Suet. *Aug.* 65.2; Dio 55.10.16); and
he called the two Julias and Agrippa Postumus his "three boils and three cancers"
(Suet. *Aug.* 65.4). Yet Julia seems to have communicated with her father from
exile: once, if Dio is to be believed, to bargain over Tiberius (55.13.1a). Her
father died leaving her out of his will and excluding both Julias from the family
tomb (Suet. *Aug.* 101); as for Tiberius, Tacitus hints that, on his accession, he
so straitened the terms of her exile as to bring on her death (*Ann.* 1.53; cf. Suet.
Tib. 50.1).

Others besides Augustus lump the younger Julia's exile for adultery in with
her mother's (Pliny *HN* 7.149; Tac. *Ann.* 3.24), and Suetonius adds that the
younger Julia's child, born in exile, was put to death (*Aug.* 65.4; see Barnes
1981).

These post-Augustan narratives all appear to be strongly colored by hindsight
and propaganda; when they mention Julia they are conscious of her spectacular
exit from Rome and her miserable end. They provide, nevertheless, some basic
facts: her strict upbringing, her immediate experience as a child and adolescent
of the realities of dynastic marriage, her exemplary fecundity as Agrippa's wife
and mother of the new heirs apparent Gaius and Lucius, the parallels between
Augustus's political progress and Julia's marriages, and the protest against her
exile by the people of Rome along with Augustus's remarkably public breast-
beating. The special position of daughters within the elite Roman family (Hallett
1984, 35–149) may explain the preoccupations of our sources. Still, as J.P.V.D.
Balsdon points out, they shy away from any description of Julia herself. Macrobius's version, Balsdon thinks, may come from the possible lost source for
Saturnalia 2: a collection of witticisms by the Augustan poet Domitius Marsus,
perhaps augmented by a slightly later collection.[7] Whatever his date, this collector
is also the only one to attribute to Julia words of her own.

Modern scholars, following the mainstream of the Roman sources, have debated what really happened in 2 B.C.: Was Julia an adulteress or a conspirator? (For a survey of arguments, see Ferrill 1980.) Thus, like their sources, they write from the end of a story that lacks her voice, only incidentally seeking Julia.[8] I would suggest that in looking at Julia's jokes in Macrobius's *Saturnalia* we are at once closer to her life, in a period before 2 B.C., and closer to the strategies by which this set of political events reached its conclusion.

JULIA'S JOKES

The *Saturnalia* is a fictional dinner party, in the tradition of symposiastic literature; its guests mostly discuss Vergil. In Book 2 they tell jokes, among which we find Julia's. The speaker, Avienus, begins with an *apologia*:

"Do you all want me to recount some sayings of his daughter Julia as well? But if I will not be thought garrulous, I want to preface this with a few remarks on the woman's morals, unless one of you has serious and edifying remarks to add here." When everyone urged him to continue with his undertaking, he began to tell about Julia with these words: "She was in her thirty-eighth year, a time of life, if her mind were still sound, verging on old age; but she was abusing the kindness of fortune as much as of her father, although otherwise a love of literature and much learning, which was easy in that household, along with a gentle humanity and a spirit in no way cruel, earned the woman great indulgence and favor, while those who were familiar with her vices marveled as well at such a contradictory personality." (2.5.1–2)

The section on Julia follows a group of stories about Augustus, and Avienus presents her as a sidetrack. He contrasts her sayings with "serious and edifying remarks" of the sort needed to critique her morals before proceeding. The anomaly of Julia's behavior apparently centers on her age; at thirty-seven (in the year of her exile) she does not conform to the rules for a mature woman. The supervisor for her behavior is her father; her audience is a double one— those whom she charms and those few who know what she really does. But this is a fiction, since those who hear the jokes are about to know all. Indeed the whole situation of vice, secrecy, and knowledge is a fiction whose purpose is to bring the audience into the circle of those who know about Julia. They all want to know, and Macrobius assumes his readers want to know, too.

So far Julia is established as a woman who acts too young, a woman who imposes on her father, a woman of education, and a woman who deceives people. Avienus continues his character sketch with an illustration:

Her father had warned her more than once, with his speech still tempered between indulgence and seriousness, that she should moderate her extravagant dress and her conspicuous entourage. Then when he had reflected on his crowd of grandsons and their likeness to Agrippa [her husband], he blushed to doubt his daughter's chastity. (2.5.3)

The text now projects Julia through the figure of her father; the conflict assumed in the signs of Julia's character reveals both what is feared and how those fears are translated. Her chastity is in question, but her father chides her only for external attributes—dress and companions—when he really means to tell her not to have sexual relations with any man but her husband. Julia's children and their resemblance to Agrippa become signs to balance against the others. Her anomalies—age, filial behavior, education, and deceit—thus combine with her dubious appearance to mark her as unchaste, while her childbearing and her father's blush mark her as chaste.

The jokes themselves, the first of which follows directly on this introduction, use the same criteria. They cover three main areas: Julia's personal appearance, including dress and hair; her relations with men, including her behavior as a daughter, marital status, affiliation with younger men, adultery, childbearing, and birth control; and her use of money and power. The series includes six stories about Julia (2.5.4–9) and one about Populia (2.5.10).

Text

(2.5.4) So Augustus cozened himself into believing that his daughter had high spirits leading to an appearance of shamelessness, but was free from guilt, and he dared to believe that, among our ancestors, Claudia had been such. And so he said among his friends, "he had two spoiled daughters, whom he had to put up with—the republic and Julia."

(2.5.5) She had come to him with a rather daring costume and had offended the eyes of her father, who said nothing. She changed the manner of her dress the next day, and embraced her father with an affectation of primness. But he, who had contained his pain the day before, could not contain his joy and said, "How much more proper this dress is for the daughter of Augustus!" But Julia was not at a loss to defend herself, with these words: "Why, today I decked myself for my father's eyes, yesterday for my husband's."

(2.5.6) Another famous one. Livia [Julia's stepmother] and Julia had diverted the attention of the populace to themselves at the show of gladiators because of the dissimilarity between their entourages; while serious and important men surrounded Livia, Julia was flanked by a flock of young men, and profligate young men at that. Her father warned her in a note that "she should notice how great a difference there was between the two first ladies." She replied elegantly, "These men with me will also become old men."

(2.5.7) This same Julia had begun to have grey hairs prematurely, which she used to pluck out in secret. Once a sudden arrival of her father surprised her dressing-maids. Augustus dissembled, though seeing that there were grey hairs on their clothing, and, drawing out the time with other topics of conversation, he introduced a mention of her age and asked his daughter "whether, after some years, she would rather be grey-haired or bald?" And when she had replied, "I would rather be grey-haired, father," he cast her mendacity up to her in this way: "Then why are those women making you bald so rapidly?"

(2.5.8) Likewise when Julia had heard a serious friend arguing that she would do better if she had modeled herself after the exemplar of her father's frugality, she said, "He forgets that he is Caesar, but I remember I am Caesar's daughter."

(2.5.9) And when those who knew of her sins used to marvel at how she gave birth to sons resembling Agrippa, when she made such public property of her body, she said, "Why, I never take on a passenger unless the ship is full."

(2.5.10) A similar quip by Populia, daughter of Marcus: To someone wondering why it is that other beasts never desire a male unless when they want to become pregnant, she replied, "Because they're beasts."

Analysis

The question of the appropriateness of Julia's appearance figures in three of the jokes—dress (2.5.5), choice of companions (2.5.6), and removal of grey hairs (2.5.7). The last is resolved to Julia's disadvantage; although this sign of old age is false, visited upon her too early, her father confronts her with a sentence to senility: She must be either grey-haired or bald. (That old women's ugliness included baldness was a commonplace in Roman jokes against women, cf. Richlin 1984.)

The jokes at 2.5.5 and 2.5.6 are resolved to Julia's advantage. In 2.5.5, improper dress is compared with proper. Augustus tells Julia that the second dress is more becoming to "the daughter of Augustus," *filia Augusti*; he emphasizes her position in his state. Her reply—the first dress was for her husband, the second for her father—redirects the emphasis to her family ties to men of different generations. She also implies that dress for the husband must naturally be too sexual for the father, pretending to speak in the conventional language of Roman kinship (cf. Hallett 1984, 102–9). But what the joke skirts (and thus stresses) must be the appeal of Julia's first dress to men besides her husband; the joke, like the dress, plays peek-a-boo with her sexual body. Augustus's euphemism allows Julia's manipulation, underscoring the hypocrisy of both participants (note her "affectation of primness"). She makes a fool of him.

In 2.5.6, Julia's entourage poses a similar problem. While her stepmother surrounds herself with elder statesmen (*graves viri*), Julia chooses profligate young men (*iuventus luxuriosa*). She resolves this, with insolent absurdity, by saying that her followers will also turn into old men (*senes*), here again changing the grounds from chastity to generational differences. Augustus's phrase *principes feminas*, "first ladies," like his *filia Augusti* in 2.5.5, only raises the stakes—a woman should be chaste, a royal woman all the more so. By sidestepping this issue, Julia belittles it; her answer belittles her elders as well.

Each joke asks: What behavior is appropriate for a grown daughter of an emperor. Dress, hair, and even companions serve as signs, and Julia's father attempts to make her abandon the signs of sexuality (the open body) for those of asexuality (the closed body). As at 2.5.3, promiscuity and illegitimate children form the unspoken signified. Julia hangs on to her sexuality by translating "sexual" as "younger" and "asexual" as "older," associating her father with asexuality. He only wins by associating her with age (2.5.7).

Julia's evasions here succeed because she (ab)uses the male generational categories in which Augustus thinks (resemblance of sons to father comforts grandfather); she subverts Augustus's discourse. The joke at 2.5.9 opens up his discourse along with Julia's body: On the one hand, she bears children who look like Agrippa; on the other, "she made such public property of her body." Her own resolution affirms this objectification. She calls her womb, pregnant with Agrippa's child, a full ship; her adulterers, apparently numerous and random, are anonymous "passengers"; she reduces the child to an implied cargo, merely a prerequisite for the taking on of passengers. Her metaphor not only adopts and transforms the common erotic image of woman as ship;[9] more radically, it shows that the signs on which the father most relies are unreliable (cf. 2.5.3).

Julia's attitude toward her children here parallels Populia's in 2.5.10, where Populia defines the dependence of sex on procreation as bestial. In Augustus's terms, legitimate children betoken a wife's chastity, and the point of chastity is the production of legitimate children. Julia's joke undercuts Augustus's system, making chastity unnecessary and legitimate children no proof of anything, not only a possible disguise for adultery but also a positive means of allowing adultery without fear. The shock of 2.5.9 and 2.5.10 comes (on the surface) from two noblewomen's rejection of the roles of daughter, wife, and mother, against the wishes of a father (cf. Hallett 1984); at a deeper level, surely the shock emanates from the claim of these female figures to control their bodies and their bloodline for their own sexual pleasure. Pregnancy normally signifies one of two things in histories of Roman women: either fulfillment of the role of wife, or evidence of unchastity, as was possibly the case with Julia's daughter and was certainly the case with Galla Placidia's daughter.[10] Julia and Populia assign unorthodox meanings to pregnancy—a serious iconoclasm in a society of ancestor worshipers. The joke's identification of Populia by her patronymic ("daughter of Marcus") reminds us that she, like Julia, throws doubt on the very assumptions underlying patronymics.

At the same time, the text denies the sexuality of women in previous generations. Augustus himself compares Julia with her ancestor Claudia (2.5.4), whose chastity had been doubted but vindicated, and contrasts her with her stepmother Livia (2.5.6). The text suppresses the scandal that surrounded the marriage of Augustus to the divorced and pregnant Livia (Suet. *Aug.* 62.2; *Claud.* 1.1); she here takes on the asexuality attributed to the older generation by Julia.[11] She does not even have any wifely sexual relations with Augustus, nor are her two children or Julia's mother Scribonia mentioned. Like Augustus's marriage laws, the jokes concern themselves with the regulation of women's sexuality only up to a certain age.

The figure of Julia only accepts being *filia Augusti* when this signifies an increase in power, rather than a limit. The joke at 2.5.8, which reproves Julia for her lack of frugality, is resolved by her statement that her father forgets that he is Caesar, while she remembers she is Caesar's daughter. She here literally entitles herself to money and power. The phrase *Caesaris filiam* recalls the loaded words of 2.5.5, *filia Augusti*, and of 2.5.6, *principes feminas*. But in the earlier jokes, where her father emphasized *Augusti*, Julia emphasized *filia*. Here, where his rank gives her privilege, she accepts it, though rejecting him as a model and reducing their relationship to a dynastic one. Once again the joke works by Julia's play with emphasis, and again she belittles Augustus and his values.

Thus we have a series of *dicta* attributed to Augustus's daughter, in which she embodies and arrogantly espouses behavior Augustus was seeking to thwart, both in the state and in his family. Whose icon is this Julia?

DOUBLE CONTEXT: FIRST CENTURY B.C.

Assuming these jokes go back to an Augustan source, we can set Macrobius aside for the moment and examine them first in an Augustan context. We can begin with the question of their origin and audience and ask whether the jokes may be anti-Augustan, and whether they may be women's humor. Then, considering the events of Julia's life and the rhetoric of Augustus's political career, and adducing some nonverbal evidence, we can look for an idealized picture of Julia against which to set these jokes. Finally, we can apply Ortner's hypothesis and consider what "unattainable status" may have been represented by the purity of this emperor's daughter.

The first joke (2.5.4) suggests the level of signification present here. Augustus is said to have drawn an analogy between Julia and the republic as his two "spoiled" (*delicatas*) daughters; the language comes from the warm affect of Roman father-daughter relations (Hallett 1984). But Augustus's head-shaking indulgence towards Julia in this joke actually signifies his control over her and his desire that she conform without coercion; likewise for the country as a whole, hence his moral legislation (for a summary, see Brunt 1971; 558–66; Richlin 1981; cf. esp. Dixon 1988; 71–103). Augustus was, in the year of Julia's exile, proclaimed *pater patriae*, "father of the fatherland"; the daughter becomes a living metaphor for the state. A Roman audience would find such a metaphor the more ominous in that Roman private law gave the *paterfamilias* power of life and death over all members of his household, a power that would be used especially to punish breaches of moral codes. The mapping of the morals of the body politic onto a woman's body was a common feature in literature of the Augustan regime, and the early books of Livy's history are littered with corpses of women whose living bodies had threatened to let corruption into the state (see Joshel 1991). This perhaps begins to suggest who listened to the jokes when they were new, and why they survived Julia's outlawry; to people who did not wish to be controlled, her obstinacy may have represented freedom.

We can, of course, not know whether the obstinacy was really hers. The figure of Julia in the jokes counters the figure of Augustus so outrageously that the stories seem a little unreal. But, from what Suetonius says about her girlhood, and from the simple facts of her birth, marriages, and pregnancies, the content of the jokes is consistent with Julia's experience. The ostentatiously strict upbringing results in a taste for display; the chain of broken marriages results in cynicism about the purpose of marriage; Augustus's incentive plan for marriage and childbearing is matched by an alternative plan. If these *dicta* were really spoken by the real Julia, she calls forth our sympathy as do few other Roman wits. (And, as a wit, she rubs shoulders with Cicero.) But the force of jokes goes far beyond the figure to whom they are attributed; though here the real Julia seems to stir within her icon, it is the icon that remains for us to examine.

There is some evidence within these jokes as to who told them, or who is supposed to have told them. The internal audience is restricted to those at Rome, usually to Julia's immediate circle. In 2.5.4, Augustus talks with his friends; while 2.5.6 concerns public behavior and comment by the *populus*, the real dialogue consists of a written message from Augustus to Julia, and her reply; the interlocutor in 2.5.8 is one of Julia's friends; 2.5.9 mentions "those who knew of her sins" (*conscii flagitiorum*). The only participants in 2.5.5 are Julia and her father; while in 2.5.7 the only other participants are Julia's maids.

The evaluative words used in the jokes define an audience that recognizes the norms Julia is breaking. The puritanical, old-fashioned plainness that Augustus wished to revive in Rome is associated with the behavior Julia usually rejects: Her stepmother's companions are *graves viri* (2.5.6), the friend who lectures her in 2.5.8 is *gravis amicus* and recommends *paterna frugalitas*. When Julia plays the role expected of her in 2.5.5, she embraces her father "with an affectation of primness," *affectata severitate*. Her normal behavior is associated with pejorative terms: "spoiled" (*delicatas*, 2.5.4), "rather daring" (*licentiore*, 2.5.5), "profligate" (*luxuriosae*, 2.5.6), "her sins" (*flagitiorum*), "such public property of her body" (*tam vulgo potestatem corporis*), the analogy between her body and a ship (2.5.9).

Yet, with all this, the joke teller and his audience do not make Julia the butt of the joke; in most cases (2.5.4, 5, 6, 8, 9), she gets the better of her father. There is a sense of being in on her secrets, one of the select circle who knew what she really did; with *qui vitia noscebant* ("those who knew of her vices," 2.5.2), compare *secrete* ("secretly," 2.5.7), "those who knew of her sins" (2.5.9). Moreover, those who comment on her anomalous behavior often do so with admiring wonder, never with disgust: *mirantibus* (2.5.2), *mirarentur* (2.5.9), with which compare Populia's interlocutor, *miranti cuidam* (2.5.10). Most telling of all, Avienus characterizes her retort in 2.5.6 with the epithet *eleganter*, an attitude Macrobius may well be picking up from his source.

The jokes that include Augustus manifest the joke teller's desire to control Augustus's behavior while allowing Julia free rein. In 2.5.3, he moderates his reproof of her, and then regrets having said anything at all. In 2.5.4, he fools himself and only speaks of her to his friends, and then indulgently, rather than chiding her. In 2.5.5 he holds himself in at first; in 2.5.6 he chides her only in a mild note, not face to face; in 2.5.7 he reserves his comment for a later time. On the other hand, in 2.5.7 he does have the last word, and the joke depends on the circumstance that he walked in on her while she was dressing.

The original audience for these jokes, then, is made up of people who wished Augustus had less power to interfere with *mores* than he did but were familiar with the wide range of his actual power and desire to interfere. They had internalized the values Augustus wished to enforce, but could tolerate infringement of these values. They seem to have been decidedly of Julia's generation, or younger, seeing Livia's friends as *senes* and Augustus as past sexuality. They wished to seem to be in the know about goings-on in court circles. And of course the jokes may have originated outside the court, among people who were watching it for signs of their own fate. All these things considered, it seems quite possible that these jokes were told, and spread, by the senatorial and equestrian women of Rome.

And if the jokes were indeed collected by Domitius Marsus, this would set them in an all-too-familiar context—the social and literary circles that surrounded both Julias. A protégé of Maecenas who wrote a lament for Vergil and Tibullus, remembered by Ovid in exile, classed by Martial with Catullus for the lasciviousness of his epigrams (1.intro.), Domitius also wrote an epic on the Amazons which Martial characterizes as both *levis* ("facile" or "sophisticated/graceful/light") and long (4.29.8). This makes it an apt companion piece for his book *De Urbanitate*, a careful study of the theory of humor. His poem on the Amazons might well have appealed to those who told the jokes about Julia—and perhaps also listened delightedly to Ovid's *Ars Amatoria*.[12] And such a circle might equally have inspired the description of Julia in Avienus's introduction, with its emphasis on her "love of literature and much learning," and on how her (Julian) virtues ("gentle humanity," "a spirit in no way cruel") "earned the woman great indulgence and favor." Marsus also praised the literary acumen of Caecilius Epirota, whose suspected seduction of Agrippa's first wife Augustus had found seriously unamusing (Suet. *Gramm*. 16); the publication of a collection that included these jokes may well have been intended to embarrass the *princeps*.

But perhaps the *princeps* could not only tolerate the jokes but could actually use them. He did cultivate a reputation for tolerance of such things (Sen. *De Clem*. 1.10.3; Macrob. *Sat*. 2.4.19), and this would certainly make their survival easier to understand.[13] After all, the jokes damn Julia's morals thoroughly, and out of her own mouth, while Augustus remains benevolent and indulgent throughout, at worst paternal. Moreover, no matter how the jokes side with Julia, we can assume that such a publication of her vices (and shadow on her sons' paternity) would have pleased her stepmother Livia, especially after 2 B.C.—as it would have continued to suit Livia's son Tiberius to have Julia remembered as a wanton betrayer of Augustus.[14] Avienus (2.5.2) begins his narrative by placing Julia in the year of her exile—a more than convenient time for her character to be painted black. We recall the public outcry for her return. The date may well have been grafted onto the jokes, either by Macrobius or by an earlier collector. For the situation portrayed in the jokes is not that of Julia's last year in Rome. Three times mention is made of Agrippa, or of a husband (2.5.3, 5, 9); 2.5.3 concerns children, 2.5.9 actual pregnancy. Conceivably the jokes may have been circulated in written form at the time of the exile, but a joke about Julia and Agrippa must come from his lifetime. Whoever collected and published them, pro- or anti-Julia, was using them outside their original context.

If the jokes really favor Julia, does anything, apart from the question of *cui bono*, mark them either as women's humor or as radical humor? The very existence of subversive humor has only recently been theorized; Julia's jokes provide an extremely rare Roman test case. Without native informants, we must rely on comparison and extrapolation, using social science models. First of all, it is a commonplace in anthropological theory that jokes that oppose social rules in fact reinforce them, since stories of outrageous behavior sharply define what is normal.[15] Yet this does not account for the possibility of genuinely revolutionary humor. Why is a joke about the powers that be different from a joke about powers about to be ousted? One recent study differentiates on the basis of the degree of power imbalance within the joke. Where common jokes about authority figures (e.g., policemen) are conservative, jokes about inflated authority figures who brutalize the protagonist of the joke (e.g., policemen as "pigs" beating demonstrators) are radical (Webb 1981). But surely such humor does little more than recognize an emphasized hierarchy; and in any case, Julia's jokes are not so extreme. They protest in the manner of any oppressed group.

But Julia's jokes certainly differ from the usual Roman jokes about women, which create and deride a consistently negative stereotype (Richlin 1984; cf. Chapman and Gadfield 1976), or blacken a noted woman's reputation to get at her family (Skinner 1982, esp. n. 33). Julia's behavior may be bad, but, within the joke, she is admired. She is verbally adroit; the point is not so much her promiscuity as her strength. And she gets the better of her father. The Hellenistic collections of the witticisms of famous Greek prostitutes—preserved in Athenaeus *Deipnosophistae* 13, in Alciphron, and recalled in Lucian's *Dialogues of the Courtesans*—remind us of Julia's jokes. In Latin, only in comedy do we see a woman have the last word like this. Odd company for the emperor's daughter; the parallels only heighten the contrast.

So although Julia's jokes may not have been revolutionary, they are likely to have been repeated by those who rejected traditional female norms. Joanne Cantor's 1976 studies of gender and joking found that most people surveyed disliked jokes in which a woman wins out over a man; the only exceptions were active feminists. Men and traditional women found jokes in which men bested women much funnier (Cantor 1976; cf. Neitz 1980). The late first century B.C. had no women's movement, but it was certainly a time when tradition became politicized (cf. Hamer 1988).

Does the content or structure of the jokes mark them as female rather than male? It has been suggested that women's oral humor follows patterns unlike those of male humor.[16] And it would be pleasant if we could believe that the hostility and machismo of mainstream humor were counterbalanced by a humor showing "female" traits—a humor without aggression. Marie Maclean (1987) summarizes arguments for the existence of "oppositional practices" by which the weak subvert the power of the strong; she attributes these especially to women's oral narrative (cf. Davis 1975). Cantor's study suggests, however, that human acculturation is so male biased that most women take on a male viewpoint in their humor preferences, incorporating self-hatred into "femininity." Co-optation must always weigh against subversion.

Still, Julia's jokes do without physical aggression, while she is decidedly assertive and opposed to norms. If the women's humor described by Green and by Johnson (n. 16) can be aligned with joking of other underclasses, which satirize their victimage as a sort of survival training (see also Walker 1988), then Julia's jokes suggest that assertiveness in jokes rises with the amount of perceived power—as, in Cantor's study, feminist women were able to perceive female dominance as funny. That is, the degree of assertiveness in a social group perceived as funny by any member of the society will rise according to the amount of control exercised by that group. So, for Julia's jokes to have been popular at all, women in Rome must have been feeling their strength, and men in Rome must have recognized it.

Of course, there is no happy ending; Julia died in exile. The jokes are a curiosity for Rome: an example of the deliberate use of a traditionally negative stereotype to represent something positive, here self-assertion in the house of a *princeps*. They must have been told in the period of her marriages, before her exile—coexisting with the many positive images of Julia, perhaps reacting against them—by a group that expected to survive and prosper. The exile of the real Julia shows who really controlled the stereotypes.

What were Julia's positive images? On July 4, 13 B.C., with Agrippa ensconced in the imperial favor as father of the heirs apparent, Augustus consecrated the site for the Ara Pacis. He still stands there, carved on its side, *en famille*, amid emblems of Julian and Roman fecundity.[17] In that same year, two of the three moneyers give prominent space to Agrippa, while Julia herself is thought to appear on three coins of the moneyer C. Marius. Especially pertinent here are *RIC* 404 and 405 (plate 7), on which Julia's head appears beneath a wreath, flanked by the heads of her sons Gaius and Lucius; the obverse of these coins depicts Augustus (Sutherland and Carson 1984, 72). This constitutes a remarkable honor paid to an achievement of the real Julia by the year 13 B.C.—her production of the imperial heirs. Even Livia, who is often claimed to appear on coins of Tiberius in allegorical guise (e.g., Giacosa n.d., 24; cf. Sutherland and Carson 1984, 87, 96), makes no monetary appearance *in propria persona*. A Tiberian coin with the legend *SPQR Iuliae August.* shows only a *carpentum* (*RIC* 51, plate 12), the two-wheeled carriage that was the sign of a respectable *matrona*.[18] Instead we find her buttressing the political message of the Ara Pacis with a shrine to Concordia, dedicating this temple of wifely affection on the Roman equivalent of Mother's Day (Flory 1984).

In this firmament shone Julia's star, her face stamped onto money in her role as *genetrix*. Suetonius tells us how her father's clothes attested that she spent time spinning and weaving (*Aug.* 73); courtly poetry inscribed her maiden betrothal to Marcellus (Cameron 1980). Later, the dead and perfect wife Cornelia, in a poem by Propertius, imagines Augustus mourning her as worthy to be Julia's sister (4.11.59; Hallett 1984, 53–54). Thus the authorized version in the period before the exile portrays Julia, with enormous publicity, as playing the role expected of her. For Augustus she was an important icon of wifehood and motherhood, in a state in which he had just made adultery a criminal offense. For some Romans, this was a joke.

As summarized by Gordon Williams (1978, 68–69), the rhetoric of 2 B.C. conforms with the iconography of Julia before her fall as much as it conflicts with the iconoclasm of Julia's jokes. The "emphasis on home and family" in Messalla's speech bestowing the title of *pater patriae*—a title inscribed on the porch of Augustus's house—tallies with Augustus's insistence on public exposure and on listing the public places desecrated by his daughter. Rome has become his house, public space has merged with private, a letter to the Senate and an assembly of the people of Rome take the place of the family council. The temple he dedicated in the year of her exile was to Mars the Avenger, and "housed the deities of Mars, Venus Genetrix, and Divus Julius—a symbol of the family . . . that had brought him to power." If, as Williams suggests and seems likely, Augustus had been planning Julia's exposure for some time, the gods he installed in 2 B.C. make a fit trinity to supervise it: Mars the Avenger, father of the Roman people; Mother Venus, mother of Aeneas; and the deified Julius Caesar, who in turn was Aeneas's descendant and Augustus's adoptive father. The temple officially closed (and marked) his debt to the slain Caesar; but in effect this temple was a shrine to Augustus's ancestors—all gods.

This context perhaps suggests what "unattainable status" was represented by Julia's purity, and also what "overclass" the emperor's daughter could possibly marry into. As he tried to make her life conform with the *mos maiorum*, the "way of the ancestors," so she is to continue the divine line of Caesars. Reaching childbearing age in fact catapulted Julia into the divine, into the future of the dynasty, and into the past of the *maiores*. The human sexual level was not for her; the jokes, as well as the tales of her enormities, represent the opposite extreme of ideology (cf. Populia's "because they're beasts").

DOUBLE CONTEXT: FIFTH CENTURY A.D.

To return to our text with a double context: What were these jokes doing in Macrobius's book? It seems safe to assume that Pulcheria, in Byzantium, would have been "not amused" by Julia's jokes; how far were such attitudes prevalent in the West? What is the meaning of a nostalgia that includes this sort of emperor's daughter? And were there any fifth-century equivalents of Julia's jokes and Julia's coins?

In light of the nature of the *Saturnalia* and its participants, the presence of the jokes about Julia in this text is at first surprising. Alan Cameron's discussion (1966) fixes the *Saturnalia* in the tradition of the nostalgic dialogue, set in a revered past at a poignant date just prior to the death of the chief participant—in this case Praetextatus, leader of the last great generation of Roman pagans (for a description of this group and their history, see Bloch 1963). The text thus has a redoubled context, that of the date of publication (probably the early 430s A.D.) and that of the dramatic date, December A.D. 384. Despite the quiet and apolitical tenor of the conversation, the setting two years before Flavianus's suicide at the Frigidus bespeaks a political intent. Yet the conquered who rule this Saturnalia stand for no unbridled license; as Robert Kaster has shown (1980), the structure, the protocol, and the content of the *Saturnalia* manifest a rigid hierarchy, an insistence on continuity between past and present, and a high-minded morality, all encapsulated in the virtues of *verecundia* ("modesty/chastity") and *diligentia*. A less likely setting for Julia's jokes can hardly be imagined, unless we bear in mind the object of the *Saturnalia's* nostalgia: the Augustan past and the heritage of the pagan aristocracy.

Macrobius introduces the whole section of jokes in the *Saturnalia* (2.2–2.7) as a memento of "ancient and noble men" (2.1.8), and indeed, as Kaster points out, it is the first barrage of jokes (2.2) that demonstrates the *ordo* ("protocol") of the dialogue (1980, 228). Their presence would seem to foster hierarchy, then; but what of the subversive content of Julia's jokes? The speaker, Avienus, starts out in the dialogue as a doubter of the value of the past, a brash young man who learns better, unlike others at the table.[19] Avienus tells most of the jokes (2.4–2.7), and, as Cameron notes (1967, 396), wins only praise from the other guests (2.8.1). His jokes both provide a Saturnalia's obligatory *lascivia* and represent a beginner's effort at reverence for the past.

Macrobius clearly feels some unease about Julia's jokes; we recall the apology he puts into Avienus's mouth at 2.5.1–2. He later again marks the series as a departure from the other jokes in Book 2 (all of which, in fact, have male protagonists), sharply demarcating the end and unity of the section with the words of Avienus which open 2.6.1: "But, that I might revert from women to men and from lewd (*lascivis*) jokes to respectable (*honestos*) ones." The alignment of women with lewd jokes and men with respectable ones is clear. Symmachus had initiated the whole series at 2.1.8 with the suggestion that the guests make "sprightliness without lewdness"(*alacritatem lascivia carentem*) the subject of their after-dinner conversation (he specifically decries vulgar humor). The jokes continue through 2.7.19. Of all 105 jokes, only six besides Julia's concern women at all; in five of these (2.2.5, 6, 9; 2.4.12, 20), the point is that the women are adulterous, while the sixth (2.2.11) concerns the high prices of the prostitute Lais. But none of these jokes has a protagonist like Julia; despite the label *lascivis*, her jokes stand out from the other, more stereotypical jokes.

In fact Roman anecdotes featuring a single female protagonist are altogether unusual. The other series of jokes in Macrobius *Sat.* 2 feature men, most notably Cicero (2.3.1–16) and Augustus (2.4.1–31). Women do appear in moral *exempla* and *ainoi*, but most are one-shots, which describe either paradigmatically good behavior (Cornelia: "These are my jewels," Valerius Maximus 4.4.*pr.*) or paradigmatically bad behavior (Claudia: "I wish my brother were alive to lose another fleet," Valerius Maximus 8.1.4). As we have seen (above, n. 11) the sayings of Livia emphasize virtues the reverse of Julia's vices. The jokes about Julia constitute the only extant series of stories with a clever woman as protagonist. Of all the stories Macrobius had to choose from, why preserve these?

It was emphatically not the case that the tradition of praise and blame of women, with its rigid list of virtues and vices, had fallen into abeyance (see Lefkowitz 1981; cf. Atkinson 1985 on the construction of St. Monica). In looking backward, Macrobius could call on a list of exemplary empresses that stretched from the women of Trajan's house to Dio's encomia of Julia Domna to the much-praised Christian empresses, from Helena to his contemporary, Pulcheria (sources above, n. 2). Even for commoners, the ideal of the *univira* ("woman married only once"), such a feature of late Republican moral praise, flourished in fifth century Rome (Williams 1958; Lightman and Zeisel 1977). We can see the ideals of Macrobius's own characters in the famous epitaph of Praetextatus and his wife (*CIL* 6.1779), which gives her a list of virtues that would be at home in the Republic, and certainly includes chastity: "putting her husband before herself"; "chaste, faithful, pure in mind and body, kind to all, useful in her home"; "kindling of modesty, chain of chastity"; "with the *pietas* of a mother, the dearness of a spouse, the closeness of a sister, the deference of a daughter"; "helping her husband, cherishing him, ornamenting him, caring for/ worshiping (*colens*) him." But for Christian women, another ideal was becoming important: asceticism.

In fact, in the late fourth and early fifth centuries, we find a split between various ideas of correct female behavior even more traumatic than the division induced by Augustus's moral legislation. As described by Peter Brown, the aristocratic families of Rome who accepted Christianity did so largely through their female members, who eventually began to adopt asceticism, even, as in the case of the younger Melania, to the detriment of their pregnancies and patrimonies. Melania was active in the 430s, the decade that saw the *Saturnalia* published (Brown 1961, 1988; Corrington 1986; and cf. McNamara 1984 on these women's self-empowerment through asceticism, refusal to bear children, and female bonding—especially mother-daughter). But not all Roman women pursued these goals, and Christian moralists found women to frown upon who were unsatisfied with one or no husband; Ambrosiaster complains that now, since Julian's edict, women have the power to divorce their husbands, and are doing so "daily."[20] What we see here is that not only have the traditional Roman female virtues survived, they have been exceeded and subverted by the new

Christian female virtues. Women's behavior is now scrutinized and prescribed not only by an Augustus (or Theodosius), but also by a Jerome.

To the pagan aristocracy, the ideals of asceticism were extremely threatening, undermining as they did the old ideals of fecundity, transmission of patrimony, and coupled unity. Julia as a figure from the venerated Augustan past might have much to appeal to the audience of the *Saturnalia*: the "love of literature and much learning" on which Avienus lays stress; her "humanity" and lack of cruelty, perhaps a contrast with Christian rigidity; her skill in the art of safe dissent; her fulfillment of her dynastic role, even if on her own terms; and her ultimate fate. Like Flavianus, she is a rebel in the old style. Her jokes recall an ancien régime.[21]

The effect of the Christian model for female behavior on the ruling women of the Eastern court has been described at length by Kenneth Holum (1982). Where Flaccilla and Eudoxia justified themselves by producing heirs to the dynasty, and Eudocia attempted to do the same, Pulcheria identified herself with and drew her power from the sexless motherhood of Mary. But Macrobius, in the West, had before him a different *exemplum* of imperial womanhood, whose life recalled pagan aristocratic traditions and the life of Julia. Galla Placidia, born to Theodosius I by his second wife in 388 or 389, came to the West and the court of her half brother, Honorius, as a child of six.[22] A dynastic marriage would have been expected for her; by 398 there were courtly hints of her marriage to Stilicho's son Eucherius (Cameron 1970, 47, 154). Instead, she became a hostage of the Visigothic leader Athaulf, whom she married in 414; her husband and their infant son died in 415, and she was returned to Ravenna and married off to Constantius III in 417. Their daughter Justa Grata Honoria was born in 418; a son, Valentinian, in 419. By 423 she had been named Augusta, Constantius had died, and her constant siding with the barbarian elements in Ravenna had forced her to flee with her children to Constantinople. She had returned by 425 and spent the last decades of her life as a pillar of the church. Meanwhile, her unmarried daughter Honoria was found to be pregnant; this was seen to pose the threat to her lover's rise to power (cf. both Julias' rumored involvement in coups), and so he was killed and Honoria was exiled to the custody of Pulcheria, or at least sequestered. (She supposedly then wrote a love letter to Attila the Hun.[23])

Like Julia's daughter, Honoria found out what it meant to be pregnant at the wrong time; Galla Placidia, who had produced a legitimate heir, was attacked after Constantius's death by insinuations that she was committing incest with her half brother Honorius (Matthews 1975, 377; cf. Oost 1968, 171). Yet after her restoration we find on coins icons of both women as Augustae, as impressive as any images of their Eastern sisters: Galla Placidia on a solidus, crowned by the hand of God; on a gold multiple, wearing a diadem and chlamys, just like the emperor's regalia—and, on the reverse, enthroned; and Justa Grata Honoria on a solidus, wearing the regalia.[24] Galla Placidia also left public religious monuments behind her; moreover, we have the letters she wrote to Theodosius and to Pulcheria on the monophysite controversy and Theodosius's reply to her (Migne, *Patrologia Latina* 54.859–62, 863–66, 877–78). They contain little more than formalities, but it is something to see those formalities attested.[25] St. Peter Chrysologus (bishop of Ravenna 432–50) himself addressed her in a sermon with these words:

Indeed, there is present the mother herself of the eternal and faithful Christian empire, who, while she follows and imitates the blessed Church in honor of the Trinity by faith, by works of mercy, by sanctity, has merited to give birth to, to embrace, and to possess the august Trinity. (Migne. *Patrologia Latina* 52.556–57)

The direct analogy here between Galla Placidia and the Church is less startling in the context of the sermon as a whole, which begins with an invocation of *Ecclesia mater* in bridal garb, and goes on to describe the children of this mother (i.e., Christians), whose conception is (like that of Jesus in Mary) "unknowing of sex, knowing of conception, aware of birth, unaware of corruption, of unbroken chastity, of closed unbrokenness, chaste in its children, diffuse in its fecundity." In the Church, sex and gender have become active metaphors for power relations; alluding to Galla, the bishop turns this around, claiming to see these power relations enacted in the real sexuality of the empress. As mother of the emperor, but also as Augusta, Galla Placidia has become an analog of the Church itself; the bishop can even proclaim in her, Augusta and mother and wife of Augusti, a kind of Trinity (Oost 1968, 266–67). The contrast between this eulogy and the earlier attacks on Galla—both centering on her sexual body—strongly recalls the contrast between the two versions of Julia.

On the content of the *Saturnalia*, Cameron remarks, "In a sense ... this antiquarianism *was* bound up with the traditions of the pagan past. But there is no suspicion of polemic, nothing at all to offend the most narrow-minded Christian" (1966: 35). I would submit that even a broad-minded Christian would have found Julia's jokes shocking and the epithet *eleganter* applied to her witticisms unthinkable, and he or she would have been horrified at the suggestion that such words from an emperor's daughter were in any way admirable, even though she came to a bad end. I think we must posit here a connection between the figure of Julia in these jokes and the changing images of Galla Placidia and her daughter. The revival of the jokes in Macrobius's *Saturnalia* constitutes recognition of an empress's power in the early fifth century A.D. and its source: her ability to control her bearing of children. The concurrent ideal of female purity recalls Julia's uncomfortable proximity to the gods; Pulcheria aims at the "unattainable goal" of entry into heaven. Sabine MacCormack comments:

A canon of virtues and deeds for emperors had been laid down during centuries of Roman politics and public life. In late antiquity, it became possible for empresses to be represented in art in the light of this canon, as was Galla Placidia . . . , but this defined their role only very partially. For, while the figure of the emperor remained caught in debates as to the nature of the imperial power which carried over from the pagan into the Christian empire, it was possible to catalogue and expound the virtues of a Christian empress independently of this legacy of the past. In this new context, the virtues and deeds of an empress were directed not merely toward the manifold contingencies of this life, but toward the ultimate goal of the life to come. (1981, 263–64)

I would postulate that the virtues of emperors' female kin, and of all women who rule, had been measured by similar criteria long before emperors were Christian.

CONCLUSIONS

Julia's jokes work similarly in both of their contexts, the early principate and the fifth century A.D. In both cases, the live models have idealized images against which their negative images react. All the images concern sexuality, especially childbearing, and this focus not surprisingly reappears in the recorded events of these women's lives. But both life and icons are manipulated for political ends, with a strong identification between the woman's body and the health of the state.

This study suggests some general rules. Jokes about the sexual impurity of women in power must normally represent a mediation of that power, perhaps a translation of that power in terms of the class fiction Ortner describes.[26] Julia's jokes, if they are an exception to this rule, owe their survival to it; they are seen as "jokes about Julia" rather than as "Julia's jokes" (cf. Walker 1988, 120–22). Moreover, if, as Ortner claims, female purity is the key to class movement upwards, purity disparaged will cancel this out, hampering the claims to superiority of the women's male kin. On reflection, the phenomenon must be, as Ortner suggests, inherent in the patriarchal state: If you invent the sepulchre, someone is bound to point out that it is whited; if you have a Caesar, you must suspect Caesar's wife. Such a phrase is inherently loaded, like *Augusti filia*.

Contemplation of the icons of Roman ruling women leaves us with the uncomfortable feeling that we can hardly know the real women inside them at all; we seem to be looking at a long series of constructs, remade whenever women arrived at a certain kind of power. Did Livia really set herself in the first lady mold? And is that icon of her merely the one that survived, while another one of Livia the adulteress disappeared? After all, we have conflicting images not only for Julia, Galla Placidia, and Justa Grata Honoria, but for many other ruling women. What of pre-Hellenistic women? More questions arise. Natalie Kampen points out how Julia Domna's images rely on Livia's; do icons validate themselves by reference to other icons? Is a sort of interreferentiality among past, present, and future characteristic of such images (cf. Atkinson 1985; Hamer 1988)? And are icons also invented for the past at the convenience of the present? Livy's story of Lucretia and the Tarquins' wives begins to sound like only a variant of Julia's joke about her followers versus Livia's.

Was Horace looking for the real woman within the icon of Cleopatra when he saw her refusing to be led in the triumph—*non humilis mulier*? Is history a branch of poetry? When we look at texts and objects to discover reality, it is as if we looked at a scene through a screen on a window; as we become interested in the screen and its properties, we suddenly notice that the scene is in fact painted on the screen itself. What lies beyond is unknown. Perhaps there are principles that determine the projection and interpretation of reality onto the screen; if so, the study of ideology serves in the search for them.

NOTES

My thanks to the Women's Classical Caucus of the American Philological Association, who heard an earlier version of this chapter; to Sandra Joshel, Natalie Kampen, Lydia Speller, and Gordon Williams for help and comments; to Suzanne Morrison for assistance in research; and to Suzanne Dixon, Pauline Allen, and Barbara Garlick for their warm hospitality and patience as editors.

1. See Austin 1981, document nos. 151, 156, 158, 185, 217; also Theocritus, *Idyll* 15; Pomeroy 1984, 3–40. On the phenomenon in Victorian England, see Auerbach 1982, 35–62. Of course, this is an extension of the praise of good women for which Greek examples go back to Homer's Penelope.

2. On the Trajanic women, see Temporini 1978; on Julia Domna and her sister and nieces, see Dio, Books 75–80 passim; Cleve 1988; Kampen 1985.

3. On Pulcheria, see Holum 1982, 79–111, 147–216, and esp. 139–45, 153–74, and the idea that through her asceticism she would " 'receive the king of the universe in her womb' " (142, quoting Atticus, bishop of Constantinople, A.D. 406–425). See also Fisher 1984; Herrin 1983, with sources.

4. The phrase *meretrix augusta*, "empress whore," comes from Juvenal (*Satire* 6.118), in his tale of Messallina, but the figure is common in historians of the empire (Suetonius, Tacitus, Dio; cf. Richlin 1983, 81–104; 1984); it continues through Procopius's *Secret History* (see Pauline Allen, chapter 5 in this volume). For a model comparable to the present one, see Wyke (forthcoming) on the Augustan construction of Cleopatra; Hamer 1988 on the use of Cleopatra in the fifteenth to seventeenth centuries (unreliable on ancient evidence). On Dido and Cleopatra, see Carney 1988.

5. For a (non-Western) example of a positive view of the use to a female ruler of bearing children to several fathers, see Hoffer 1974.

6. This and all subsequent translations are my own.

7. Balsdon 1962, 82; full discussion of the sources on Julia, 68–88. Hallett 1984 describes the kinship/gender/political systems of Julia's world. On the sources of Macrobius 2.2–2.7, see Wessner 1928; on Domitius Marsus, see Skutsch 1905. The overlaps between Macrobius and Quintilian 6.3.1–112 anchor the jokes in the early first century A.D., and at any rate it seems natural to assume they were contemporary with their protagonists. See below on the audience for the jokes about Julia.

8. For discussion of the development of the study of female historical figures, with sources, see NEH 1983, 100–8. Studies that share the concerns of the present chapter include Fisher 1984; Skinner 1983. See Walcot 1987 for a recent example of an old-style dragon-lady history, invoking Freud's "Femininity"; compare Cleve 1988, who champions the Severan women's power under the title "Some Male Relatives of the Severan

Women" and winds up explaining how they took their power by "manipulating all of their male relatives," "using the same tools and techniques employed by male politicians of their time—albeit with much more subtlety . . . , because they had to rule 'behind the scenes' " (cf. n. 13).

9. For woman as ship in Aristophanes, see Henderson 1975, 164–65 (here men also are ships); and cf. especially *Palatine Anthology* 5.204. For the image in Latin, see Adams 1982, 89, 167.

10. On the signification of Julia's daughter's pregnancy, see Barnes 1981; on Justa Grata Honoria, below, page 82 and note 23. See Williams 1962 for the importance of procreation in the ideology of Horace's praise of Augustus's marriage legislation, esp. *Odes* 4.5.23, *laudantur simili prole puerperae* ("women in childbirth are praised for children resembling [their husbands]").

11. Livia apparently had her own stories, which directly counter Julia's. Dio says (58.2.4): "Various well-put sayings (*apophthegmata*) of hers are recorded," and gives two: (58.2.4) how she spared the lives of some men who had crossed her path naked and so were to be executed, saying that to chaste women (*sōphronousais*) such men are no different from statues; (58.2.5) that she explained her hold over Augustus by saying she herself was scrupulously chaste, cheerfully did what seemed best to him, did not meddle in his business, and pretended not to hear of or notice his love affairs.

12. On Julia's known circle, see Williams 1978, 63–70; also P. Green 1982. For sources on Domitius Marsus, see Skutsch 1905.

13. See Zijderveld 1968, esp. 306–7, on the "manipulatory use of joking" by political leaders.

14. See Levick 1975 for a discussion of the factions angling for the succession; she emphasizes the dynastic importance of Julia's progeny and depicts Julia's history entirely in political terms—the "lovers" are Julia's political clique. "Behind the scenes" lurks the "dark figure" of Julia's mother, Scribonia, who cannot forgive her ousting by Livia and promotes Julia's children against Livia's son Tiberius; Livia is at the center of the opposing faction.

15. For example, Fine 1976; Makarius 1970; Turner 1969, 47 and passim; Zijderveld 1968, esp. 297–98; also Barber 1959.

16. See R. Green 1977; Johnson 1973. Some empirical support is provided by C. Mitchell 1985. Nancy Walker 1988 argues that American women's humor is marked by its domestic content (she does not consider structure) and that it incorporates a veiled and subversive protest against patriarchy; related arguments on Victorian women's writing in Gagnier 1988. Both follow Apte 1985 and Eco 1984. On women cartoonists, see D. Mitchell 1981; Robbins and yronwode 1985.

17. See Kleiner 1978 for an update on who (including Julia) is where on the Ara Pacis, with special consideration of the place of women and children on the monument; Galinsky 1969, 219 on Venus in the Ara Pacis. Cf. Dixon 1988, esp. 71–103, for in-depth treatment of the ideology of maternity in the early principate and for women of the imperial house thereafter.

18. See discussion of a *sestertius* of Caligula showing Agrippina with a *carpentum* on the reverse, in Breglia 1968, 46 and facing plate.

19. Kaster 1980, 242–48, 240, n.64; cf. Cameron 1967 for the identification of Avienus with the fabulist Avianus who dedicated his book to Macrobius around A.D. 430.

20. Ps.-Aug. *Quaestiones* 115.12, 16, = *CSEL* 50.322, 323; Brown 1961, 7 n.50

takes the passage to refer to a relaxation of divorce laws for *clarissimae feminae* (women in the elite social class), but the question is vexed.

21. I owe these insights to the helpful reading of my colleague, Martha Malamud.

22. For a full, if dramatic, account, see Oost 1968; also Matthews 1975, 224, 248, 316–18, 354–55, 377–80.

23. Holum 1982, 1; Oost 1968, 282–85; but cf. *PLRE* 2: 568–69.

24. Galla Placidia, in MacCormack 1981, 228 and plates 59 and 60; Justa Grata Honoria, in Holum 1982, figure 14, and discussion of all the coins, 129–30.

25. Oost 1968, 290 sees the letter to Pulcheria as a "less formal" sharing of religious feeling.

26. Compare P. Green 1982, who sees the accusations of sexual misconduct against both Julias as camouflage for accusations of political conspiracy in which the women served as tools; Hallett 1984, 141–42, 328, who sees Roman fathers' concern with their daughters' chastity as stemming from "paternity anxiety."

REFERENCES

Ancient Authors

The author has in all cases consulted the original texts and has given her own translations in the chapters and notes. The following information about translations is provided for the convenience of readers unfamiliar with the ancient authors.

Dio, *Roman History*. Translated by E. Cary, 1924. Cambridge, Mass.: Harvard University Press.

Macrobius, *Saturnalia*. Translated by Percival Vaughan Davies, 1969. New York: Columbia University Press.

Suetonius, *The Twelve Caesars*. Translated by Robert Graves, rev. 1979. Harmondsworth, England: Penguin.

Tacitus, *The Annals of Imperial Rome*. Translated by Michael Grant, rev. 1975. Harmondsworth, England: Penguin.

Modern Works

Adams, J. N. 1982. *The Latin Sexual Vocabulary*. Baltimore: Johns Hopkins University Press.

Apte, Mahadev L. 1985. *Humor and Laughter: An Anthropological Approach*. Ithaca, N.Y.: Cornell University Press.

Atkinson, Clarissa W. 1985. " 'Your Servant, My Mother': The Figure of Saint Monica in the Ideology of Christian Motherhood." In *Immaculate and Powerful: The Female Sacred Image and Social Reality*, edited by Clarissa W. Atkinson, Constance H. Buchanan, and Margaret R. Miles, 139–72. Boston: Beacon Press.

Auerbach, Nina. 1982. *Woman and the Demon*. Boston: Harvard University Press.

Austin, M. M. 1981. *The Hellenistic World from Alexander to the Roman Conquest*. Cambridge: Cambridge University Press.

Balsdon, J.P.V.D. 1962. *Roman Women: Their History and Habits*. London: Bodley Head.

Barber, C. L. 1959. *Shakespeare's Festive Comedy*. Princeton, N.J.: Princeton University Press.

Barnes, T. D. 1981. "Julia's Child." *Phoenix* 35:362–63.

Bloch, Herbert. 1963. "The Pagan Revival in the West at the End of the Fourth Century." In *The Conflict between Paganism and Christianity in the Fourth Century*, edited by Arnaldo Momigliano, 193–218. Oxford: Clarendon Press.

Breglia, Laura. 1968. *Roman Imperial Coins: Their Art and Technique*. Translated by Peter Green. New York: Praeger.

Brown, P.R.L. 1961. "Aspects of the Christianization of the Roman Aristocracy." *Journal of Roman Studies* 51:1–11.

———. 1988. *The Body and Society: Men, Women, and Sexual Renunciation in Early Christianity*. New York: Columbia University Press.

Brunt, P. A. 1971. *Italian Manpower 225 B.C. to A.D. 14*. Oxford: Oxford University Press.

Cameron, Alan. 1966. "The Date and Identity of Macrobius." *Journal of Roman Studies* 56:25–38.

———. 1967. "Macrobius, Avienus, and Avianus." *Classical Quarterly* n.s. 17:385–99.

———. 1970. *Claudian: Poetry and Propaganda at the Court of Honorius*. Oxford: Oxford University Press.

Cameron, A[lan] D. E. 1980. "Crinagoras and the Elder Julia: *AP* 6.345." *Liverpool Classical Monthly* 5,6:129–30.

Cantor, Joanne R. 1976. "What Is Funny to Whom? The Role of Gender." *Journal of Communications* 26:164–72.

Carney, Elizabeth. 1988. "*Reginae* in the *Aeneid*." *Athenaeum* n.s. 66:427–45.

Chapman, Antony J., and Nicholas J. Gadfield. 1976. "Is Sexual Humour Sexist?" *Journal of Communications* 26:141–53.

Cleve, Robert L. 1988. "Some Male Relatives of the Severan Women." *Historia* 37:196–206.

Corrington, Gail P. 1986. "The 'Divine Woman'? Propaganda and the Power of Chastity in the New Testament Apocrypha." *Helios* 13:151–62.

Davis, Natalie Zemon. 1975. "Women on Top." In *Society and Culture in Early Modern France*, 124–51. Stanford, Calif.: Stanford University Press.

Dixon, Suzanne. 1988. *The Roman Mother*. Norman: Oklahoma University Press.

Eco, Umberto. 1984. "Frames of Comic 'Freedom.' " In *Carnival!*, edited by Thomas A. Sebeok, 1–9. Berlin: Mouton.

Ferrill, Arthur. 1980. "Augustus and His Daughter: A Modern Myth." In *Studies in Latin Literature and Roman History*, edited by Carl Deroux, II, 332–46. Brussels, Belgium: Latomus.

Fine, Gary Alan. 1976. "Obscene Joking across Cultures." *Journal of Communications* 26:134–40.

Fisher, Elizabeth A. 1984. "Theodora and Antonina in the *Historia Arcana*: History and/or Fiction?" In *Women in the Ancient World*, edited by John Peradotto and J. P. Sullivan, 287–313. Albany: State University of New York Press.

Flory, Marleen Boudreau. 1984. "*Sic Exempla Parantur*: Livia's Shrine to Concordia and the Porticus Liviae." *Historia* 33:309–30.

Gagnier, Regenia. 1988. "Between Women: A Cross-class Analysis of Status and Anarchic Humor." *Women's Studies* 15:135–48.

Galinsky, G. Karl. 1969. *Aeneas, Sicily, and Rome*. Princeton; N.J.: Princeton University Press.

Giacosa, Giorgio. n.d. *Women of the Caesars: Their Lives and Portraits on Coins*. Translated by R. Ross Holloway. Montclair, N.J.: Numismatic Fine Arts.

Green, Peter. 1982. "*Carmen et Error*: *Prophasis* and *aitia* in the Matter of Ovid's Exile." *Classical Antiquity* 1:202–20.

Green, Rayna. 1977. "Magnolias Grow in Dirt: The Bawdy Lore of Southern Women." *The Radical Teacher* 6:26–31.

Hallett, Judith P. 1984. *Fathers and Daughters in Roman Society*. Princeton, N.J.: Princeton University Press.

Hamer, Mary. 1988. "Cleopatra: Housewife." *Textual Practice* 2:159–79.

Henderson, Jeffrey. 1975. *The Maculate Muse*. New Haven, Conn.: Yale University Press.

Herrin, Judith. 1983. "In Search of Byzantine Women: Three Avenues of Approach." In *Images of Women in Antiquity*, edited by Averil Cameron and Amélie Kuhrt, 167–89. Detroit: Wayne State University Press.

Hoffer, Carol P. 1974. "Madam Yoko: Ruler of the Kpa Mende Confederacy." In *Woman, Culture, and Society*, edited by Michelle Zimbalist Rosaldo and Louise Lamphere; 173–87. Stanford, Calif.: Stanford University Press.

Holum, Kenneth G. 1982. *Theodosian Empresses*. Berkeley: University of California Press.

Johnson, Robbie Davis. 1973. "Folklore and Women: A Social Interactional Analysis of the Folklore of a Texas Madam." *Journal of American Folklore* 86:211–24.

Joshel, Sandra. 1991. "The Body Female and the Body Politic: Livy's Lucretia and Verginia." In *Pornography and Representation in Greece and Rome*, edited by Amy Richlin, 112–30. New York: Oxford University Press.

Kampen, Natalie Boymel. 1985. "Julia Domna and the Program of the Severan Arch at Leptis Magna." Tenney Frank Lecture, University of Kansas, Lawrence.

Kaster, Robert. 1980. "Macrobius and Servius: *Verecundia* and the Grammarian's Function." *Harvard Studies in Classical Philology* 84:219–62.

Kleiner, Diana E. E. 1978. "The Great Friezes of the Ara Pacis Augustae: Greek Sources, Roman Derivatives, and Augustan Social Policy." *Mélanges de l'École Française de Rome—Antiquité* 90:753–85.

Lefkowitz, Mary R. 1981. "Men and Women on Women's Lives." In *Heroines and Hysterics*, 26–31. New York: St. Martin's Press.

Levick, B. 1975. "Julians and Claudians." *Greece & Rome* 22:29–38.

Lightman, Marjorie, and William Zeisel. 1977. "*Univira*: An Example of Continuity and Change in Roman Society." *Church History* 46:19–32.

MacCormack, Sabine G. 1981. *Art and Ceremony in Late Antiquity*. Berkeley: University of California Press.

Maclean, Marie. 1987. "Oppositional Practices in Women's Traditional Narrative." *New Literary History* 19:37–50.

McNamara, Jo Ann. 1984. "Cornelia's Daughters: Paula and Eustochium." *Women's Studies* 11:9–27.

Makarius, Laura. 1970. "Ritual Clowns and Symbolic Behaviour." *Diogenes* 69:44–73.

Matthews, John. 1975. *Western Aristocracies and Imperial Court* A.D. *364–425*. Oxford: Oxford University Press.

Mitchell, Carol. 1985. "Some Differences in Male and Female Joke-Telling." In *Wom-*

en's Folklore, Women's Culture, edited by Rosan A. Jordan and Susan J. Kalčik, 163–86. Philadelphia: University of Pennsylvania Press.

Mitchell, Dolores. 1981. "Humor in California Underground Women's Comix." In *Women's Culture: Renaissance of the Seventies*, edited by Gayle Kimball, 72–90. Metuchen, N.J.: Scarecrow.

NEH Humanities Institute on Women in Classical Antiquity. 1983. *Women in Classical Antiquity: Four Curricular Modules*. New York: Hunter College Department of Classical and Oriental Studies.

Neitz, Mary Jo. 1980. "Humor, Hierarchy, and the Changing Status of Women." *Psychiatry* 43:211–23.

Oost, Stewart Irvin. 1968. *Galla Placidia Augusta: A Biographical Essay*. Chicago: University of Chicago Press.

Ortner, Sherry B. 1978. "The Virgin and the State." *Feminist Studies* 4:19–35.

Pomeroy, Sarah B. 1984. *Women in Hellenistic Egypt*. New York: Schocken.

The Prosopography of the Later Roman Empire. 1971. Edited by A.H.M. Jones, J. R. Martindale, and J. Morris. Cambridge: Cambridge University Press.

Richlin, Amy. 1981. "Approaches to the Sources on Adultery at Rome." In *Reflections of Women in Antiquity*, edited by Helene P. Foley, 379–404. New York: Gordon and Breach.

———. 1983. *The Garden of Priapus: Sexuality and Aggression in Roman Humor*. New Haven, Conn.: Yale University Press.

———. 1984. "Invective against Women in Roman Satire." *Arethusa* 17:67–80.

Robbins, Trina, and catherine yronwode. 1985. *Women and the Comics*. Forestville, Calif.: Eclipse Books.

Skinner, Marilyn B. 1982. "Pretty Lesbius." *Transactions of the American Philological Association* 112:197–208.

———. 1983. "Clodia Metelli." *Transactions of the American Philological Association* 113: 273–87.

Skutsch, O. 1905. "Domitius Marsus." Pauly-Wissowa *Realencyclopaedie* Vol. 5, 1430–32.

Sutherland, C.H.V., and R.A.G. Carson. 1984. *The Roman Imperial Coinage*. Vol. 1 (rev.). London: Spink and Son.

Temporini, H. 1978. *Die Frauen am Hofe Trajans*. Berlin: De Gruyter.

Turner, Victor. 1969. *The Ritual Process*. Chicago: Aldine.

Walcot, Peter. 1987. "Plato's Mother and Other Terrible Women." *Greece & Rome* 34:12–31.

Walker, Nancy A. 1988. *A Very Serious Thing: Women's Humor and American Culture*. Minneapolis: University of Minnesota Press.

Webb, Ronald G. 1981. "Political Uses of Humor." *Et cetera* 38:35–50.

Wessner, P. 1928. "Macrobius." Pauly-Wissowa *Realencyclopaedie*, Vol. 14, 184.

Williams, Gordon. 1958. "Some Aspects of Roman Marriage Ceremonies and Ideals." *Journal of Roman Studies* 48:16–29.

———. 1962. "Poetry in the Moral Climate of Augustan Rome." *Journal of Roman Studies* 52:28–46.

———. 1978. *Change and Decline*. Berkeley: University of California Press.

Wyke, Maria. Forthcoming. "Augustan Cleopatras: Female Power and Poetic Authority."

In *Augustus and the Poets*, edited by Anton Powell. Bristol, England: Bristol Classical Press.

Zijderveld, Anton C. 1968. ''Jokes and Their Relation to Social Reality.'' *Social Research* 35:286–311.

5

Contemporary Portrayals of the Byzantine Empress Theodora (A.D. 527–548)

Pauline Allen

Although the powers of the Byzantine empress were never constitutionally defined in an unequivocal manner, she clearly enjoyed more influence than her subjects.[1] Her status was usually acquired partly on her marriage to the emperor and partly by virtue of her motherhood, although there were highly significant exceptions to this rule. Several Byzantine empresses were powerful and influential in their own right;[2] some of them ruled without a consort.[3] However, in general it is true to say that in the Byzantine period, as in other cultures and eras, the role of the royal woman was vague and often ceremonial, and the channels open to her for exercising political power were limited and unofficial ones.[4]

Bearing this in mind I turn to the Empress Theodora, the wife of the Emperor Justinian I (527–565), and to the portrayals given of her by the contemporary historian Procopius of Caesarea. In his works *Wars* and *Buildings* we have what resembles an official history of the reign of Justinian and Theodora, while in his monograph, known as the *Secret History*, an example of abusive pamphleteering that is hard to match in the ancient world, the origins, private life, and morals of Theodora and her husband receive exhaustive attention.[5] The techniques employed by Procopius in representing the empress in the *Secret History* are the concern of this chapter. These techniques, because of their variety and overlap, make a reconstruction of the historical Theodora particularly difficult.

Before one begins to examine the portrayal of Theodora in the *Secret History*, however, for the sake of completeness three passages in *Wars* and *Buildings* in which Theodora figures substantially should be considered briefly. The first of these occurs in *Wars* I.24 during Procopius's narrative of the Nika riot in 532 A.D. in Constantinople, when, in the face of an uprising, Justinian had to consider the possibility of flight. Here the historian has Theodora deliver a speech before the Senate, in which she resolutely puts the point that *she* at any rate intends to stand her ground and, if necessary, to die in the purple. While there can be little doubt that this address was composed by Procopius himself in accordance with one of the tenets of classical historiography,[6] what we need to take cognizance of is the fact that he is casting Theodora in the role of a woman who acts publicly, taking the unusual step of speaking in the Senate in order to safeguard her own position.[7] In a second passage, *Wars* I.25.4–7, John the Cappadocian, an influential man in the imperial court, is said to have slandered the empress to her husband, not taking into account the emperor's great devotion to his wife. On hearing of this episode, according to Procopius, Theodora planned to do away with John, who consequently went about in great terror. Extrapolating from both these passages we conclude that for Procopius the power and influence of Theodora were real and sometimes public. A final passage, from *Buildings* I.11.8–9, should be taken into account here for the contrast it provides with Procopius's representation of Theodora in the *Secret History*. Describing a statue of the empress in Constantinople, Procopius writes:

There also the Empress Theodora stands upon a column, which the city in gratitude for the court dedicated to her. The statue is indeed beautiful, but still inferior to the beauty of the Empress; for to express her loveliness in words or to portray it in a statue would be, for a mere human being, altogether impossible. (I.11.8–9)[8]

It has been recognized that these words are "ominous as well as fawning" (Fisher 1984, 301).

However, although on reading between the lines of these passages one may come to the conclusion that the conservative and aristocratic Procopius found strong females offensive,[9] there is no overt bias against Theodora. The *Secret History*, on the other hand, is so explicit in its denunciation of the empress that Procopius's authorship of the work was long disputed (Cameron 1985, 49–50). Here the focus is on two couples: Theodora and Justinian and the general Belisarius and his wife Antonina. For her part Theodora is characterized venomously as the daughter of a keeper of circus animals in Constantinople, an experienced harlot who had prostituted herself throughout the Byzantine empire before Justinian conceived an overwhelming passion for her and made her his mistress. Her vulgarity defied description, her lust was insatiable, and she practiced abortion regularly. If Procopius is to be believed, she was universally hated and feared by her subjects. Together with her husband she adopted the aim of destroying an old and mighty empire, an aim which, during their joint regency, they achieved largely through a *Doppelspiel*, a disingenuous policy of divide and rule.

At the outset the main commonplaces in Procopius's presentation of Theodora in the *Secret History* should be isolated. The best known of these is the emphasis he places on her sexuality, describing her supposedly highly promiscuous and deviant behavior before she met Justinian. As a small girl she acted as a kind

of male prostitute (9.10) before becoming an actress (9.13),[10] a profession reserved for the lowest levels of society; at dinner parties she had intercourse with
all the guests and then with the servants as well (9.16); she was the concubine
of a governor of Libya and worked her way back from that country to Constantinople by prostitution (9.27–28). It does appear, in fact, that Theodora had been
both an actress and a prostitute before she met Justinian. Procopius records in
embroidered fashion at 9.51 that Justinian even had his uncle, the Emperor Justin
I, enact a law enabling a person of his rank to marry an actress.[11] However, the
exaggerated and prurient account of her exploits by Procopius must be seen as
pertaining to that stereotype that links female power with rampant sexuality, that
attempts to blacken both the prominent woman and those associated with her.[12]

For Procopius it is Theodora who is the dominant and forceful partner in the
imperial duo, a reading that serves primarily not to indict her weak and wavering
husband (as he is depicted), but rather to show to what degree Theodora exceeds
acceptable norms. The empress is denounced for acting toward both subjects
and foreign diplomats as if she were in control of the empire,[13] apparently an
intolerable thought for a patrician like Procopius. Justinian is enslaved to her
through blind passion on his part and magic on hers (9.31; 22.28); she can lead
him by the nose into any of her schemes (13.19); he must seek her approval in
every matter (15.10). Justinian's marriage to her, given her origins and her past,
reveals his moral sickness—the marriage, according to Procopius, was "both
interpreter, witness and chronicler of the course he followed" (10.4:90).

As previously mentioned, the power and prestige of empresses in Byzantium
were more often than not manifested in oblique ways. Even so, Procopius's
insistence on portraying Theodora in her private, domestic role must be seen as
part of the stereotype that trivializes or neutralizes female power. Even the public,
ceremonial role of the empress is reduced by Procopius to a situation in which
Theodora acts in an autocratic, domineering manner (30.21–24).[14] Consistently
throughout the *Secret History* her role in palace politics is stressed. Here her
whimsicality, personal motives, scheming, and meddling all receive attention.
She is said, for example, to have maintained a private prison in the cellars under
the palace, where those who fell from her favor were incarcerated and tortured.[15]
She is portrayed as meddling in the private lives of others, especially in her self-
appointed role as matchmaker, where by exaggeration she is accused of arranging
all marriages in the realm as if by divine right;[16] even the composition of juries
is decided by her (15.21). According to Procopius, Theodora had armies of spies
who informed her of everything that went on in the capital city (16.14). Criticism
of Justinian she takes as criticism of herself (4.5); forever working behind the
scenes, she can arrange for the punishment of existing generals (4.6–8) or the
creation of new ones (3.19).

These devices, used by Procopius in portraying Theodora, are what we might
call traditional stereotypes applied to women who were as active in the sphere
of power or politics as contemporary strictures allowed, and the present volume
bears testimony to their striking consistency throughout Western political

thought. Procopius, however, is too astute and too thorough to allow his case against Theodora to rest there. Literary devices existed on which this educated writer could also draw for his portrait of the empress and her husband. The rhetorical schools in which Procopius was trained had set rules for the writing of invective, as for other literary genres (Tinnefeld 1971, 29–33). Exaggeration is a first *desideratum* in invective: thus in the *Secret History* Theodora is described as "double-dyed with every kind of horrible pollution, and guilty over and over again of infanticide by wilful abortion" (10.3:89–90); absolutely nothing or no one can persuade her to abate her wrath to any degree at all (15.1–5); and since human beings first appeared on earth no tyrant was ever regarded with such fear (16.13). Procopius's generous use of superlatives throughout the work is also part of this rhetorical technique. Generalizations are called for as well. Of the magistrates who come to consult Theodora in the palace and are shabbily treated it is said: "[O]n every occasion they all had to await her pleasure, waiting like slaves in a small, stuffy anteroom all the time" (15.13:115). Similarly, when the empress supposedly has a suppliant removed by force from his place of asylum, Procopius comments: "There was not one inviolable spot that ever remained beyond her reach; and in her eyes violence done to sacred things of any and every kind was nothing at all" (3.25:55). A further literary device at Procopius's disposal is repetition, such that by the accumulation of incidents in which Theodora confiscates property[17] or has her enemies tortured, mutilated, or removed,[18] the particular point is driven home.

In addition to these literary devices, there were also prescribed elements for the writing of invective, of which we find the following in the *Secret History*: the origins of the person under attack, his or her education or upbringing and physical appearance, deeds indicative of character, and comparison.[19] Theodora, as we have already mentioned, is said by Procopius to have been the daughter of a keeper of circus animals in Constantinople (9.2), a social position that would not have commanded respect.[20] In Procopius's pamphlet her education takes place not at home but on the stage and in the brothel, and from an early age: "Such, then, was the birth and upbringing of this woman, the subject of common talk among women of the streets and among people of every kind" (9.29:86). It is in this section dealing with Theodora's upbringing that Procopius concentrates on his pornographic portrait of her, the portrayal of the subject's sexuality being a common feature of invective.[21] The emperor, for his part, is introduced as the nephew of the previous emperor Justin, an illiterate farmer from the provinces who is said to have been "uncouth in the extreme, utterly inarticulate and incredibly boorish" (6.18:70). In the description of the physical appearance of each of the imperial pair—a theme beloved of Byzantine writers whether treated in a positive or negative manner[22]—Procopius is more restrained. According to him, Theodora "had an attractive face and a good figure, but was short and pallid, though not in an extreme degree, for there was just a trace of colour. Her glance was invariably fierce and intensely hard. If I were to attempt a detailed account of her life upon the stage, I could go for the rest of time"

(10.11–12:91). Apparently little negative comment could be made about Theodora's outward appearance, and Procopius trails off into a weak generalization, giving the impression that he knows much more than he actually does—a ploy that has many parallels in the *Secret History*.[23] Justinian himself is depicted in fairly neutral terms, but the clever comparison made between him and the Emperor Domitian (8.12–21), considered by many Christians as the anti-Christ, is damning.[24]

Whereas the rhetorically prescribed elements of origins, education, and physical appearance of both Theodora and her husband are treated in a block by Procopius, the categories pertaining to their deeds and characteristics are dealt with consistently throughout the work. By her supposed deeds Theodora is characterized as extremely malicious (9.26), jealous (16.1), rapacious (4.17), self-indulgent (15.6–9), vindictive, unscrupulous, and domineering.[25] The portrayal of Justinian primarily as destructively innovative, unstable, and chaotic in administration[26] is useful for Procopius when it comes to making comparisons with Theodora, a practice that extended throughout the whole work. For Theodora is compared consistently with Justinian, and vice versa, and the impression deliberately created by their attacker is that between them they embody every fault or vice. Theodora is also compared with Antonina, who is said to be "an inseparable friend of the Empress" (4.18:58),[27] just as the disgraced and foolish general Belisarius (5.27) evokes Justinian (Evert-Kappesowa 1964). The interweaving of these four personalities in a sustained, many-sided comparison in the *Secret History* is both one of the central techniques in the work and a device which the author has ingeniously made his own.

Let us examine in some detail how Procopius uses the element of comparison. Since it is his aim to show that Theodora and Justinian between them destroyed the ancient and powerful Roman Empire root and branch, he must make his case as comprehensive as possible. Stereotypes associated with female power, and literary and rhetorical ploys alone, are insufficient. Above all it is imperative for him to convey the constant, concerted efforts made by the imperial pair to devise the ruin of their subjects, and to stress their singleminded collusion. "Neither did anything apart from the other to the end of their joint lives," maintains Procopius (10.13:91); "the pair of them were almost indistinguishable in their aims," he says elsewhere (13.9:106), claiming that all the time they took "everything into their hands to the detriment of their subjects" (30.30:193). Despite their different attitudes and way of life, according to Procopius, they were as one in their rapacity, bloodlust, and disregard for the truth (15.19). While Justinian espouses stargazing and foolish theologizing (18.29), Theodora practices sorcery; and they are portrayed as a pair of demons (12.13–32).[28] If this staunch partnership is to be used effectively by Procopius it must admit of no chinks. To make outright accusations of estrangement or infidelity, for instance, between Theodora and her husband would serve his purpose ill. On the other hand a treatment of Theodora's sexuality is an indispensable part of his abusive pamphlet. It is therefore a tribute to Procopius's ingenuity that, while relegating her profligate and deviant behavior to the period in her life *before* she met Justinian, by innuendo and association he has succeeded in besmirching her character as empress. But meanwhile the collusion between the imperial couple remains intact.[29]

The thoroughgoing evil embodied in Theodora and Justinian is denounced to the reader on another level. While they acted in unison, Procopius says, and were almost indistinguishable in their aims, "where there did happen to be some real difference in their characters they were equally wicked, though they displayed exactly opposite traits in destroying their subjects" (13.9:106–7).

By comparing them in this manner Procopius is able to suggest that between them Theodora and Justinian contain almost every known vice. The empress is implacable, whereas the emperor is frequently said to be unstable;[30] she is unapproachable and formidable, he is affable in the extreme and too easygoing (15.11–18); she is too fond of bathing, eating, and sleeping, he is an ascetic insomniac who uses his sleepless hours to devise his subjects' perdition.[31] Theodora is presented as forceful and domineering, Justinian as being easily led by her.[32] This misrepresentation is carried even farther by Procopius, who asserts that for a long time,

it was universally believed that they were exact opposites in their ideas and interests; but later it was recognized that this false impression had been deliberately fostered to make sure that their subjects did not put their own differences aside and rebel against them, but were all divided in their feelings about them. (10.14:91)

Thanks to this disingenuous behavior Theodora and her husband are able to outwit and control religious groups, circus factions, the Senate, and contestants of legal suits.[33] While Theodora pursues a policy contrary to his own, the emperor is said to turn a blind eye.[34]

It will be obvious that this sustained contrast between the couple's united front, on the one hand, and the polarity of their characteristics, on the other, makes a reconstruction of Theodora as a public figure hazardous. However, Procopius's representation of the *Doppelspiel* played by Theodora and her husband may well reflect contemporary views of their administration, particularly with regard to religion. A later contemporary of Procopius, the Church historian Evagrius Scholasticus, who as a student of law in Constantinople would have been familiar with details of the reign, reports that the empress supported the monophysites while her husband resolutely championed the Chalcedonians, either because these were their real beliefs or because they had privately agreed to behave in this way. Neither made concessions to the other, according to Evagrius.[35] There is abundant evidence from other contemporary writers of the esteem in which Theodora was held by the monophysite party: Theological tractates were addressed to her (Van Roey 1989); she housed deposed monophysite bishops in her palace; and she dispatched monophysite missionaries to Nubia. Meanwhile her husband upheld Chalcedonian orthodoxy and persecuted monophysites.[36] The idea that this opposing stance was deliberately devised was perhaps a natural one, and it seems to stem not simply from Procopius but from opposition literature in general, of which the *Secret History* is the most vicious example.[37] The propaganda in favor of the reign, of which, it has recently been argued, there are traces in the contemporary chronographer John Malalas (Scott 1985), contains no evidence that can be regarded as a counterargument to the *Doppelspiel*, or which enables us to reconstruct the public role of Theodora.

But let us return to Procopius's multifaceted use of comparison in the *Secret History*. In the introduction to the work Procopius explains that for the information of posterity he is going to recount "the contemptible conduct of Belisarius and . . . the equally contemptible conduct of Justinian and Theodora" (1.10:39). In fact the book opens with a description of Belisarius's wife Antonina, and it is easy to see why. Her origins, it is alleged, were lowly; her mother is said to have been an actress of easy virtue. In a vague sentence Antonina herself is described as living a loose kind of life. She is skilled in the use of magic; before her marriage to Belisarius she was already the mother of many illegitimate children (1.11–13). A little later her cruelty is depicted (1.27), as well as her domination of her husband (4.29–30). The implicit comparison with Theodora cannot be missed, especially as Antonina is said to be her close friend and collaborator (1.13;4.18). Unlike the empress, however, Antonina does not desist from profligacy after her marriage; on the contrary, she even has intercourse in public with her husband's adopted son (1.14–18). By association the infidelity and sexual excess of the one friend are transferred to the other, but not in such a way that Theodora's own fidelity to her husband is called into question. Similarly, Belisarius's counterpart is Justinian. The easygoing general turns a blind eye to the doings of his wife (1.35;1.20), to whom he is held in servility through a passion he cannot control (4.30.31); he lets Antonina have her way in everything (5.14). Procopius's dismissal of him early in the work as a hopeless fool (4.41) prefigures the indictment of Justinian later on (8.23). By using on various levels the element of comparison from the genre of invective, both explicitly and by innuendo, Procopius deftly rounds out his misrepresentation of Theodora and her husband into a comprehensive defamation.

CONCLUSIONS

We have seen how in his thoroughgoing vituperation of the Empress Theodora in the *Secret History* Procopius avails himself in the first place of the stereotypes traditionally applied to political women. To be sure, he uses these techniques viciously and unscrupulously in order to trivialize the influence of Theodora; but it must also be admitted that, since the political role of the empress in Byzantium was never explicitly defined and she was consequently obliged to act indirectly, he could hardly avoid depicting her, for example, as involved in palace politics. The devices and elements of classical invective, which include stereotypes, are also marshalled by Procopius in his denunciation of Theodora.

The element of comparison is built on extensively, and the result is the *Dop-pelspiel* between Theodora and her husband, in which the couple Antonina and Belisarius are also used to highlight and complement the actions and character-istics of the imperial pair. Although Procopius's presentation of Theodora in the *Secret History* is the best example we have in Greek, Roman, and early Byzantine literature of the depiction of a political woman by one author, its complexity, together with Procopius's cleverness and lack of scruple, makes a sound recon-struction of Theodora as public figure difficult. Nor do other contemporary sources enlighten us substantially. We must conclude, however, that the dis-gusting portrait of Theodora in the *Secret History* is not there simply to indict Justinian by association, and that while the political power and the public role of Byzantine empresses were on the whole never spelled out, for Procopius, at least, Theodora's power and influence, chiefly exercised though they were within the bounds of contemporary social and political norms, were only too threatening and real.

NOTES

1. On Byzantine women in general see, with bibliography, Grosdidier de Matons 1974, Beaucamp 1977, Laiou 1981, Herrin 1983. On the Byzantine empress see Runciman 1972; Grosdidier de Matons 1974, 20–23; Bensammar 1976; and Missiou 1982. The constitutional position of the empress is discussed by Bosch 1982; cf. Maslev 1966. For the paradoxical situation of royal or elite woman in two societies see Pomeroy 1984, 11 (Hellenistic queens) and Hallet 1984, 3–34 (elite Roman women).

2. For example, Aelia Eudoxia (395–404), Aelia Pulcheria (413–453); cf. Holum, 1982, 48–111; and Richlin, chap. 4 in this volume; Sophia (565–578); cf. Cameron 1975.

3. For example, Irene (797–802), cf. Runciman, 1978; Zoe (1042) and Theodora (1042,1055–1056); cf. Psellus, *Chronographia* I.108–24 and II.72–82 (Penguin tr. 155–62, 261–71).

4. On this point see Lefkowitz, 1983 and cf. Elshtain, 1981, 14, n. 11.

5. On Procopius of Caesarea in general see Rubin 1953, 1960; and Cameron 1985. For the *Secret History* (*S.H.*) in particular see Rubin 1951, 1953, 1960, 197ff; Tinnefeld 1971, 29–36; Cameron 1985, 49–83. All references to the *S.H.* are to the Leipzig edition of 1963, followed, where necessary, by reference to the Penguin translation by G. A. Williamson.

6. *Pace*, e.g., Baldwin 1982, who takes the speech at face value. Cf. Cameron 1985, 69.

7. See Fisher 1984, 300–301 on the significance of the passage.

8. Tr. Dewing-Downey, 89–91.

9. This is argued convincingly and in detail by Fisher 1984.

10. I have preferred to retain the word "actress" because women who entered the acting profession were regarded as morally loose.

11. Even by John of Ephesus, a bishop of the outlawed monophysite party championed by Theodora (see below), she is said to be "from the brothel": *Lives of the Eastern Saints*, 189. On the legislation see *Codex Iustinianus* 5.4.23 and Daube 1967.

12. On this stereotype in Cicero see Skinner 1982, 207; contrast Richlin, chap. 4 of this volume.

13. *S.H.* 2.32–36; 15.8–9; 17.27; 30.24.

14. On a ceremonial role of the empress depicted in Ravenna see MacCormack 1981, 259–66.

15. *S.H.* 3.9–11; 3.21–22; 4.7–12; 16.25–26.

16. *S.H.* 5.18–22; 17.28–31.

17. *S.H.* 4.17.31; 10.20–23.

18. *S.H.* 3.8; 16.11; 17.18–21.44.

19. On the elements, see Tinnefeld 1971, 33–35, supplemented by Struthers 1919; Levy 1946, 1948; Nisbet 1961, 192–97. Cf. Cameron 1970, 68–69, 83–84.

20. Low social origins in themselves, however, did not constitute a bar to becoming empress. The consort of Justinian's uncle, Lupicina/Euphemia (A.D. 518–527), was herself a former slave. See Grosdidier de Matons 1974, 21.

21. See Cameron 1985, 59; Baldwin 1987; cf. Richlin 1983, 105–43 (Roman literature).

22. See Head 1980, 1982; Baldwin 1981.

23. Cf. *S.H.* 8.27; 12.11; 14.1; 15.39; 21.8; 27.1.32; 29.19.26; 30.20.

24. For a discussion of the comparison, see Rubin 1960, 445–48; Cameron 1985, 57.

25. *S.H.* 1.13; 3.29; 15.1–4 (vindictive); 3.21–26; 5.11; 16.22 (unscrupulous); 2.32–36; 4.13; 15.8–9.17; 17.27; 30.24 (domineering).

26. *S.H.* 6.21; 14.1; 29.19 (innovative); 7.31–32; 8.3; 13.19; 15.17–18 (unstable); 7.7; 11.1; 14.1; 18.11–12 (chaotic).

27. On Antonina and her husband, see Evert-Kappesowa 1964.

28. This portrayal is discussed by Rubin 1951 and Cameron 1985, 56–57.

29. In 16.11ff., there is a suggestion that Theodora had an affair with a certain Areobindus, but the point of the story is rather the cruelty with which she flogged and disposed of him because he had offended her (cf. 15.39). Similarly in a throwaway line Justinian is said to have had "a demonic passion for the pleasures of Aphrodite" (12.27:104). While suggesting a great deal in a vague manner, in order to leave no stone unturned in his attack on Theodora and her husband, Procopius manages this without detracting substantially from his depiction of them always and in all things acting in unison.

30. *S.H.* 15.1–5 vs. 7.31–32; 8.3; 13.19; 15.17–18.

31. *S.H.* 15.6–9 vs. 13.28–33.

32. For example, *S.H.* 13.18–19; 15.10.

33. *S.H.* 10.15; 27.13 (religion); 10.15–18 (factions); 14.7–10 (Senate); 10.19 (litigants).

34. *S.H.* 10.22; 16.10; 17.45.

35. *Historia Ecclesiastica* IV.10; ed. Bidez-Parmentier, 160. For a discussion of the passage, see Allen 1981, 182–83.

36. For a discussion of the sources, see Cameron 1985, 75–80.

37. See Rubin 1953; Allen 1981, 182–83; 194–96; 206–7.

REFERENCES

Allen, P. 1981. *Evagrius Scholasticus the Church Historian* (*Spicilegium Sacrum Lovaniense* 41). Leuven: Peeters.

Baldwin, B. 1981. "Physical Descriptions of Byzantine Emperors." *Byzantion* 51:8–21.
———. 1982. "An Aphorism in Procopius." *Rheinisches Museum* 125:309–11.
———. 1987. "Sexual Rhetoric in Procopius." *Mnemosyne* 4(40): 150–52.
Beaucamp, J. 1977. "La situation juridique de la femme à Byzance." *Cahiers de civilisation médiévale* 20:145–76.
Bensammar, E. 1976. "La titulature de l'impératrice et sa signification. Recherches sur les sources byzantines de la fin du VIIIe siècle à la fin du XIIe siècle". *Byzantion* 46:243–91.
Bosch, U. V. 1982. "Fragen zum Frauenkaisertum." *Jahrbuch der Österreichischen Byzantinistik* 32(2):449–505.
Cameron, Alan. 1970. *Claudian Poetry and Propaganda at the Court of Honorius*. Oxford : Oxford University Press.
Cameron, Averil. 1975. "The Empress Sophia." *Byzantion* 45:5–21.
———. 1985. *Procopius and the Sixth Century*. London: Duckworth.
Cameron, Averil, and A. Kuhrt, eds. 1983. *Images of Women in Antiquity*. London: Croom Helm.
Daube, D. 1967. "The Marriage of Justinian and Theodora. Legal and Theological Reflections." *Catholic University Law Review* 16:380–99.
Elshtain, J. B. 1981. *Public Man, Private Woman : Women in Social and Political Thought*. Princeton, N.J.: Princeton University Press.
Evagrius Scholasticus. [1898] 1964. *Ecclesiastical History*. Edited by J. Bidez and L. Parmentier. London: A. M. Hakkert.
Evert-Kappesowa, H. 1964. "Antonine et Bélisare." In *Byzantinische Beiträge*, edited by J. Irmscher, 55–72. Berlin: Akademie Verlag.
Fisher, E. A. 1984. "Theodora and Antonina in the Historia Arcana: History and/or Fiction?" In *Women in the Ancient World*, edited by J. Peradotto and J. P. Sullivan, 287–313. Albany: State University of New York Press.
Grosdidier de Matons, J. 1974. "La femme dans l'empire byzantin." In *Histoire mondiale de la femme*, vol. 3. Edited by P. Grimal. 11–43. Paris : Nouvelle Librairie de France.
Hallett. J. P. 1984. *Fathers and Daughters in Roman Society. Women and the Elite Family*. Princeton, N.J.: Princeton University Press.
Head, C. 1980. "Physical Descriptions of the Emperors in Byzantine Historical Writing." *Byzantion* 50:226–48.
———. 1982. *Imperial Byzantine Portraits. A Verbal and Graphic Gallery*. New York: Caratzas Brothers.
Herrin, J. 1983. "In Search of Byzantine Women: Three Avenues of Approach." In *Images of Women in Antiquity*, edited by Averil Cameron and A. Kuhrt, 167–89. London: Croom Helm.
Holum, K. G. 1982. *Theodosian Empresses*. Berkeley: University of California Press.
John of Ephesus. [1923] 1974. *Lives of the Eastern Saints, Patrologia Orientalis* 17. Paris and Turnhout: Brepols.
Justinian. 1963. *Codex Iustinianus*. Edited by P. Krueger. *Corpus Iuris Civilis* II. 13th ed. Berlin: Teubner.
Laiou, A. 1981. "The Role of Women in Byzantine Society." *Jahrbuch der Österreichischen Byzantinistik* 31:233–60.
Lefkowitz, M. R. 1983. "Influential Women." In *Images of Women in Antiquity*, edited by Averil Cameron and A. Kuhrt, 49–64. London: Croom Helm.

Levy, H. L. 1946. "Claudian's In Rufinum and the Rhetorical Psogos." *Transactions of the American Philological Association* 77:57–65.

———. 1958. "Themes of Encomium and Invective in Claudian." *Transactions of the American Philological Association* 89:336–47.

MacCormack, S. G. 1981. *Art and Ceremony in Late Antiquity*. Berkeley: University of California Press.

Maslev, St. 1966. "Die staatsrechtliche Stellung der byzantinischen Kaiserin." *Byzantinoslavica* 27:308–43.

Missiou, D. 1982. "Über die institutionelle Rolle der byzantinischen Kaiserin." *Jahrbuch der Österreichischen Byzantinistik* 32 (2):489–98.

Nisbet, R.G.M., ed. 1961. *M. Tulli Ciceronis in L. Calpurnium Pisonem Oratio*. Oxford: Clarendon Press.

Pomeroy, S. R. 1984. *Women in Hellenistic Egypt. From Alexander to Cleopatra*. New York: Shocken Books.

Procopius of Caesarea. [1963]. *Opera Omnia*. Edited by J. Haury and G. Wirth. 4 vols. Leipzig, Germany: Teubner.

———. [1966]. *The Secret History*. Translated by G. A. Williamson. Harmondsworth, England: Penguin.

———. [1971]. *Buildings*. Translated by H. B. Dewing and G. Downey. Cambridge, Mass.: William Heinemann.

Psellus, Michael. 1966. *Fourteen Byzantine Rulers*. Translated by E.R.A. Sewter. Harmondsworth, England: Penguin.

———. 1967. *Chronographia*. Edited by E. Renauld. 2 vols. Paris: Les Belles Lettres.

Richlin, A. 1983. *The Garden of Priapus*. New Haven, Conn.: Yale University Press.

———. 1984. "Invective against Women in Roman Satire." *Arethusa* 17:67–80.

———. 1992. "Julia's Jokes, Galla Placidia, and the Roman Use of Women as Political Icons," chap. 4 in this volume.

Rubin, B. 1951. "Der Fürst der Dämonen." *Byzantinische Zeitschrift* 44:469–81.

———. 1953. "Zur Kaiserkritik Ostroms." *Studi Bizantini e Neoellenici* 7 *Atti der VIII congresso internazionale di Studi Bizantini*, 453–62. Roma: Associazione Nazionale per gli Studi Bizantini.

———. 1960. *Das Zeitalter Iustinians I*. Berlin: W. de Gruyter & Co.

Runciman, S. 1972. "Some Notes on the Role of the Empress." *Eastern Churches Review* 4:119–24.

———. 1978. "The Empress Irene the Athenian." In *Studies in Church History*. Subsidia I. *Medieval Women*, edited by D. Baker, 101–18. Oxford: Basil Blackwell.

Scott, R. D. 1985. "Malalas, *The Secret History*, and Justinian's Propaganda." *Dumbarton Oaks Papers* 39:99–109.

Skinner, M. B. 1982. "Pretty Lesbius." *Transactions of the American Philological Association* 112:197–208.

Struthers, L. B. 1919. "The Rhetorical Structures of the Encomia of Claudius Claudian." *Harvard Studies in Classical Philology* 30:49–87.

Tinnefeld, F. H. 1971. *Kategorien der Kaiserkritik in der byzantinischen Historiographie von Prokop bis Niketas Choniates*. Munich, Germany: W. Fink.

Van Roey, A. 1989. "Unedited Monophysite Documents of the Sixth Century." *Studia Patristica* 20:76–80.

6

Women and Power in the Scandinavian Sagas

Margaret Clunies Ross _____

Most of the surviving vernacular writing of medieval Scandinavia comes from Iceland. We cannot prove it, but it seems likely that the medieval Icelandic sagas[1] were written by men, largely about men and their world, but for an audience that would have comprised both men and women. Some scholars think that saga writers may have been mainly men in orders, although we also know of several nonclerical writers of the Middle Ages, and it seems sensible to hypothesize that saga writing was not restricted to churchmen (see Lönnroth 1976 for a discussion of saga audiences). Certainly, however, those people who composed the sagas that have come down to us from the Middle Ages, largely of thirteenth-century date, were Christians, yet the nature of their subject matter and their own cultural pride led them to compose stories about persons and events that took place in the pre-Christian age of Scandinavia just as much as in the period after the conversion, which in Iceland occurred in A.D. 1000.

The subjects of Icelandic sagas are varied, but they all have a historical dimension, whether they are set in the legendary past, the early period of the settlement of Iceland (late ninth to the end of the tenth century), Norway and its colonies during the Viking Age, or northern Europe including Iceland during the twelfth and thirteenth centuries. The chronological dimensions of *Orkneyinga saga* (The history of the Orkney Islanders) stretch from the late ninth century to the beginning of the thirteenth. The saga in its preserved form probably dates from the third decade of the thirteenth century, though an earlier version may have been in existence in the 1190s (Pálsson and Edwards 1978, 10; Guðmundsson 1965, vii–ix). There is good reason to believe that it was composed in Iceland, though probably from the testimonies of Orkney Islanders. It is this saga that I have chosen to analyze in my examination of the relationship between women and power in early Scandinavian saga writing, partly because it covers a long period of time and partly because it falls between the genre known as the family saga and that of royal biography, largely of the kings of Norway. It concerns the jockeying for power within the family of a dynasty of hereditary earls of the Orkney Islands, whose title was originally granted to them by the Norwegian king. Norway was the motherland of this Viking Age colony, though the inhabitants also formed strong political alliances with the Celtic world, particularly with the kings of Scotland and the local rulers of parts of northern Scotland, especially Caithness, which is separated from the islands by the Pentland Firth.

The saga concentrates on relationships of political power and on the continual tension between the desire of the Orkney earls to remain independent of the successive kings of Norway and, to a lesser extent, of Scotland, and the frequent necessity they found to petition these rulers for help in internal political rivalries, largely initiated by other members of their own family. It must be stated at the outset that no female member of the family inherited the earldom. Tenure of office was usually patrilineal, although, in three cases within the saga—those of Rögnvaldr Kali, Haraldr Maddaðarson, and Haraldr the Young—it was transmitted through a female member.

Wider political and governmental issues in Orkadian history are not central to this saga. For example, important farmers on the islands had the distinctive name of gæðingar, meaning "men endowed with goods," and probably enjoyed both rank and responsibilities similar to those of the "landed men" in Norway (Foote and Wilson 1980, 131–32). On the islands these responsibilities included the maintenance of ships and of beacons on each island as part of the defense system, but these matters only become part of the saga narrative when they are involved in the political intrigues of members of the ruling family, as the lighting of the beacons does in chapters 69–71. Individual characters, too, appear in the saga only to the extent that they are involved in the dynastic struggles of the earls, and this applies to both men and women. However, as these struggles typically take place in the public arena of journeyings abroad, fights, oath takings, pilgrimages, and so forth, in which women traditionally did not participate, there are fewer opportunities for female characters to appear in the saga narrative, which has a frankly masculine point of view. Thus the nature and extent of female characterization in this saga may give some indication of the degree to which women were regarded as proper political agents in the culture from which the saga author came. Moreover, cultural attitudes and expected norms of female behavior may be deduced both from the range of female characters deployed and from the value judgments about them that are perceptible in the text.

The relationship between what one can crudely call "literature" and "life" in the genesis of the Scandinavian sagas continues to be a point of contention in saga scholarship and has been productive of new approaches to these texts. In the earlier part of this century scholars came to discredit the strict historicity of many Icelandic sagas (Nordal 1940; Andersson 1964, 41–64), but within the last two decades opinion has shifted to admit that these texts, while in some cases unreliable in terms of chronology or accurate representation of older beliefs and practices, may give us access to customary behavior and unconsciously held societal attitudes. One difficulty that this approach runs into, however, is that societal attitudes changed over time, particularly as a result of the introduction of Christianity to Scandinavia. So we must be careful to take account of the Church's desire to reform heterosexual behavior, for example, when assessing saga writers' accounts of matters such as marriage and divorce (Jochens 1986a). And yet most studies of early Scandinavian collective states of mind (e.g., Meulengracht Sørensen 1983), including this chapter, assume a cultural continuity in matters of custom and community attitudes that existed as something distinctively Scandinavian in the medieval European context. Thirteenth-century texts and the traditions they were based on formed part of the conceptual universe of the saga writer (or writers) and his audience; some of those traditions were purely native ones, some were formulated by Christian churchmen.

A work like *Orkneyinga saga* has its basis in transpired events, as the classical view maintained that history should (Smalley 1974, 15–25), but many people's views of just what the facts were and of what was important within them contributed to the version of history that has been recorded in the extant manuscripts. Michael Chesnutt (1981) has shown, for example, how the concluding chapters of the saga probably derive from the personal reminiscences of a prominent Caithness man. One can assume that the contributors also held common values that are perceptible in this historical narrative, and that one such set of values related to the place of women in political history.

In a strict sense, women had no direct role in the political process in medieval Scandinavian societies outside the influence they might exert as private persons on their male kin and acquaintances. Women could not exercise secular power in any public arena in their own right; they could not plead cases in the law courts and assemblies; they could not act as officials of the *þing* or assembly in Iceland (Hastrup 1985, 121); they were not normally heads of households. They did not prosecute blood feuds in person, although they might act as inciters of male kin, and often did, if we are to believe the Icelandic family sagas.

There is an apparently puzzling discrepancy between the presentation of women's involvement in Icelandic feuding in the family sagas, which relate events that are supposed to have taken place in Iceland during the age of settlement, and their much smaller involvement in the feuds, litigations, and battles of the so-called contemporary sagas, those that deal with Icelandic politics of the late twelfth and the first half of the thirteenth centuries. In the family sagas women appear frequently as inciters of feuds and as goaders of their men (Heller 1958, 98–123). Though they may not fight themselves, they try very hard to get their men to take vengeance for family wrongs, and they frequently succeed, though often at considerable personal cost. In contemporary sagas, of which the compilation *Sturlunga saga* is the prime example, women are rarely represented as participating directly in feuds and have a very small presence in politics generally. The situation in *Orkneyinga saga* is closer to *Sturlunga saga* than to the family sagas.

Jenny Jochens (1986b) has recently tried to explain the difference between the roles women play in the two types of saga as reflecting policies and attitudes of the Church to marriage and women's conditions generally. She holds that the family sagas (but presumably not the contemporary sagas, which she sees as more "realistic") are to be read didactically, as advocating mutual consent between marriage partners, even though this is unlikely to have been historically accurate. She and Roberta Frank (1973) have observed how often in the family sagas marriages contracted against the woman's will or without consulting her end in disaster and lead to feuding between the families concerned. According to this argument, the ideal of consent is absent from the more realistic contemporary sagas because it was not a reality in Iceland until well after the thirteenth century.

Some problems are associated with this argument. First, not all cases in which women appear as inciters of their men in family sagas have to do with frustrated marriage plans. Second, and more important from the perspective of the history of ideas in Scandinavia, female inciters appear in Old Norse heroic poetry, which is unlikely to be the vehicle for Christian didacticism. Furthermore, their opposite, the "peace weaver," as the Old English poem *Beowulf* calls the type of woman who seeks to calm down opposing tribal groups and family parties, exists in early Germanic poetry alongside the figure of the inciter. They are both archetypes of female roles in the politics of the heroic age, as that period is represented in early Germanic poetry (Clunies Ross 1977).

To find female inciters in the family saga is therefore to perceive a conceptual continuity with heroic literature rather than an innovation. It may also indicate that the family sagas are not centrally concerned with the politics of feuding *tout court* (*pace* Byock 1982) but rather with what Theodore Andersson has called the displacement of the heroic ideal (1970). Their major preoccupations, which include the role of women in family and community politics, are with what these struggles are all about, not with the political system itself. To understand them, as Jesse Byock (1982) has demonstrated most effectively, requires one to understand the Icelandic political process, but the focus of these sagas is on the conceptual underpinning of a society of displaced heroism, on concepts of honor and social status, on the proper roles of men and women in such a society and, conversely, on improper behavior judged by Icelandic mores, and on breaches of honor.

By contrast, the contemporary sagas assume the operation of an honor and shame society as the background to their accounts of multifarious political intrigues, fights, property disputes, and marriage arrangements. On the whole, they are concerned with the operation of the political system rather than with what makes it work. *Sturlunga saga*, given the fact that medieval Iceland was a commonwealth rather than a society ruled by kings and hereditary nobles like the rest of contemporary Europe, is the history of a de facto political dynasty, the Sturlungar. It is the history of a family that dominated Iceland in the late twelfth and the first part of the thirteenth century. It is not to be expected that women, who were largely excluded from the public sphere of litigation, fighting, traveling abroad, and so forth, would play a dominant role in such a political narrative, nor that they would initiate political action. And on the whole they do not.

Another reason for the disparity in the presentation of the supposedly active, inciting women of the family sagas and their less active counterparts in the contemporary saga may be that Christian authors were attempting a historical overview of male-female relations from a Christian point of view. They represent active women as characteristic of pre-Christian society, just as Saxo Grammaticus does in his *Gesta Danorum*, because they knew that this sort of behavior was not proper to the Christian view of women as subservient to men. Birgit Strand (1981, 150–51) has noted how the Christian part of the *Gesta Danorum* contains "colourless and shadowy women," whereas the heathen section is full of colorful, active ones. The disparity between the family and contemporary sagas probably reflects the same sense of difference between Christian and pre-Christian society, at least as an ideal.

Orkneyinga saga shares with *Sturlunga saga* a central concern with issues of political power. Melissa Berman (1985) has called this and two other sagas of events in Norse Viking colonies the "political sagas" because of their concentration on the users of political power and on the relationship between a colonial society and the major power from which it struggled to gain independence, while at the same time often drawing on its political support. Like *Sturlunga saga* also, *Orkneyinga saga* is a dynastic history; it tells of those men who came to power in each generation of the family of the earls and of whether they ruled alone or shared the earldom with a kinsman. In many cases men were unable to tolerate a co-ruler and either murdered their rivals themselves or had them killed by others. Thus Þorfinnr was responsible for the death of his father's brother's son Rögnvaldr and Hákon Pálsson for his father's brother's son St. Magnús. Erlendr Haraldsson is killed by his father's sister's son, Haraldr Maddaðarson, and his father's father's brother's daughter's son, Rögnvaldr Kali. Haraldr the Young is killed by Haraldr Maddaðarson, but their kinship was a more distant one on the mother's side.

These murders within the family are carried out more often by kinsmen whose relationship to their victims is patrilineal rather than matrilineal, as such kinsmen, usually cousins, constituted a direct dynastic threat. On many occasions the saga writer details the disruption to Orkadian society brought about by intrafamilial rivalry, and the saga is not free from a Christian sense of sin at such acts. The killing of Magnús Erlendsson, in particular, is attended by an authorial sense of outrage, and Magnús himself is represented as a saintly figure who gives himself up to his cousin Hákon in an act of martyrdom rather than continue the family strife. It is generally reckoned that a separate hagiographical account of the death and miracles of Magnús, who came to be regarded as a saint in Orkney, underlies these chapters (Guðmundsson 1965,xliii–lix).

Turning now to the female characters of *Orkneyinga saga*, we may distinguish first of all those women who appear in largely passive roles. This group includes women whose involvement in the narrative comes about through the acts of men—through arranged marriages, or because a male protagonist calls at an inn run by a woman (chap. 60), or because another male character comes to a certain farmhouse to pick up his concubine and her clothing and gets killed while she is inside the house saying goodbye (chap. 61). Of course, some female characters whose primary inclusion in the narrative derives from the fact that they are married to one of the protagonists may become active characters, pursuing their own interests or those of their kin, which may include both their family of origin and their children or kinswomen's children.

Most of the nonpassive female characters in *Orkneyinga saga* belong to this latter group, and they fall into a small number of easily recognizable character types both in Icelandic saga literature and more generally in literature representing politically active women. There are only two female characters of any importance in *Orkneyinga saga* who do not marry into the earls' family. The first of these is the exotic Ermingerðr of Narbonne, whom Earl Rögnvaldr Kali encounters on his pilgrimage east to the Holy Land. Rögnvaldr is mightily impressed by this foreign woman, and indeed her advisors indicate that they would look favorably upon an offer of marriage from him for this beautiful lady who was her father's sole heir (chap. 86). Nevertheless, in spite of her various attractions and in spite of a series of verses Rögnvaldr composes, with their focus half on her and half on his military campaign (Frank 1978, 167–68), we hear no more of her in the saga. In political terms, such a marriage would have been of little use to a ruler of the Orkneys, for alliances with such a distant power and such an exotic culture would have counted for little in the North Atlantic. So for all Rögnvaldr's possible attempts at troubadour verse (Andersson 1969), his adventure with Ermingerðr is just that, a sexual exploit, and that is also how it comes across in his poetry.[2]

The second female character who is an independent agent in the saga and has no relationship by marriage with the Orkney earls is the presumably widowed woman farmer, Ragna, who runs a farm with her son Þorsteinn on the outermost of all the Orkneys, North Ronaldsay. She had a second estate on Papey (chap. 67). First introduced in chapter 56, she is described as a distinguished mistress of a household (*göfug húsfreyja*). Later, during a visit of Earl Páll Hákonarson to North Ronaldsay (chap. 67), she arranges a feast for the earl and makes a speech, urging him to seek reconciliation with his kinsman, Earl Rögnvaldr and the powerful commoner Sveinn Ásleifarson. She ends her address with the sententious reminder that really distinguished men look after the interests of their friends and thereby increase their own support and popularity (Guðmundsson 1965, 157). Ragna is the type of disinterested commoner, an honest farmer of independent means, who dares to give political advice to a ruler.

Páll rebukes Ragna for her outspokenness and presumption: "You are a wise woman (*vitr kona*), Ragna, but it hasn't been your lot to have the name of earl in the Orkneys; you must not control the government of the country here" (my translation; Icelandic text in Guðmundsson 1965, 157). He shows little inclination to follow her wise advice; instead, he indicates his resolve to fight his relative Rögnvaldr. The narrator's report that many people thought this unwise though no one else was brave enough to contradict him indicates the normative point of view, which coincides with Ragna's.

Ragna is involved in another scene (chap. 81) in which she demonstrates her superior discernment in a matter of political judgment over another of the Orkney earls, Rögnvaldr Kali. Significantly, this matter is a question of his estimation of the quality of a visiting Icelandic poet. Poetry was a skill for which Rögnvaldr himself had a considerable reputation. To be a fine poet was linked in the Icelandic mind with a range of manly virtues, as Rögnvaldr proudly claimed of himself in a verse, quoted in the saga in chapter 58:

I am quick to play at tables,
I am master of nine accomplishments;
I'm often busy with my hands and books,
I know how to glide on skis,
I shoot and row pretty well;
I understand both the arts
Of harp-playing and of poetry.
(Author's translation; for the Icelandic, see Guðmundsson 1965, 130)

The incident with Ragna involved an Icelander, Hallr Þórarinson, who had come to seek service with Earl Rögnvaldr.[3] We know from sources external to *Orkneyinga saga* that the two men composed a poem together, called *Háttalykill* or "Key to the Meters," a sort of Icelandic *clavis metrica*, and a version of this poem has survived (Helgason and Holtsmark 1941). The scene of chapter 81 operates in the saga to introduce a reference to *Háttalykill* and the narrating voice's knowledge of it, thereby deepening the audience's perception of Rögnvaldr's importance as a poet and patron of poets. But it also develops the character of Ragna as a woman of greater shrewdness than her male rulers. In fact, the scene illustrates perfectly two stanzas of the Old Norse wisdom poem *Hávamál* (132–33), which first urge that one should not mock or scorn a guest or a traveller and then give the reason—that those who are sitting inside a hall can only have a superficial knowledge of the characters of those who visit them. Appearances are often deceptive, and so it proves with Ragna.

We are told in chapter 81 that Ragna's son Þorsteinn and Hallr first go together to seek a place for the Icelander with Earl Rögnvaldr, but they fail to impress him. In fact, according to a verse of Hallr's quoted in the text, Rögnvaldr makes derogatory references to Icelanders as a group of sausage eaters, a common enough medieval jibe. Ragna decides to visit Rögnvaldr herself to plead for

Hallr and she does so dressed rather oddly. Instead of the silk or linen headdress women usually wore, Ragna had on an outlandish red headdress (*gaddan*) made of horsehair.[4] This seeming impropriety of dress annoyed and offended Rögnvaldr, and in a verse he complained that Ragna had slighted him and had failed to dress in the manner customary for women at his court. He also assumed that, being a woman, her headdress was made from the hair of a mare.

Evidently, Ragna had carefully prepared her apparel to transmit confusing semiotic messages to the earl and to trick him into recognizing that women can play male roles as well as men can and that they should therefore be listened to. Headdresses may have a variety of cultural meanings, depending on their nature and symbolic value, and the identity and gender of their wearers. Sometimes, as with a crown, they may denote the authority of their bearers, but when a head covering is worn by members of a particular social group, say, monks or married women, it serves to distinguish them as members of that group rather than as individuals, and it often connotes their deference to more authoritative figures in society. Such was probably the case with the *höfuðdukr* or tall headress that married women used in medieval Scandinavian societies to cover their hair, which they wore gathered up in a knot, by contrast with the loose, unrestrained hair of a young unmarried woman who wore no headdress (Foote and Wilson 1980, 174).

In his verse to Ragna, Rögnvaldr admits that he has been angered by her failure to adopt the usual headcovering of high-born women. By implication, her behavior makes a mockery of him and his court. Her substitution of a headdress apparently made from a mare's tail (*marar tagl*) flouts his authority by its lack of decorum (signaled by animal hair rather than woven cloth) and at the same time draws attention to the headdress as a badge of femininity. And this is just the point that Ragna wishes to subvert, for she has deliberately made her headdress out of the tail of a stallion (*hestr*), not a mare. She scores a double point here: First, she puts Rögnvaldr at a disadvantage by proving him wrong, and second, she demonstrates that his error is precisely in the area of what we would nowadays call sex-role stereotypes. What she proves is that a woman can be as wise and intelligent (*vitr*) as a man, or more so, in comparison with men like himself who are fooled into trusting appearances. Her message is, of course, that Rögnvaldr would be a greater fool if he did not take her advice and accept Hallr þórarinson as a member of his retinue. The earl eventually does so, and the narrator's reminder to the audience that the two of them composed *Háttalykill* indicates that, judged empirically, Ragna gave the right advice, as the poem was still famous many years after it had been composed.

Ragna's rather bizarre play with semiotic codes was made possible by two underlying medieval Icelandic assumptions. The first of these is not peculiar to Icelandic society, but was widely held there, to judge by a variety of extant medieval texts: Women's judgment is basically unsound because women are fickle and changeable by nature. This view is expressed in another stanza of *Hávamál* (chap. 84): "No one should trust a maiden's words nor what a wife says, because their hearts were made on a turning wheel, and fickleness placed in their breasts'' (my translation; for the Icelandic text see Evans 1986, 56). The second assumption has to do with the symbolic significance of mares and stallions in Icelanders' thinking about what they perceived as the essential differences between men and women and the chief qualities they associated with each sex.

Male sexual performance was intimately bound up in Icelandic consciousness with notions of bravery and masculinity generally; conversely, cowardice and effeminacy were two dimensions of the same thing (Meulengracht Sørensen 1983). To call a man effeminate or to suggest that a woman was behaving like a man were insults of the highest seriousness, called *níð*, and was a major offense at law. Many of the almost stereotyped insults cited in the law codes and sagas involve animal imagery, particularly references to mares or stallions to indicate female or male sexuality and all that was associated with it. By wearing a headdress made from a stallion's tail, therefore, Ragna signaled that she was playing a male role, that of Wise Counsellor (Lönnroth 1976, 62–63). Hence the game she played with Rögnvaldr was not without its dangers, though her status as an independent landowner may have freed her from the likelihood of being charged with unfeminine behavior. Nevertheless, according to the saga, Ragna took a *silkidúkr* or silk kerchief and tied it upon her head immediately after she had made her point to the earl, thus indicating her essential femininity, even while giving him sound advice in a role more usually played by men.

To turn now to a consideration of the female characters associated by marriage with the Orkney earls, we may distinguish those who are mere names from those who are more developed as literary characters. The latter belong to a set of fairly stereotyped female figures in saga literature, and the motives given for their engagement in politics are likewise stereotyped.

It must first be said that, in the society depicted in *Orkneyinga saga*, men aimed where possible to marry a woman of higher social status than themselves or at least, if they were of the highest class, to marry a woman who was not their social inferior. The Orkney earls, like many medieval European rulers (Stafford 1978, 1983), had to look abroad for suitable wives who could bring with them powerful political alliances.

Most of the Orkney earls obtained their wives from Norway or Scotland. In some cases the paramount political significance of such a union was underlined by the fact that the saga writer never mentions the woman by name, but refers to her only as the daughter of an important foreign king or nobleman (cf. Jochens 1987). Sigurðr the Stout, for example, married an unnamed daughter of Malcolm, King of Scots (chap. 12), and Páll þorfinnsson married an unnamed daughter of Earl Hákon Ivarsson of Norway and of Ragnhildr, daughter of King Magnus the Good. In a few cases, no mention is made at all of the mother of a particular earl's children, in some cases certainly, in others possibly, because she was slave born (cf. Karras 1990). Examples here are the mother of Torf-Einarr, the first earl; the wife or concubine of Earl Rögnvaldr Kali; the mother of Earl Páll Hákonarson; and the wife or mistress of Earl Haraldr the Smooth-tongued.

Women are also given in marriage by powerful political leaders as rewards to their followers for faithful service or in compensation for the loss of a kinsman in battle. In chapter 42 King Magnús Ólafsson "Bare-legs" gives Earl Erlendr's daughter Gunnhildr to one of his important retainers, Kol, in compensation for his father's death. Her dowry consisted of some property in Orkney, including a farm on Papley. It was by this marriage that Kol's son Rögnvaldr Kali was able to claim a share in the Orkney earldom. Another example of an opportunistic political match arranged by King Magnús concerned the childhood betrothal of his son Sigurðr to the five-year-old daughter of a King of Connaught (chap. 41). We hear not long afterwards in the saga that when Sigurðr hears of his father's death in Ulster, he abandons his Irish bride and hurries back home to Norway to claim the throne.

In *Orkneyinga saga* women are, on the whole, assessed as either assets or liabilities in male political activities. The figure of a Ragna is as striking as it is rare. Thus in chapter 61 trouble between two families in Norway is settled by the king by bestowing the daughter of one principal on the other in marriage. The friendship between two important men in Orkney politics, þorbjörn Clerk and Sveinn Ásleifarson, is strengthened by þorbjörn's marriage to Sveinn's sister (chap. 77), but as soon as their friendship breaks up, so does the marriage, and in chapter 82 we are told that ill-will between the two men leads þorbjörn to declare himself divorced from Ingigerðr and to send her back home to Sveinn. That act dishonored Sveinn and led to full-blown enmity between the two men.

Apart from the figures of Ermingerðr and Ragna, there are only five other women characters in *Orkneyinga saga* who are in any way developed. Three of these women are wives of Orkney earls, one is the daughter of an earl and later the mother of another, and the fifth is the sister of a woman whom one of the earls had taken as his concubine. With one exception, these women, who are represented as active and independent in furthering their own interests or those of their children, are given a bad press.

Ragnhildr, the daughter of the notoriously cruel Norwegian king Eiríkr Blood-axe and his sorceress wife Gunnhildr—they appear in a number of Icelandic sagas—wreaks havoc among the sons of Earl þorfinnr (chap. 9) by marrying one, then having him murdered when she tired of him, marrying a second and then a third brother, while causing further murders within the wider family of the earls by playing on the dynastic ambitions of the male kin. Such a stereotype of the sexually active, politically dangerous, not to say murderous, woman is also to be found in the writings of the Danish historian Saxo Grammaticus (Strand 1980, 1981) and in the works of many other medieval authors. In many cases, as in the representation of Eðna (Eithne), daughter of King Kjarval of Ireland, wife of Earl Hlöðvir and mother of Earl Sigurðr, the ingredient of magical powers or sorcery is added to the other dangerous character traits attributable to active saga women. Eðna manufactures a banner embroidered with the figure of a raven; it is fairly clear that her ability to endow the banner with the power to bring victory to the man it was carried before and death to him who carried it is seen as a kind of sorcery (chap. 11). The saga writer's Christian perspective on Eðna's powers makes it evident, however, that the predicative power of the raven banner does not preempt the action of fate—it merely signals when an earl's power is on the wane, when, that is, he can no longer force others to carry his banner but must carry it himself.[5]

It has often been noted by anthropologists (e.g., Fortes 1980, xviii) that sorcery, witchcraft, and "the anger of the heart" are conceived of as the products of impulses and motives that are secret or are repressed by cultural definition. Those who are said to harbor such impulses are frequently culturally oppressed. Their oppressors attribute to them, in the form of magical powers or murderous impulses, the kinds of acts that they would ordinarily find difficult to accomplish. Thus it would ordinarily have been difficult if not impossible for a medieval Scandinavian woman to cause the deaths of men in battle, as Eðna is supposed to have done.

The women of the family of Moddan of Caithness, introduced into the saga in chapter 53, are typical examples of malevolent, politically active female figures. It is clear that the saga writer at this point introduces a certain bias against the Caithness faction which here marries into the dynasty of the earls of Orkney, even though, according to Chesnutt (1981), the final chapters of the saga look at events from a pro-Caithness viewpoint. It can be seen that the offspring of Earl Hákon by his concubine Helga Moddans-daughter, together with Helga's sister Frakökk, form a rival dynastic group to the descendants of Hákon's paternal uncle's children, who include St. Magnús (who himself as a Christian saint remained chaste even though married) and his sister Gunnhildr, mother of Rögnvaldr Kali. The prejudice against the descendants of Moddan is concentrated on the female line, thus leaving the males relatively free of blame, which would be improperly heaped on those who inherited the earldom. By contrast, Magnús is represented as a Christian saint, as is his sister's son Rögnvaldr Kali and the latter's daughter's son Haraldr the Young. Though the last-named of these three men is not said to have been canonized, the account of his death in chapter 109 reads like a piece of hagiography (Pálsson and Edwards 1978, 220; Guðmundsson 1965, 292). It is significant that both Magnús and Gunnhildr were the children of Earl Erlendr Þorfinnsson and Þóra, an Icelandic woman, who was a descendant of Hallr of Siða, one of the first men in Iceland to adopt the Christian faith.

Just as the female descendants of Moddan are systematically vilified in *Orkneyinga saga*, especially Frakökk and Margrét, daughter of Earl Hákon Pállsson and mother of another earl, Haraldr Maddaðarson, soÞóra is the only woman member of the family of the earls whose active role in family affairs is represented in a positive light, almost certainly because of her strong Christian connections with one of the first Icelandic Christians and with the holy St. Magnús. Even so, the one scene (chap. 52) in which Þóra appears in her own right concerns her action on behalf of her son Magnús, who has been murdered by his kinsman Hákon, who refused to allow the dead body to be buried in consecrated ground.

She appeals to Hákon's mercy with tears and pleads with him to consider her as his mother and so grant her wish to bury Magnús properly. Such an appeal does not breach the norms of female behavior.

The saga records clear disapprobation of Frakökk Moddans-daughter and her sister's daughter Margrét. Frakökk and her sister Helga are represented as having far too much to say in the government of the latter's son Haraldr (chap. 54) and of plotting to kill Haraldr's brother Páll (perhaps by a different mother). They make a magically destructive white linen cloak, with which they intend to kill Páll. Unfortunately Haraldr cannot resist putting on the splendid cloak, and he dies instantly (chap. 55). Frakökk later brings up Erlendr, son of Haraldr, back in Caithness and for a period is in alliance with Rögnvaldr Kali (chap. 63). She appears resourceful and powerful, marrying off her sister's daughter Margrét to Maddaðr, earl of Atholl, and, with her daughter's son Ölvir "Brawl," leading an army. There is a certain ambivalence in the saga portrait of Frakökk: On the one hand, she is a powerful matriarch, who at one point is described as *djúpvitr*, "deeply wise" (chap. 63); on the other hand, she is acknowledged to be a great troublemaker (chap. 74) and is finally burnt in her house by Sveinn Ásleifarson, a punishment which is said to be more severe than she deserved (chap. 78).

Her niece Margrét is an example of a woman whose sexual attractiveness and willful self-regard (as the saga represents it) cause a lot of trouble for the men around her. She first acts most cruelly toward her brother Páll in the interests of her young son Haraldr (chap. 75) and is said to have arranged Páll's torture and death, although this allegation is left as a rumor. We next hear (chap. 91) that she is very beautiful but full of pride (*svarkr mikill*); this judgment evidently has something to do with her pursuit of illicit sexual relationships that may not be in the best interests of her male kin. We hear in chapter 92 that Sveinn Ásleifarson's brother Gunni fathered a child on Margrét, which caused her son Haraldr, then earl, to make Gunni an outlaw, and which led to bad feelings between Haraldr and Sveinn. We do not hear of Margrét's feelings in the matter. Again, in chapter 93, it is related that a certain Erlendr the Young abducted Margrét, whether willingly or unwillingly we are not told, to the Broch on Mousa in Shetland.[6] Earl Haraldr pursued them to Shetland and laid siege to the Broch; eventually the two men were reconciled, Erlendr promising to support Haraldr, and Haraldr marrying his mother to Erlendr. Again, we hear nothing of Margrét's opinion of these political deals.

It is clear that *Orkneyinga saga* on the whole represents the relationship between women and political power in much the same way as most other medieval Scandinavian writings do, and in ways not dissimilar to many of the world's other literary traditions. The saga is predicated on an opposition between the male and the female that aligns the male with dominance and power, and so with political centrality, and the female with subordination and marginality. Hence female incursions into the public, political arena are likely to be represented as threatening, suspicious and, above all, as actions of the self-seeking individual female will. By contrast, male individualism, being the norm, is never fundamentally questioned, even when it becomes repressive in the exercise of political power and harsh in its effect on society as a whole.

In *Orkneyinga saga* female desires and activities that affect the body politic are consistently represented as either purely personal, as when þóra the Icelander appeals to Earl Hákon to let her bury her son Magnús, or as sinister and malevolent, as in the cases of Eðna, Frakökk, and Helga. A third variation of female willfulness is Margrét's rampant sexuality and the damage it is said to cause to the network of political relations between men. The saga's treatment of Margrét lays bare the nexus between female assertiveness and the ever-present threat to male honor.

Male honor required that women be subordinate to men and that women's domain not extend—at least in theory—beyond the household. It followed that all political behavior by women infringed upon the norms of feminine behavior and this infringement could be expressed on several symbolic levels, as nymphomania, as sorcery, or as malevolent destructiveness. It so happens that these three imputed qualities were exactly those that were thought to characterize the female invert, a role always expressed in a sexual idiom (Meulengracht Sørensen 1983, 20–32).

There was some room in Old Icelandic literature for the assertive woman, particularly the cleverly assertive one like Ragna who turned the idiom of sexual role-playing on its head. This was because, as Meulengracht Sørensen has observed, the masculine ideal was so dominant that it could be admired—at least to an extent—in a female as well as in a male. However, this admiration is inconsistent with the more insistent tenet of male dominance and female subordination. In narrative terms, the admired "masculine" woman always has to be conquered, sometimes, as we have seen with Ermingerðr of Narbonne and Earl Rögnvaldr Kali, by marrying the "maiden king" to her wooer or, as in this case, by suggesting they might be married but for the tyranny of distance and culture. Alternatively, as in Frakökk's case, we find a mixture of admiration and disapprobation in the narrator's expressed position toward his character and of the other saga characters toward her. It could hardly be otherwise, given the pervasive antithesis between what was regarded as appropriate male and female behavior in early Scandinavian society.

NOTES

1. *Saga* is an Icelandic word meaning "that which is said, story." The saga was a prose form, often containing a considerable amount of verse, which was attributed to the saga characters in most cases. In citing Icelandic words and the Icelandic forms of personal names, I have used the runic letters þ and ð, which are both *th*-symbols, and the ligature æ.

2. The episode of Rögnvaldr's visit to Ermingerðr is reminiscent of some of the patterns of male-female encounters in Icelandic versions of romances (*riddarasögur*) and in the fantastic legendary sagas (*fornaldarsögur*). Here we find that the foreign heroine is often a "maiden king" (Wahlgren 1938), a woman who acts as a man in fighting or ruling on

her own behalf, in the absence of male kin. Ermingerðr is like a "maiden king" in being her father's sole heir; she is not, however, aggressive toward the hero, Rögnvaldr, probably in deference to the saga author's perceptions of the concept of courtly love.

3. Hallr may well have been a distant kinsman of Earl Rögnvaldr's on his mother's side; cf. Guðmundsson 1965, 182–83, n. 7.

4. *Gaddan* may have been a Celtic-style headdress; cf. Guðmundsson 1965, 184, n. 1.

5. The motif of the raven banner appears in other Icelandic sagas (see Guðmundsson 1965, 25, n. 4) and also in the Old English *Anglo-Saxon Chronicle* s.a. 878 (MSS B,C,D,E) (Whitelock 1979, 195), where King Alfred is said to have fought against a Viking band equipped with a raven banner. The *Annals of St. Neots*, reporting the same event, says that the raven banner was woven by the daughters of the famous Viking leader Ragnarr Loðbrok. As the raven was particularly associated with the deity Óðinn, god of war and of sorcery, its presence on the banner Eðna makes reinforces the audience's perception of her as sorceress.

6. The broch, or iron-age stone tower on the island of Mousa, is also mentioned in *Egils saga*, chap. 32, as a place to which a woman was abducted from Norway. It is hard to know whether this coincidence represents literary convention or actual practice.

REFERENCES

Andersson, Theodore M. 1964. *The Problem of Icelandic Saga Origins: A Historical Survey*. Yale Germanic Studies, 1. New Haven Conn.: Yale University Press.
———. 1969. "Skalds and Troubadours." *Medieval Scandinavia* 2:7–41.
———. 1970. "The Displacement of the Heroic Ideal in the Family Sagas." *Speculum* 45:575–93.
Berman, Melissa A. 1985. "The Political Sagas." *Scandinavian Studies* 57:113–29.
Byock, Jesse L. 1982. *Feud in the Icelandic Saga*. Berkeley; University of California Press.
Chesnutt, Michael. 1981. "Haralds saga Maddaðarsonar." In *Specvlvm Norroenvm. Norse Studies in Memory of Gabriel Turville-Petre*, edited by U. Dronke, G. P. Helgadóttir, G. W. Weber, and H. Bekker-Nielsen, 33–55. Odense, Denmark: Odense University Press.
Clunies Ross, Margaret. 1977. "Women in Early Scandinavian Myth and Literature." *Refractory Girl* 13/14:29–37.
Evans, David A. H., ed. 1986. *Hávamál*. Text Series VII. London: University College Viking Society for Northern Research.
Foote, Peter G., and D. M. Wilson. 1980. *The Viking Achievement*. Sidgwick and Jackson Great Civilizations Series. 2d. ed. London: Sidgwick and Jackson.
Fortes, Meyer. 1980. "Preface" to *Sacrifice*, edited by M.F.C. Bourdillon and M. Fortes. London: Academic Press.
Frank, Roberta. 1973. "Marriage in Twelfth and Thirteenth Century Iceland." *Viator* 4:473–84.
———. 1978. *Old Norse Court Poetry. The Dróttkvaett Stanza*. Islandica XLII. Ithaca, N.Y.: Cornell University Press.
Guðmundsson, Finnbogi, ed. 1965. *Orkneyinga saga*. Íslenzk Fornrit XXXIV. Reykjavík, Iceland: Hið Íslenzka Fornritafélag.

Hastrup, Kirsten. 1985. *Culture and History in Medieval Iceland*. Oxford: Clarendon Press.

Helgason, Jón, and Anne Holtsmark, eds. 1941. *Háttalykill enn forni*. Bibliotheca Arnamagnaeana I. Copenhagen, Denmark: Munksgaard.

Heller, Rolf. 1958. *Die literarische Darstellung der Frau in den Isländersagas*. Halle, Germany: VEB Max Nieweyer Verlag.

Jochens, Jenny M. 1986a. "Consent in Marriage: Old Norse Law, Life and Literature." *Scandinavian Studies* 58: 142–76.

———. 1986b. "The Medieval Icelandic Heroine: Fact or Fiction?" *Viator* 17:35–50.

———. 1987. "The Politics of Reproduction: Medieval Norwegian Kingship." *American Historical Review* 92:327–49.

Karras, Ruth Mazo. 1990. "Concubinage and Slavery in the Viking Age." *Scandinavian Studies* 62: 141–62.

Lönnroth, Lars. 1976. *Njáls saga. A Critical Introduction*. Berkeley: University of California Press.

Meulengracht Sørensen, Preben. 1983. *The Unmanly Man: Concepts of Sexual Defamation in Early Northern Society*. Translated by J. Turville-Petre. The Viking Collection 1. Odense, Denmark: Odense University Press.

Nordal, Sigurður. 1940. *Hrafnkatla*. Studia Islandica VIII. Reykjavík, Iceland: Munksgaard.

Orkneyinga saga. The History of the Earls of Orkney. 1978. Translated by Hermann Pálsson and Paul Edwards. Harmondsworth England: Penguin.

Smalley, Beryl. 1974. *Historians in the Middle Ages*. London: Thames and Hudson.

Stafford, Pauline. 1978. "Sons and Mothers: Family Politics in the Early Middle Ages." In *Medieval Women*, edited by D. Baker, 79–100. Oxford: Blackwell for The Ecclesiastical History Society.

———. 1983. *Queens, Concubines and Dowagers: The King's Wife in the Middle Ages*. Athens: University of Georgia Press.

Strand, Birgit. 1980. *Kvinnor och Män i Gesta Danorum*. Kvinnohistoriskt arkiv nr. 18. Göteborg, Sweden: Göteborgs Universitet Historiska institutionen.

———. 1981. "Women in Gesta Danorum." In *Saxo Grammaticus. A Medieval Author between Norse and Latin Culture*, edited by K. Friis-Jensen. Copenhagen, Denmark: Museum Tusculanum Press.

Wahlgren, Erik. 1938. *The Maiden King in Iceland*. Ph.D. diss., University of Chicago. Private ed. Chicago: University of Chicago Libraries.

Whitelock, Dorothy, ed. and trans. 1979. *English Historical Documents*, vol. 1. 2d. ed. London: Eyre Methuen.

7

Imperial Women in the History of the Ming Dynasty (1368–1644)

Ellen Soullière

Emperors and Prominent Imperial Women of the Ming Dynasty

Temple Name	Reign Title and Dates	Prominent Imperial Women
T'ai-tsu	Hung-wu (1368–1398)	Ma, Sun, Kuo
(Hui-tsung)	Chien-wen (1398–1402)	Ma
T'ai-tsung (Ch'eng-tsu)	Yung-lo (1402–1424)	Hsü
Jen-tsung	Hung-hsi (1424–1425)	Chang
Hsüan-tsung	Hsüan-te (1425–1435)	Hu, Sun, Wu
Ying-tsung	Cheng-t'ung (1435–1449) T'ien-shun (1457–1464)	Ch'ien, Chou
Tai-tsung	Ching-t'ai (1449–1457)	Wang, Hang
Hsien-tsung	Ch'eng-hua (1464–1487)	Wu, Wang, Wan, Shao
Hsiao-tsung	Hung-chih (1487–1505)	Chang
Wu-tsung	Cheng-te (1505–1521)	Hsia
Shih-tsung	Chia-ching (1521–1567)	Ch'en, Chang, Fang, Tu
Mu-tsung	Lung-ch'ing (1567–1572)	Ch'en, Li
Shen-tsung	Wan-li (1572–1620)	Wang, Cheng
Kuang-tsung	T'ai-ch'ang (August to September 1620)	Kuo, Li, Wang
Hsi-tsung	T'ien-ch'i (1620–1627)	Chang, Liu
Ssu-tsung (Chuang-lieh ti)	Ch'ung-chen (1627–1644)	Chou, T'ien

The case of imperial women in traditional China is a variation on the theme of the portrayal of actively political women as essentially nonpolitical. It gives a new twist to the political distinction between public and private spheres, and it provides an example of an exceptionally well-organized and often successful system for the exclusion of women from participation in political life.

Two important aspects of the intellectual landscape that influenced Chinese thinking about the political relations between men and women were yin-yang theory and Confucian theories of ethical behavior. Yin-yang theory which originated even before the first Chinese empire was established in 221 B.C., held that natural phenomena were the result of the alternation of yin and yang. These two fundamental principles were associated respectively with female and male, darkness and light, passivity and activity, and other similarly paired attributes. Ideally, the forces were balanced and complementary, but at the same time, the subordination of yin to yang was always assumed. The theory went through numerous permutations during the course of the imperial era, but the idea of an unequal balance between the forces was regularly used to support the view that women should remain in a subordinate, domestic role and not "interfere" in the politics of the state. It was the duty of the emperor to limit both the number and the influence of the women of his household. Whenever conflict arose involving the women of the palace, a yin-yang imbalance was likely to be cited as the cause.

Even more important than yin-yang theory in molding attitudes to the participation of women in politics was Confucian thought. Confucianism stressed the importance of ethical behavior within a series of linked, hierarchical relationships, among which the father-son relationship was central. Within the family, status, wealth, and the power to make decisions were allocated according to the criteria of generation, age, and sex. In this system, then, a woman who outlived her husband and became the senior member of her generation could achieve a position of dominance within her family. For the most part, however, Confucian prescriptions of male dominance were borne out in social practice. Kinship was patrilineal; marriage was usually patrilocal, and, within the family, power customarily lay in the hands of the senior males. The system was made tolerable for women by the hope of living to become the senior surviving member of their generation and, more immediately, by the desire to advance the interests of their own children.

The family was the most important organizational unit in China's traditional agrarian society. Indeed, apart from the family and central government, there were remarkably few social organizations of any kind. The family and the state were often portrayed as analogous to each other, with the emperor and the empress cast as father and mother to the people. Officials owed them loyalty in the same way that sons owed loyalty to their parents. In China's traditional history, the imperial family was also set the task of serving as an exemplary model to the families of the elite and, on a steadily decreasing scale of grandeur, to the lesser families of the empire.

The imperial family of the Ming dynasty (1368–1644) provides us with an opportunity to study the interplay between family and state politics at the highest level. It shows how the officials and historians who served the state worked together to contain the political activities of imperial women and to devalue their achievements.

The founding of China's Ming dynasty in 1368 ushered in nearly three centuries of unprecedented political and social stability and economic growth. The dynasty's founder was Chu Yuan-chang (1328–1398), the peasant leader of a millenarian rebellion. Chu succeeded in defeating and driving out the Mongols, who had ruled China for most of the previous century. Intellectually, the early Ming was characterized by a desire to redefine and reassert Chinese values in the face of the markedly divergent customs of the Mongols. Socially, the remarkable social mobility seen at the time of the founding, when a penniless peasant became emperor of China, was to a certain extent institutionalized in early efforts to redistribute land and to prevent the reemergence of entrenched local and imperial elites. The examination system, as administered under the Ming, produced the highest levels of social mobility up into the official ruling elite ever achieved in traditional China (Ho Ping-ti 1962, 260).

At the beginning of the dynasty, the Ming economy was poor, impoverished by the many rebellions which finally succeeded in putting an end to Mongol rule. By the early seventeenth century, a new and highly sophisticated economy had developed, whose features included specialized trade and marketing systems, the increased use of money as a medium of exchange, and the emergence of merchants as a distinct and influential class. Increased agricultural production and the introduction of new world crops contributed to a burgeoning population, whose numbers had reached 100 million by the beginning of the seventeenth century, more than twice the probable level of 1368.

Politically, the dynasty's record was mixed. It succeeded in preventing the decentralization and regional fragmentation of power that had troubled the three preceding dynasties. Non-Chinese peoples on the empire's borders were, for the most part, kept under control without the costly and dangerous appeasement policies that the Sung had found it necessary to adopt. But these successes were not achieved without cost.

As part of his campaign of centralization, the Ming founder concentrated imperial power in his own hands in unprecedented ways. In 1380 he abolished the office of prime minister, which in earlier dynasties had served both to advise the emperor and to share in the exercise of imperial power. The vacuum created by the abolition of this office was filled in several ways, most notably by the institution of the Grand Secretariat. The grand secretaries, usually four in number, were selected from the Hanlin Academy and were at first intended to serve as the emperor's private secretaries. From about 1425, however, they often assumed prime ministerial responsibilities, although they lacked the formal authority to do this with a full measure of legitimacy.

A second group, the eunuchs, were also able to share in the power of the emperor. The basis of their power was the fact that they transmitted all the documents exchanged between the emperor and his civil officials. In reigns where the emperor took insufficient interest in affairs of state, the eunuchs were sometimes able to use their access to state documents to exercise imperial authority on the emperor's behalf. Imperial women and their families were a third group which periodically succeeded in obtaining access to imperial power. The tension between these "inner court" groups, whose power derived from their proximity to the emperor, and the civil officials of the "outer court" was one of the major unresolved problems of the Ming political system.

The Ming dynastic institution depended for its continuity on the ability of emperors to produce sons to succeed them. Like earlier dynasties, the Ming sought to ensure the necessary continuity by providing each emperor with one principal wife and a very large number of secondary wives and lesser female attendants. It was hoped that this would maximize his prospects of having a surviving male heir. The extravagant provision of women for the emperor was also intended to mark his high status and to set him apart from all other men. The thousands of women who belonged to the Ming imperial household were organized with these goals in mind.

The high level of centralization attempted in Ming governmental institutions created problems not only for relations among those at the center of power, but also for relations between the center and the regions. Neither communication systems, transport systems, nor systems of local government were adequate to implement the high levels of centralization and control that were theoretically prescribed. This was one reason why the rituals of the state and Confucian ideology, as codified and perpetuated in the examination system, were so important for the cohesion of the empire (Huang 1976, 6–12). Both served to inspire the elite with ideals that served the needs of the central government.

Confucian ideology also permeated the writing of history. Chinese historians were always profoundly aware of the links between the interpretation of the past and the control of events in the present. Each dynasty undertook the task of writing the history of its predecessor with a view to assigning "praise and blame" (*pao-pien*) to individuals and their achievements. This and the fact that history was viewed as the record of cycles of ascendancy and decline gave much traditional historical writing a stereotyped quality. In writing about members of the imperial family, such stereotypes are particularly pervasive. Nevertheless, traditional sources make it possible both to provide a general account of the political activities of the women of the Ming imperial household and to evaluate the intentions of the official historians in recording them.

THE WOMEN OF THE IMPERIAL HOUSEHOLD

In 1353, when Chu Yuan-chang was twenty-five years old, he married a twenty-year-old woman whose surname was Ma. She was a member of the household of Chu's military superior, Kuo Tzu-hsing (d. 1355), and the marriage was designed to cement the alliance between the two men. Empress Ma was a capable and energetic person, who had probably had little opportunity as a young girl to acquire an education. She managed to become functionally literate, however, and in the early years of Chu's rise to power she was in charge of all the records and documents kept in his household. Her official biography records that if Chu needed to see one of these documents, "she immediately located it and presented it to him. She never made a mistake" (*Ming Shih Lu* [*MSL*] 1962, chap. 147, 2303). On several occasions, she saved Chu's life by providing him with food and by interceding for him when he fell foul of Kuo Tzu-hsing. She once also assumed a quasi-military role, leading the wives of Chu's subordinates across the Yangtze river, while battle raged around them.

As Chu's prestige, status, and power increased, so too did his household, and he began to acquire secondary wives. In 1367, just before he finally defeated his rivals for power, Chu began the construction of a palace at Nanking. The palace was intended to house the women, young children, and servants of his household and his growing staff of eunuchs, and to serve as the administrative center of the new empire. In the same year Chu began to establish institutions to control his expanding household. He established six bureaux, staffed by female officials (*nü kuan*) and charged with governing the imperial household. The following year was proclaimed the first year of the Ming dynasty, and work continued on the development of its institutions.

Official Chinese sources do not state the total number of women who lived and worked in the palace in the Ming period. There were probably between 50 and 100 female members of the imperial family living in the palace at any given time. The structure of the six bureaux in the mature Ming system called for a staff of 283, and these numbers were maintained after the capital was moved to Peking and a new palace constructed there in the early 1400s. There were several hundred laundresses, wet nurses, and chair bearers. The *Collected Statutes of the Ming Dynasty* (*Ta Ming Hui-tien*) also mentions entertainers, musicians, dancers, mourners, and minor ritual functionaries who took part in the many rituals that marked each stage of the Ming calendar year (Shen Shih-hsing 1976, chap. 92, 1453–55). There must also have been hundreds of women who served as cooks, cleaners, seamstresses, and ladies' maids.

Fu-lin, the first emperor of the Manchu Ch'ing dynasty, which replaced the Ming in 1644, stated that at the end of the Ming the palace had been staffed with 9,000 women and 100,000 eunuchs. Fu-lin's purpose in making these figures public, however, was a political one. He wished to contrast the modesty of his own requirements with the extravagance of his predecessors. His own establishment, he went on to say, was not to exceed 400 or 500 persons.[1] The late Ming European observer, Jesuit priest Álvaro Semedo, estimated that there were 3,000 women and 12,000 eunuchs living in the Ming palace in about 1626 (Semedo 1655, 113–14). Semedo's estimates can only have been based on hearsay, but, because they were made without political intent, they are probably more reliable than Fu-lin's.

Information, not only on the numbers of imperial and palace women, but also on all other aspects of their lives within the palace walls, is difficult to obtain. The most important reason for this is that the emperor's private life was thought to have moral and political significance and important implications for his ability to rule wisely and well. A good emperor was able to manage his household harmoniously. A bad emperor and in particular a "bad last" emperor, whose behavior could be blamed for the downfall of a dynasty, was one who recruited too many women for his harem, overindulged in sexual pleasure, and neglected affairs of state. Criticism of an emperor's sexual activities was also, by implication, criticism of his fitness to rule the empire. It was for this reason that Chinese emperors sought to prevent information on the women of their households from being transmitted to the outside world.

The physical freedom of imperial and palace women was restricted even more rigidly than the flow of information. The 1381 edition of the *Ancestral Instructions*, attributed to the Ming founder himself, treats it as a matter of course that women could routinely leave the palace. The work contains a regulation stating that palace women who were going out could ride in their palanquins as far as the *Hsi-hua* gate. There, they were to descend from their palanquins and walk through the gate, reentering the palanquins on the other side to continue their journeys (Chu Yuan-chang 1381). The same early text also states that doctors could enter the palace to treat palace women, provided two eunuchs and two elderly matrons were present throughout all consultations. In the later, printed version of the text, however, both these statements have been changed. The regulation about the departure of women from the palace has been removed entirely, and the regulation on doctors has been altered to state that doctors must prescribe medication for women of the imperial household solely on the basis of a description of the symptoms, without seeing the patient (Chu Yuan-chang 1395, woodblock).

Imperial women of the highest status, the empresses and dowager empresses, did occasionally leave the palace to visit the Ming tombs north of Peking or to conduct rituals. They did so, however, only under conditions of the most extraordinary security. When the wife of the Chia-ching emperor led the women of the imperial household and the wives of the highest officials in offering sacrifice to the First Sericulturalist in the early 1530s, for example, 10,000 troops lined the route from the palace to the ritual altar (Shen Shih-hsing 1976, chap. 92, 1453–1455).

During the early Ming and again in 1465 and 1526 lower ranking women who had served in the palace for a number of years were released. The reason generally given for this release was that the women had grown old and it was time to make way for new recruits. The late Ming eunuch, Liu Jo-yü, however, records that in the seventeenth century old women and women who had committed crimes were sent to the "Hall of Peaceful Happiness" (*An-lo t'ang*) within the palace. There they were kept for some time before being sent to the Laundry Bureau (*Wan-i chü*) outside the palace walls. The Laundry Bureau was under the direction of eunuch supervisors, who kept the women supplied with rations of rice and salt until they died of natural causes. The women were usually not allowed to leave the Laundry Bureau alive "in order to guard against the divulging of secrets" (Liu Jo-yü, chap. 16, 38). Semedo notes that these separate palaces for "old and penitent" women were popularly called *Leng-kung* or "the cold palaces" (Semedo 1655, 112).

European observers of late Ming China confirm that the court's custom of keeping women in seclusion was echoed in urban society at large. Semedo, who spent most of his time in South China, writes:

The retirement of the women is very great. There is not a woman to be seen in the streets, although in yeares; or never so blameless in her life; neither are men suffered to visit them in their houses. That part of the house where they inhabit is, as it were, a sacred place, for their sakes. It is enough to tell anyone who entereth unwillingly that there are women there to make him stop presently. The men servants may enter thither only when they are little boys. Into the very chamber where they are, not so much as their kindred are allowed to come, unless they be the younger brethren of the husband, of very small age. . . . If women go out to visit their parents they are carried in a sedan chair and this is the custom of all their women, even to those of the most ordinary quality. If they go on a pilgrimage and go part of the way on foot they cover their faces with a veil. In some parts of China ordinary women go about as among us, but the women of quality always observe the style of retiredness. (Semedo 1655, 31)

The Ming court set standards of behavior that reduced women from a condition of considerable freedom of movement at the beginning of the dynasty to a state of near total domestic seclusion by its close. In urban centers, at least, these standards seem to have been widely observed by women who held or aspired to elite status.

THE ORGANIZATION AND FORMAL POWERS OF THE WOMEN OF THE IMPERIAL HOUSEHOLD

There is some evidence that at the beginning of the dynasty Chu Yuan-chang intended the powers of the women officials to function as a counterweight to those of his growing eunuch organization (Shen Te-fu 1959, 814). In the early Ming the women officials acted as private secretaries, scribes, and court scholars to the empress. Although the activities of the women officials were later largely overshadowed by those of the eunuchs, they continued to be the custodians of the seals that authorized the use of goods and services within the imperial household (Liu Jo-yü, chap. 16, 18b). They played an important part in imperial rituals throughout the dynasty. Despite the formal status of the powers of the women officials, none of these women emerged in a position of political prominence during the course of the dynasty.

The powers of the consorts and concubines, the lesser wives of the emperor, were not formal, legitimate powers. They derived solely from the proximity of these women to the emperor and their consequent ability to influence him. The powers of these women were usually fairly limited and consisted mainly in the power to persuade the emperor to confer salaried military positions and the revenues from imperial estates on their male relatives. An exception was the Lady Wan, favorite consort of the Ch'eng-hua emperor (r. 1465–1487). Together with a number of eunuchs, she is said to have sold civil offices and imperial patents and favors (Mote 1987, 346). Occasionally, these women were able to persuade the emperor to depose his principal wife and to install one of them in her place.

The powers of the empress (*huang-hou*), the principal wife of the emperor, were also for the most part informal. However, empresses had greater opportunities than consorts to obtain access to the emperor and to persuade him to act as they desired. The biography of Empress Ma, the wife of the founder, makes it clear that they shared a domestic routine that kept them in frequent close proximity to one another. They ate together and together discussed the affairs of their family and the state. On six separate occasions Empress Ma intervened in the cases of men who were on the point of being executed or severely punished by her suspicious husband. The most dramatic of these cases was that of Sung Lien (1310–1381). Sung had been one of Chu's most senior advisers since 1360, serving in the historiography office of the Hanlin Academy, as senior tutor to the heir apparent and as tutor to several of Chu's younger sons. In 1380 Sung's grandson, Sung Shen, was accused of having been an associate of Hu Wei-yung (d. 1380), the prime minister whom Chu Yuan-chang executed on false charges of having plotted to overthrow him. Sung Shen was executed, along with thousands of other people, and Chu Yuan-chang had decreed that Sung Lien should share the same fate, even though he had been living in retirement away from the court since 1377. Empress Ma argued that Sung should be pardoned because of this and because he had been their sons' tutor. Even commoner families respected their children's teachers, she told him. "What of the Son of Heaven?" (*Ming Shih* [*MS*] 1974, chap. 113, 3506).

The emperor refused to listen to her and allowed plans for Sung's arrest and execution to go ahead. Then, when they were dining together, the empress refused to touch any wine or meat. When asked her reason for this, she replied that she was abstaining on behalf of Sung Lien. The emperor became distressed, threw down his chopsticks and left the table, but the following day he withdrew the execution order and had Sung demoted and banished instead (*MS* 1974, chap. 113, 3506).

Empress Ma interceded not only for individuals known to her, but also for convicted criminals whom she did not know personally and for the people. She argued for the humane treatment of the convicted criminals who were working on the construction of the city walls of Nanking, and she regularly expressed her concern for the sufferings of the people. Whenever there was a drought, she led the women of the palace in following a vegetarian diet and in assisting at prayers for rain. When the harvest was poor, she established centers for dispensing coarse porridge and vegetable soups. She enjoined the emperor not only to provide relief measures, but also to see that adequate stores were accumulated so that famine would not occur (*MS* 1974, chap. 113, 3507).

In all of these cases, the source of Empress Ma's power was the closeness of her relationship to her husband and his willingness to allow her to influence his decisions. Despite this, both the officials and the official historians regarded her political acts as legitimate. An empress's legitimacy derived primarily from her position as the senior woman of the emperor's own generation in the imperial family. On these grounds alone she was owed a high level of ritual deference. The civil officials also readily accepted the necessity of conferring high noble and military titles and the revenues from imperial estates on the male relatives of empresses. This was done on a vastly greater scale than in the case of the male relatives of lesser consorts, but the officials seldom protested, while exercising constant vigilance to ensure that the emperor's lesser women did not overstep the bounds of their positions. A Ming empress could enhance her claim to the legitimate exercise of a measure of power if she were able to represent her activities as echoes of the exemplary acts of empresses of former times. These women are remembered for having advised their husbands and sons on matters of moral principle which, in traditional China, always had political implications. Every effort was made to prevent consorts and concubines from casting themselves in a similar light.

The powers of the dowager empresses (*huang t'ai-hou*) were greater than those of any other imperial women. The dowager empresses were the mothers of reigning emperors, and their powers were not only legitimate, but had a formal, institutional basis. For example, when it was time to select a wife and consorts for their sons, they had the power to issue orders directly to the Ministry of Rites to begin the selection process. They also had another, related power, which was very much more important for the political life of the dynasty. Whenever the succession was in doubt, it was the dowagers who issued the edict enthroning the new emperor. In every dispute about the succession, the dowager empresses had an important role to play. In several cases, they were able to exert a decisive influence on the resolution of the crisis.

INSTITUTIONAL RESTRICTIONS ON THE POWER OF MING IMPERIAL WOMEN

A number of institutional factors combined to limit severely the powers of Ming imperial women. First of all, the founder's *Ancestral Instructions* contains a general prohibition on the participation of imperial women in political affairs. Much more important, however, was Chu Yuan-chang's decision, also codified in the *Ancestral Instructions*, that only the daughters of families of no social consequence should be recruited as wives for the heir apparent and the imperial princes. Despite the fact that political marriages were an important part of Chu's strategy for founding the dynasty, he had ample opportunity during his long reign to reflect on possible sources of danger to the state he had established. As a student of history, he became aware of the dangers that could arise when the emperor's wives came from families that were important in their own right.

Traditionally the imperial family had selected spouses for its members from families of great prominence. These families were deemed worthy of the privilage because of their aristocratic heritage or because of the recent achievements, usually military, of their members. In Chinese dynasties before the Ming the marriages contracted by the imperial family were part of an elaborate, inter-locking system of relationships that linked the imperial family to a social elite. In both the T'ang and Sung periods it is possible to observe complex social networks involving families who enjoyed elite status because male members of the families occupied important civil or military positions while female members achieved high rank within the imperial family. In both cases the women who became empresses were members of an elite, which attempted to perpetuate its high status through marriages contracted with the imperial family and through intermarriage with other elite families. The court attempted to use these rela-tionships to reward and control elite families. The families used them to enhance their own status, wealth, and power within society. Occasionally, as in the Han and T'ang dynasties, such families became strong enough to pose a serious threat to the power of the state.

Had they not been reversed, the early policies of the founder of the Ming dynasty of marrying his children to the children of his military and civilian supporters could have led to the emergence of a new, imperial elite similar to that of Sung. As it was, Ming imperial women were prevented from serving as links between the court and prominent families, or as part of a network of such families. The Ming policy of selecting spouses for members of the imperial family from families of no social importance broke a traditional connection between the power of imperial women and the power of an elite with imperial connections. Ming imperial women, as a result, never attained the levels of power that had belonged to their well-connected predecessors in earlier dynasties.

For women who occupied the position of empress, an important consequence of the abandonment of the traditional system of selection of imperial spouses was that they were frequently and rather easily deposed. Lacking practical ex-perience of politics, the empresses were ill-equipped to defend themselves. Nor could they rely on their fathers and brothers to defend their interests. These imperial in-laws had been suddenly lifted from a condition of real social obscurity to positions of great wealth and prominence. They often held high noble or military rank, but this had been granted solely as a result of imperial favor, at the time when their female relative became empress. In general, this made them unlikely to be able to act successfully in the complex arena of court politics. They were also fully aware that, if their female relative died or lost the emperor's favor, their downward mobility would be as sudden and as striking as their rise to eminence.

A second major reason for the weakness of Ming empresses in comparison to those of earlier ages may be found in the dynastic institutions codified in the *Ancestral Instructions*. Here, the Ming founder stipulated that only the son of an emperor by his principal wife could inherit the throne. The idea that the throne should pass to the eldest son of the empress, even if the emperor had older sons by other women, was firmly established as a dynastic principle by Han times (T'ao-T'ien-yi 1978, 175). Parallel distinctions between the sons of the principal wife (*ti*) and the sons of concubines (*shu*) were maintained in noble households. When the empress had no son, it was also traditional practice for the throne to pass to the reigning emperor's eldest son by any of his wives. Chu Yuan-chang deliberately sought to put this precedent aside and to replace it with a system of his own devising in which the sons of lesser women were absolutely barred from inheritance. He made no provision, however, for what was to happen if the empress should have no surviving son.

In the reigns of the first four Ming emperors the position of empress was stable and secure. Empress Ma, the wife of the Ming founder, and Empress Hsü, the wife of the Yung-lo emperor, both died before their husbands' reigns were half over. Although both men subsequently formed new attachments and continued to father children, neither appointed a new empress. The two emperors certainly intended their gesture to be an expression of their high regard for the women who had aided them in establishing the dynasty and consolidating their control over the empire. Even more important, however, their actions displayed respect for the idea that, just as there is only one emperor in each generation, so there can be only one empress. From 1429 onward, however, the position of empress was never again secure.

The principal source of the insecurity of empresses after the early Ming was that they seldom had sons. There is some controversy over the question of whether Empress Ma had any surviving male children.[2] The Chien-wen, Yung-lo, and Hung-hsi emperors all had sons by their principal wives and so there was no conflict about the designation of the heir apparent. However, the Hsüan-te emperor, who ascended the throne in 1426, did not have a son by his principal wife, Empress Hu. He chose to resolve this problem by deposing her and installing in her place Lady Sun, who was the mother of a healthy son. He explained his actions by saying that Empress Hu was often ill and barren, two of the seven traditional grounds on which Chinese husbands could divorce their wives.

The emperor's solution to the problem of his wife's childlessness complied with the letter of the *Ancestral Instructions* while violating their spirit. After this time, it was the exception, rather than the rule, for a Ming emperor to be succeeded by his principal wife's son. Only the eccentrically monogamous Hung-chih emperor and the last Ming emperor had healthy sons by their principal wives. Most Ming emperors solved the problem by following the Hsüan-te precedent and raising the status of those women who had borne them sons. Thus, from the Hsüan-te period onward, the force of the founder's injunctions combined with the natural competitive instincts of imperial women to make the conflict between the rights of the principal wife and those of the mother of the heir a perennial issue.

The Ching-t'ai, Ch'eng-hua, Chia-ching, and Lung-ch'ing emperors all deposed their first principal wives and replaced them with other women. Of the empresses who were not deposed, only the Hung-chih emperor's Empress Chang and Chuang-lieh-ti's Empress Chou had healthy sons, and only the former was not threatened by the ascendancy of a rival. From the Hsüan-te period onward, it was highly unusual for one woman to be both the rightful empress and the mother of the heir. A much more common pattern was for one woman to be empress, while another enjoyed the emperor's affection, and, in many cases, still another was the mother of the heir. This fragmentation seriously undermined the power of empresses from the early Ming until the end of the dynasty.

THE ABSENCE OF REGENCIES UNDER THE MING

In dynasties before the Ming, the institution that had provided imperial women with the greatest access to political power was the regency. In Chinese history, as in the histories of other monarchies, regents, who acted as heads of state in place of and on behalf of the ruler, were appointed when the ruler was ill, too young, or for some other reason incapable of performing his duties. Male regents were sometimes appointed, usually when aristocratic influences were strong at court. Male regents were most often members of the imperial family, often on the distaff side, and they regularly and predictably displayed a strong tendency to disrupt the succession to the throne. Female regents were much more frequently appointed in traditional China than male, and the choice almost invariably fell on the dowager empress, the principal wife of the deceased emperor.

There were two principal advantages in appointing a dowager empress when a regency was required. First of all, because she was the senior surviving member of the previous generation, she enjoyed a measure of legitimacy that none could deny. She was therefore an influence for stability when the emperor was weak and the succession was in dispute. The extent to which an empress dowager could use her authority to make decisions varied, depending on her own abilities and prevailing political conditions. In some cases, such as Empress Wu of the T'ang dynasty and Empress Dowager Tz'u-hsi of the Ch'ing, she was as much in control of the government as a powerful emperor. In others, she was merely a figurehead, delegating her authority to her relatives or to civil officials, who made decisions in her name. Most commonly, her role fell somewhere between these two poles.

There was a second major advantage in appointing female regents. The political power of imperial women was regarded as a temporary, stopgap phenomenon. One of the earliest rationales for educating women was that education prepared them to provide leadership for the family in a time of crisis until a suitable male could be found to resume control. Institutional constraints imposed on the activity of a regent empress because she was female also helped to limit her power. She could never meet her ministers face to face, for example, but instead had to transact government business from behind a lowered screen in order to maintain the prescribed ritual distance between the sexes. As a result of these limitations, it was usually not difficult to remove a female regent when her usefulness was ended and the male on whose behalf she had assumed the regency was able to rule. Despite these limitations, the Han, T'ang, and Sung dynasties, the major Chinese dynasties that preceded the Ming, all had striking examples of powerful regent dowager empresses. The Ming, by contrast, produced not a single such regency, and Ming imperial women were thus markedly less powerful than imperial women of other eras.

THE ROLE OF EMPRESS DOWAGER CHANG IN THE DEVELOPMENT OF MING INSTITUTIONS

There were several reasons for the absence of regencies by dowager empresses under the Ming dynasty. First, they were implicitly forbidden by the founder in his *Ancestral Instructions*. Second, imperial women who were recruited from families of no social standing or political experience were at a great disadvantage in the inner court. Third, the capable principal wives of the founding emperor and the Yung-lo emperor predeceased their husbands and thus did not become dowager empresses. More important than any of these factors, however, were the actions of a remarkable woman, the Empress Dowager Chang (d. 1442).

Empress Dowager Chang was the wife of the Hung-hsi emperor, who reigned for less than a year. From the time of her marriage to him in 1393, when he was Prince of Yen, she showed a firm grasp of political reality. The prince, unlike his father, did not have a martial disposition, and he was so fat that he could neither ride nor shoot. The future empress defended her weak young husband when his father thought of replacing him with one of his more active brothers. Her biography also records that during her husband's short reign as emperor she "had a thorough knowledge of the political affairs of the inner and outer courts" and that this knowledge extended to the ranking of officials (*MS* 1974, chap. 113, 3512; Ho Ch'iao-yuan 1970, chap. 30, 8b).

After her husband died on 29 May 1425, their eldest son ascended the throne as the Hsüan-te emperor. Immediately, the new emperor's uncle, the Prince of Han, rose in rebellion. The new emperor himself led troops into the field and was able to quell the rebellion. Despite the fact that the Hsüan-te emperor came to the throne as a mature man of twenty-six, his mother's biography credits her with instructing him in the art of government and says that, during the early years of his reign, "all major councils on civil and military affairs were controlled by the empress" (*MS* 1974, chap. 113, 3512; Ho Ch'iao-yuan 1970, chap. 30, 10a).

Throughout the course of her son's ten-year reign, the empress dowager continued to advise him. She also maintained a relationship with her son's senior ministers, most of whom had also served under her husband. On two occasions, she met these ministers face to face, without the use of a screen. On the first occasion she thanked them for their services to the imperial family and the state, and on the second she called upon them to support her in criticizing a eunuch who, she believed, had become too influential with her young grandson (*MS* 1974, chap. 113, 3512; T'an Ch'ien 1958, chap. 25, 1633).

When the Hsüan-te emperor died suddenly in 1435, his eldest son and heir apparent was less than nine years old. Most unofficial historical sources agree that Empress Dowager Chang wished to enthrone her own second son, the Prince of Hsiang, instead of her young grandson. She had clear motives for attempting this. She had lived through the turmoil of the Yung-lo usurpation in 1402 and had assisted her elder son in establishing his authority after the rebellion of the Prince of Han. As a result, she had every reason to fear that political conditions were still so unstable that the succession of a young child posed a serious threat to the stability of the dynasty. Furthermore, she may have feared that she would have difficulty in controlling her young grandson in the face of competition from her daughter-in-law, Empress Sun. Despite Empress Dowager Chang's undoubted political ability, she was unable to prevent the grand secretaries, aided by her daughter-in-law, from enthroning the little boy as Emperor Ying-tsung in 1435 (Soullière 1987, 355–60).

Empress Dowager Chang soon recovered from this setback, however. The grand secretaries realized that they could not govern without her consent, and, less than a month after the boy was declared emperor, they invited her to establish a formal regency. Surprisingly, she refused to do this, explaining her decision with reference to the founder's general prohibition of the participation of women in government. She also forbade her brothers, both of whom held high military and noble rank, to interfere in the affairs of the court.

Empress Dowager Chang's caution in these matters had several probable causes. First of all, she did not have the backing of an influential family with a power base independent from the court. She had also lived through succession crises and had been defeated in the most recent of these by her daughter-in-law. She had ample opportunity to consider firsthand the question of dynastic instability in relation to her own interests and those of her family. Finally, she was a literate woman and may have been influenced by the norms of self-abnegation that formed the core of all writings for the instruction of women.

After the dowager refused to establish a formal regency, the problem remained of how to authorize imperial decisions when the emperor was incapable of doing so. The solution worked out by the empress dowager and the grand secretaries was to establish an informal, de facto regency. From 1435 until her death in 1442 it was the empress dowager who provided the authority for all imperial decisions. All matters requiring a decision were first referred to the grand secretaries for deliberation. Their recommendations were then presented to the empress dowager in the form of memorials. She indicated her authorization of the decision with her great seal of office.

The formula worked out by Empress Dowager Chang and the grand secretaries for the use of power during the minority of a reigning emperor set a precedent which was followed when similar situations arose in later reigns. The informal regency established by Empress Dowager Chang for her grandson, despite its institutional irregularity, was recognized by both the inner and outer courts as having a full measure of legitimate authority. Empress Dowager Chang was the last of the three great founding empresses of the Ming imperial house. No subsequent imperial woman enjoyed comparable prestige, and none became powerful enough to assume a formal regency in violation of the precedent set by the dowager in 1435.

MING POLITICAL WOMEN AND THE HISTORIANS

Sexuality

Some features of the stereotypes imposed by historians on Ming imperial women are shared with those imposed on political women in other cultures; others are distinctively Chinese. In general, most historians who treated the subject of the sexuality of members of the imperial family concerned themselves with the emperor's sexuality. Emperors, and in particular "bad last" emperors, are characteristically accused of having recruited too many women for their harems and of having allowed sensual pleasure to distract them from affairs of state. The Ming Hung-hsi emperor was accused of having organized recruiting drives to obtain more women for his harem just when he should have been observing the three-year mourning period for his deceased father, a time when abstention from sex was ritually prescribed. The Cheng-te emperor was accused of having a sexual relationship with a woman who was pregnant by another man; and the Chia-ching emperor was said to have had sexual relations with barely pubescent children for the purpose of prolonging his own life through Taoist magic. In each case, the effect of the historians' recording of these matters was to discredit the emperor involved and to suggest that his behavior made him unsuited to hold his high position.

The historians treat the sexuality of imperial women with much greater caution. On the whole, imperial women are portrayed as the relatively passive objects of the emperor's desire. In late traditional China, women of high status were expected to be able to suppress their sexuality to an almost infinite degree for the benefit of their husbands' families. The historical record gives the impression that most high-ranking Ming imperial women were successful in this regard.

Imperial women of earlier eras were most often reproached by the historians, not for the overt expression of sexuality, but for having given vent to jealousy of their husbands' other women. In the biography of Empress Lü of the Han dynasty, for example, we learn that she had her rival's son murdered, then put out the woman's eyes and cut off her ears, cut off her arms and legs, and threw her into the privy to die slowly, calling her a "human pig." Similar tales of cruelty are told of Empress Wu of the T'ang dynasty, who is said to have drowned her rivals in a wine vat, and of Empress Dowager Tz'u-hsi of the Ch'ing dynasty, who is also said to have tortured her husband's other women to death.

In the Ming case, only lesser consorts are accused of violence because of excessive jealousy. Lady Wan, the favorite consort of the Ch'eng-hua emperor, for example, is accused of having caused abortions in "countless" cases when the emperor's other women became pregnant and she could not. She is also accused of having poisoned other women, an allegation more likely to be true in view of the level of sophistication of the Chinese pharmacopoeia of that time (*MS* 1974, chap. 113, 3524).

More direct references to the sexuality of imperial women are rare in official sources. Lady Wan's biography does make a point of stating that she was fifteen years older than the emperor, implying that his sexual relationship with her was both improper and likely to harm his masculine vitality (*MS* 1974, chap. 113, 3524). On the whole, however, the high status of Ming imperial women and the secrecy that shrouded their lives protected them from overt depictions of their sexuality by official and unofficial historians alike. All suffered from the pervasive assumption that excessive contact with them would undermine the emperor's vital energies. But broader speculation on the sexual lives of the inhabitants of the Ming palace was left to the writers of fiction.

The Public, the Private, and the Political

The distinction between public and private was effectively used by the historians to discredit lesser imperial women: the consorts and concubines. All of these women are portrayed as acting from motives of the purest selfishness and greed as they desperately try to improve their own status at court and seek military office and wealth for their natal families. A consort who was successful enough to have the original empress deposed and her own son installed as heir apparent earned the unmitigated hostility of the historians. Empress Sun, who became empress after Emperor Hsüan-tsung deposed his first wife, was, in all likelihood, slandered by the official historians. They chose to give credence to the very doubtful rumor that the new heir apparent was not her own son, but rather the child of some lesser palace woman whom she had passed off as her own (Soullière 1987, 360–65). The result of the official recording of this rumor was to disgrace and discredit Empress Sun and to deny her the fruits of the eminence of her position.

In the case of imperial women of the highest status, however, the private, domestic sphere and the public, political sphere were linked in a way that could confer both political power and legitimate authority. From very early historic times, Chinese political thinking assumed a link between an emperor's ability to govern the state and his ability to order his family. A passage from the *Great Learning*, one of the classic Four Books of early Chinese philosophy, enjoyed a great resurgence of popularity at the beginning of the Ming dynasty. It reads,

in part, "The ancients who wished clearly to exemplify illustrious virtue throughout the world first ordered well their own states. Wishing to order well their
own states, they first regulated their families. Wishing to regulate their families,
they first cultivated their persons" (Feng Yu-lan 1952, 362). This passage is
paraphrased and related to the regulation of the imperial household in the introduction to the biographies of imperial women in the official history, in which
Chu Yuan-chang orders his officials to compile works of moral instruction for
the women of his family:

> In ordering the state, first priority must be given to regulating the family. The way of
> regulating the family originates in respect between husband and wife. Although the
> empress and consorts are exemplars of motherhood to the empire, they must not be
> allowed to participate in political affairs. The activities of palace women of lesser rank
> must not exceed the fulfillment of their appointed duties, which are to wait on the emperor
> with towel and comb. If an emperor shows them excessive favour they will become
> haughty and overstep their roles. Then the distinction between superior and inferior will
> be lost. In imperial palaces throughout history, disaster has seldom been avoided when
> governmental decisions have emanated from within [the women's apartments]. Only an
> enlightened ruler can recognize the [potential sources of] such disasters before they have
> occurred. With a lesser man, there would surely be more chaos of this kind. You officials
> must compile precepts for women and accounts of virtuous consorts of former times so
> that our descendants in later ages may know what they must cling to and preserve. (MS
> 1974, chap. 113, 3503)

Within this frame of reference, the emperor fulfilled a dual role as the senior
member of the imperial family and as head of state. Symbolically, the emperor
was the father of everyone in the empire, and the empress their mother. This is
made plain in Empress Ma's biography, where it is stated that she once asked
her husband if all the people of the empire were content under his rule. He
replied irritably that this was not a matter about which she should concern herself.
She retorted, "If you are the father of the empire, then I am its mother. How
can one fail to be concerned about one's children?" (MS 1974, chap. 113, 3507).
The view of the imperial family as a microcosm of the state meant that the most
senior member of the family was potentially also the head of state. This was the
foundation of the political power and the legitimate authority of the dowager
empresses in times of dynastic crisis.

Historiography and Iconography

Chinese historians were exceptionally successful at transforming imperial
women into icons in order to regulate and control their activities. At the beginning
of the dynasty, books of precepts for women were published which codified the
norms for imperial women and prescribed the kinds of acts that would win the
approval of the officials and the official historians. At the same time, a book of
biographies of virtuous women of earlier ages was compiled and presented to

the emperor. The chapter devoted to the lives of imperial women culminated with the biography of Empress Ma, the wife of the Ming founder. Similar books were published under the auspices of imperial women in connection with almost every dispute about the succession to the throne that arose during the course of the dynasty (Soullière 1987, chap. 1).

A legitimate empress was required by these norms to exemplify feminine virtue for the benefit of all within the imperial household and the empire. She must be tolerant and without jealousy toward the emperor's other women to ensure that her husband will have many sons. She must devote herself to the ritual aspects of the preparation of food, drink, and clothing to ensure the continuation of the sacrifices to the ancestors and to set an example of industry to be followed by all the women of the empire. She must suppress the interests of her own family to prevent them from challenging those of the state. She must promote the interests of "good" officials. She must be frugal and self-abnegating. She must be familiar with the moral principles enshrined in the classics so that she can provide moral instruction for her husband and sons.

The most striking Ming example of the transformation of a legitimate empress into an icon is the biography of Empress Ma. It states that she was filial toward her parents and, after marriage, unswervingly loyal to her husband. Even after becoming empress she was so frugal that she wore clothing that "had been through many launderings" and ordered that old bow strings be boiled to recover the silk. She was magnanimous toward her husband's many other women, and, as a result, he had many children. She encouraged him to employ worthy officials and to treat them well. She repeatedly persuaded her husband to modify harsh decisions, and she instructed him in matters of morality (*MS* 1974, chap. 113, 3505–8). Almost every item in her biography echoes a theme from the biographies of exemplary empresses of earlier ages.

Empress Ma's biography also has a further social dimension, however. Her life began in conditions of extreme poverty, and she is fond of reminding her husband of the days when they both wore the cotton clothing of commoners. Her earthiness and commonsense and her clear memories of her origins are an essential part of her saintly image. Her life does not merely imitate ancient traditions of feminine virtue. It provides new interpretations of these traditions which adapt them to the needs of the newly founded dynasty. Her biography represents a fusion of elite and popular values, and she emerges from it as a new prototype of the supremely virtuous woman, reflecting the high levels of social mobility and of interaction between elite and popular culture that characterized the Ming dynasty. The power exercised by subsequent Ming empresses could never be legitimate unless they too succeeded in presenting themselves as the interpreters of this tradition.

The iconic image of the ideally virtuous empress or dowager empress worked two ways. On the one hand, it served to regulate and control the uses imperial women could make of their political power. On the other hand, because of its association with the idea of legitimacy, it actually conferred political power. A woman who succeeded in becoming the iconic embodiment of feminine norms could use her position as a screen for political activities that might be far from acceptable to the civil officials. For this reason, every empress and every consort who aspired to the position of empress sought to have her actions cast in the iconic mold. For this reason, too, after the founding of the dynasty, the official historians sought to prevent imperial women from succeeding in presenting themselves as the perfect embodiment of the ideal type.

Because of the pressing need to affirm the legitimacy of the new dynasty, the first three "founding empresses" were portrayed as totally successful realizations of the ideal. In the case of Empress Dowager Chang, the official historians deliberately concealed evidence that she planned to violate the rules of succession by placing her own younger son on the throne after the death of her elder son, Emperor Hsüan-tsung. The historians probably also concealed evidence that her support for the grand secretaries, who desperately needed her authority to legitimize their decisions, was not always wholehearted (Soullière 1987, 371).

After the dowager's death in 1442, however, no imperial woman was ever again presented in such a favorable light. In the late sixteenth century, for example, the Empress Dowager Li, mother of the Wan-Li emperor, made strenuous efforts to conform to the norms. She provided decision-making authority for grand secretary Chang Chü-cheng (1525–1582) during her son's minority. She deferred to Chang's judgment in all important matters, brought up her son to do the same, and supported the interests of the civil officials in a controversy concerning the designation of the heir apparent. Despite the dowager's extreme adherence to the norms, her official biography ends on a note of great disrespect. Instead of listing her posthumous honors and titles in accordance with the conventions for the biographies of senior imperial women, it criticizes her for having acted against Chang's wishes in the matter of donations to Buddhist institutions (*MS* 1974, chap. 114, 3514).

Through the selective recording of events and the occasional deliberate deception, the official historians were able to manipulate iconic images of imperial women. This worked to the detriment of the power of the women of the inner court in relation to that of the civil officials of the outer court. The officials and their historians were able to persuade imperial women that they should strive to conform to norms of impossible selflessness, while at the same time denying women the power and legitimacy that complete success would have conferred.

NOTES

1. These figures are cited in Hucker 1958, 10. Hucker is quoting Ting I, *Ming-tai t'e-wu cheng-chih* (Peking 1950), and Ting I is quoting Yü Chin, *Hsi-ch'ao hsin-yü*: chap. 4, 3b.

2. For the extreme view, that Empress Ma had no sons at all, see Wu Han 1935, 631–46. For a rebuttal of this view, see Li Chin-hua 1936, 3.6.1.

REFERENCES

Unless otherwise stated, all translations are the author's.

Chu Yuan-chang. 1395. *Huang Ming Tsu-hsün*. Nei-ling. Woodblock print ed. Rare Books, National Library of Peking. Microfilm roll no. 507.

————. 1381. *Huang Ming Tsu-hsün lu*. Nei-ling. Manuscript ed. Rare Books, National Library of Peking. Microfilm roll no. 507.

Feng Yu-lan. 1952. *History of Chinese Philosophy*. Vol. 1. *The Period of the Philosophers, from the Beginnings to ca. 100* B.C. Princeton, N.J.: Princeton University Press.

Ho Ch'iao-yuan. 1970. *Ming-shan ts'ang*. Taipei: Ch'eng-wen ch'u-pan she.

Ho Ping-ti. 1962. *The Ladder of Success in Imperial China: Aspects of Social Mobility 1368–1911*. New York: Columbia University Press.

Huang, Ray. 1976. "Institutions." *Ming Studies* 2 (Spring): 6–12.

Hucker, C. O. 1958. "Governmental Organization of the Ming Dynasty." *Harvard Journal of Asiatic Studies* 21:1–66.

Li Chin-hua. 1936. "Ming I wen t'ai tzu sheng mu k'ao." *Li-shih yü-yen yen-chiu so chi-k'an* 3.6.1.

Liu Jo-yü. *Cho-chung chih*. Taipei, Taiwan: Pai-pu ts'ung-shu chi-ch'eng.

Ming Shih (MS). 1974. Edited by Chang T'ing-yü. Vol 12. Chung-hua shu-chü.

Ming Shih Lu (MSL). 1962. Taipei, Taiwan: Chung-yang yen-chiu yuan li-shih yü-yen yen-chiu so.

Mote, F. W. 1987. "The Ch'eng-hua and Hung-chih Reigns, 1465–1505." In *The Cambridge History of China*, edited by F. W. Mote and D. C. Twitchett. Cambridge: Cambridge University Press.

Semedo, Álvaro. 1655. *The History of the Great and Renowned Monarchy of China*. London: John Crook. Translator not indicated.

Shen Shih-hsing, ed. 1976. *Ta Ming Hui-tien*. Vol. 3. Taipei, Taiwan: Hsin-wen feng ch'u-pan kung-ssu.

Shen Te-fu. 1959. *Wan-li yeh-huo pien*. Peking: Chung-hua shu-chü.

Soullière, E. F. 1987. "Palace Women in the Ming Dynasty." Ph.D. diss., Princeton University.

T'an Ch'ien. 1958. *Kuo Ch'üeh*. Taipei: Ting-wen shu-chü. Reprint 1958, Peking edition.

T'ao-Tien yi. 1978. "The System of Imperial Succession during China's Former Han Dynasty." Canberra, Australia: *Papers on Far Eastern History* 18 (September).

Wu Han. 1935. "Ming Ch'eng-twu sheng mu k'ao." *Ch'ing-hua hsüeh-pao* 10 (3) (July): 631–46.

8

The Virago and Machiavelli

Lenore Coltheart

The emergence of a feminist appraisal of the history of ideas in "Western" political thought has thrown a cold and revealing light on the practice of un-self-conscious political analysis that had become part of that tradition. This feminist critique of the orthodox history of ideas is sometimes aimed at inclusion in the received legacy of political thought, but sometimes questions concepts and assumptions basic to that legacy. Overviews of the tradition, such as those published by Martha Osborne (1979), Susan M. Okin (1980), Jean B. Elshtain (1981), Dale Spender (1983), and A. Saxonhouse (1985), and the substantial critique of liberal-democratic thought and practice that includes work by Zillah Eisenstein (1981) and Carole Pateman (1979, 1988, 1989) have brought this critical focus to the moment of Liberalism and the significance of the seventeenth-century theorists Thomas Hobbes and John Locke. My own curiosity has been aroused by the way in which Machiavelli was able to prepare the ground for Liberalism and thus for modern politics, and how that process can be clarified in the light of feminist theories of the function of writing and reading in the construction, maintenance, and transmission of meanings (see, for instance, Threadgold 1988). A brief review of some feminist work is provided first to show the threads that need to be drawn together to see Machiavelli in context.

Plato's concept of the ideal state, the good and just society, is the starting point for most overviews of women in political thought. That Plato allowed the authority of women to equal that of men in the elite of the guardians has recommended him to feminists. In Plato's ideal city, women realize their essential human being as do men, and women as well as men contribute to the life of the *polis*. This idea remains in vivid contrast to the exclusion of women from public life in practice, and from ethical being in theory, which became a constant in traditional Western political thought. Plato's arguments nevertheless fail to satisfy the criteria of some modern feminist theorists because the *Republic* is "a purely abstract vision" without a connection to real human life (Elshtain 1981, 39) or because Plato sees women's contribution as more feeble than men's (Osborne 1979, 32). Okin suggests that the difference between the ideal of the *Republic* and the real world of the *Laws* reflects not an ambivalence in Plato's concept of women and men as equally human, but the absence of private property and the family in the abstract world (1980, 70). An essential difference is the irrelevance of a woman's capacity to bear children in the *Republic*; in the *Laws*, this is the criterion that determines the position of a woman in the city (Saxonhouse 1985, 39, 61–62). General histories that suggest that the society in which Plato lived and developed his ideas enforced the absolute exclusion of women from public life and formal education might overstate the case, but we do not have sufficient evidence to deduce the significance among his contemporaries and colleagues of educated and influential women such as his mother Periktione and the scholar Aspasia (Seltman 1956; Saxonhouse 1985, 55–57).

Whether Plato's idea of women guardians was or was not a radical proposal at the time, feminist critiques of Aristotle's views on women vary in interpretations of the central difference between these theorists. With Aristotle there is no ambiguity, and his theory of women's nature as functional only in the private realm of family life provokes united condemnation. The misogynist attitude behind Aristotle's arguments for a separate sphere for women from which worthy men can escape is central to his theory of political justice. Elshtain points out that Aristotle sees women as among a number of groups whose "natural" disabilities suit them to serve rather than participate (1981, 51), but feminist interpretations of his arguments for women's exclusion from political life differ. As he defines woman by the capacity to bear children this is seen as the criterion that somehow prevents women from exercising their rationality as men do (Osborne 1979, 46–47; Okin 1980, 85–86). Saxonhouse points out that it is Aristotle's view of women as controlled by emotion, not reason, that is the basis of his arguments for their exclusion from the political life of the city (1985, 73–75, 88). In a recognition of the essential role of a private realm, Aristotle refutes Plato's idea of a community of women and children with the assertion that the private family is the "natural and necessary" basis for social life (see Saxonhouse 1982).

The Aristotelian theory that nature determines a hierarchical social order was in contrast with the Christian theory of divinely determined order as well as with Plato's ideal. The spiritual equivalence of the sexes integral to the Christian concept of the soul is an idea which, like Plato's republic, has not yet found its moment in history. On the contrary, in the thirteenth century, Thomas Aquinas developed a doctrine fusing the Aristotelian theory of the natural superiority of the male with the theological speculation that Eve's sin condemned women to subjection to men. Aquinas endorsed Aristotle's definition of women in arguing that the fulfillment of human being, life with God, is reached through the soul. Soul and body are not only separated, but the body is seen as a hindrance to the purpose of human being. As women are defined by the capacity of their bodies to reproduce, the activity of their rational souls is necessarily impaired. Women are thus a second level of human being, the instruments by which humankind is reproduced, and men are situated between women and God. With Aquinas the theoretical equivalence of all human souls before God is not incompatible with the argument that women have a second-class social and political status because they are defined as bodied beings who bear children. While the origin of this doctrine lies with Aquinas, symbols within medieval Christianity carried the idea of women as an obstruction to salvation (Saxonhouse 1985, 144–50; Osborne 1979, 78).

Niccolò Machiavelli was born in Florence in 1469 and died in 1527. He is generally regarded as a dividing line between the "classical" political theorists, from Plato to Aquinas, and the "modern" political theorists after Hobbes. His work is still one of the milestones in political thought as it is taught today and remains an important field for teaching and research, in which his abdication of the purpose of rule and his concentration instead on the maintenance of power are seen as the foundation of modern politics. Machiavelli's fourteen years as an influential figure in the city's government ended abruptly when the Medici returned to power in 1513 and he was arrested and tortured. After his release he retired, at the age of forty-four, to a country villa where he began the writing through which he has had such a powerful influence on modern political thought. This chapter is concerned with Machiavelli's ideas of the place of women in the life of the state and uses a modern compendium of his writings, including, as well as *The Prince* and an abridged version of the *Discourses on the First Ten Books of Titus Livius*, a selection of his letters and other writing including the novella *Belfagor, the Devil Who Took a Wife* (Bondanella and Musa 1979).

Commentary on the *Discourses* invariably refers to Machiavelli's educated, middle-class family background and usually mentions his father's copy of Livy's *History of the Roman Republic*. His faith in the authority of such classics, one reads, was "always tempered by direct observation" (Berki 1977, 120–23; Bondanella and Musa 1979, 26). The past was a chronicle of models to Machiavelli, and in this conception of human history and in his idea of human nature he was a typical product of the Renaissance. In such a view conflict is an inevitable consequence in society, to be regulated by secular law or military force rather than by divine commandment. Modern views of *The Prince* range from perceptions of the work as immoral, or amoral, to seeing it as common sense. In the latter view, Cesare Borgia is the prototype for a modern prince, and the work is an essential handbook for both politicians and bureaucrats (Plamenatz 1970, 36–41). According to Bondanella, Machiavelli has been maligned through a mistranslation of "Si guarda al fine" (*The Prince* XVIII) as "The end justifies the means." But this whole section, "How princes should honor their word," conveys the message that, although doing evil is never good, it is nevertheless often prudent and sometimes necessary for the ruler. Machiavelli points out that, "If all men were good, this precept would not be good; but because men are wretched creatures who would not keep their word to you, you need not keep your word to them'' (Bondanella and Musa 1979, 134). There is no disagreement over what constitutes the essence of Machiavelli's work—the striving for and maintenance of power—for Machiavelli was addressing the modern prince, whose rule was not constituted or enforced by tradition or custom and who had neither the legitimacy of divine right nor that of the popular will.

The justification for authority that Machiavelli proposed was the ability to wield power. This did not depend on might alone, but on the interplay of skillful action and the right moment. The characteristic most essential to the ruler was *virtù*, generally but inaccurately translated as virtue but defined as ingenuity, ability, or skill (Bondanella and Musa); vitality, energy, or courage (Plamenatz); or the exercise of any capability that fulfills the purpose of the ruler—courage and cunning, honesty and deceit, obedience to law and ruthlessness (Jones). What these definitions have in common is summed up by R. N. Berki, for whom this key concept ''stands for the masculine and warlike qualities of courage, fortitude, devotion and the pursuit of success and glory'' (1977, 121).

The fateful moment—the full tide in the affairs of the prince—is in the gift of *fortuna*. Just as *virtù* is sexed, so is *fortuna*. The best ruler is the embodiment of *virtù*—that is, he has a male body—and the matrix of the ruler's actions, *fortuna*, is interpreted as female. To Bondanella, *fortuna* is ''the classical female goddess who now replaced Christian providence'' and ''the personification of all the contingent forces in the world''; *fortuna* is ''like a woman . . . always more likely to smile upon an energetic and courageous young man'' (1979, 19–23). To Berki, *fortuna* is a woman. These modern interpretations of the central Machiavellian concepts thus set the heroic man as actor against the shifting background of capricious, yet passive, woman. The accuracy of these interpretations will be assessed later; for now we can assume that these current commentators have correctly presented Machiavelli's ideas and arguments and note how uncritically the gendered nature of his theory of effective and legitimate rule has been treated. If these theorists—we shall not call them critics—perceived the implications of this, they have apparently thought it an unimportant dimension of Machiavelli's writing. When these same men place Machiavelli as the first modern political theorist, the proto-realist who anticipates the discipline of political science, they privilege his displacement of women too—for this is not marginal to Machiavelli's politics but a vital component in his reasoning. The durability of the notion of Machiavelli's realism, which accorded him the status of the father of political science, is particularly curious given Donald McIntosh's observation that this interpretation ''simply cannot be sustained from the texts'' (1984, 184).

The Machiavellian doctrine of militarism was rationalized by the idea of *virtù*, of masculinity, courage, and independence manifest in the ruler and developed as the primary ethic of civic life. Passivity and self-interest were antithetical to his idea of good citizens and thus these traits were to be confined to the home. As Hanna Pitkin observes, ''Machiavelli invokes . . . a vision of human reality that underlies the entire body of his thought, a vision of embattled men struggling to preserve themselves, their masculinity, their autonomy, and their achievements of civilization, against almost overwhelming odds'' (1984, 169). The male-female sexual relationship is the metaphor through which the difficulties of the struggle to establish and preserve a state and the constant threat to its success are concisely conveyed by Machiavelli. Much of his reasoning in *The Prince* is devoted to strategies for outwitting or overpowering obstacles to the exercise of *virtù* expressed in these metaphorical terms. Pitkin is one of the few political theorists to take Machiavelli's view of women seriously, and it is disappointing that she diverts her analysis in arguing that his view is a result of fear of the power of women and in attempting to explain the source of his fear. We do not have the evidence Pitkin needs to make her case about Machiavelli's own infancy (Pringle 1986).

In any case, it is not Machiavelli's singularity that is at issue here, but the ways in which his metaphoric language speaks for Aristotle and Aquinas and speaks so clearly to the modern political theorist. Machiavelli's most profound achievement is his mediation of the politics of women's place by his contribution to the process of replacing the weakening meanings of medieval symbolism with a newly significant modern metaphor. He thus enables Aristotle's embodiment of ethics as male to bridge the transformation of the relation of ethics to politics, a critical point in the history of gender relations. Aristotle had taken ethics and maleness as synonymous, and Machiavelli's case for ''realism'' rather than ethics as the basis for political life could thus have disenfranchised men. It is for this reason that maleness is so heavily endorsed as the essential political virtue, and it is in this sense that Machiavelli provided the foundation for the work of Hobbes and Locke.

In such political theorization, women will never belong in the *polis* and will always be ''other,'' for this is primarily a politics of definition and only secondarily a systematic prescription for the order and preservation of a state. Despite the emphasis placed on the element of realism, until McIntosh and Pitkin questioned Machiavelli's view of women, the problem of the accuracy of his portrayal of the role of women in his society was disregarded. This acceptance is revealing, whether it arose from the view that this dimension of Machiavelli's work was insignificant, or whether his accuracy on this point was considered irrelevant. It is because of Machiavelli's supposed realism that he is now considered the first modern political theorist. We might explore whether he created or merely recorded the valorization of masculine dominance which underpins his work. Though no comprehensive response to this question can be properly developed here, its importance is such that some of the available evidence will be discussed briefly.

Machiavelli appears more open about the man-as-ruler/woman-as-wanton dichotomy than the orthodox modern commentators on his work suggest, and it certainly does not appear that they have misunderstood but only underestimated this dimension. In *The Prince* (XXV) he argues that

Fortune is the arbiter of one half of our actions, but . . . she still leaves the control of the other half, or almost that, to us. And I compare her to one of those ruinous rivers that, when they become enraged, flood the plains, tear down the trees and buildings . . . everyone yields to their onslaught, unable to oppose them in any way. . . . Fortune . . . shows her force where there is no organized strength to resist her.

In Chapter VI, Book II of the *Discourses* he asserts that, apart from a threat to life, "property and honour are the two things concerning which men take offence more than anything else. . . . And of the honours that may be taken from a man, women are the most important." Machiavelli's view of the relationship of women to civic life is concisely conveyed in the title given to Chapter XXVI of the *Discourses*, "How a State Is Ruined Because of Women."

In his published letters Machiavelli uses military metaphor to refer to sexual relationships as well as the sexual metaphor to refer to statecraft. Some of the letters offer frank statements of the political threat of women and the prescribed armament of men, else "fortune varies and commands men, and keeps them under her yoke." Whether writing in this way of woman as the symbol of political threat in a letter to his mentor, Piero Soderini; as a desired sexual object in a letter to his friend, Francesco Vittori; or as a despised whore in his letter to another close friend, Luigi Guicciardini (Bondanella and Musa 1979, 54–76), woman is invariably presented as a trap and an obstacle for right and purposeful— that is, male—action. Fortune, and women, might be outwitted, escaped, beaten, or, in both the colloquial meanings, "screwed," but never consulted, trusted, negotiated with, or treated as a partner.

The small sample from letters and from recent translations of *The Prince* and *Discourses* quoted above indicates that the commentaries discussed earlier are an accurate transmission of Machiavelli's ideas about women. The sexual element in the vilification of women, implicit in these letters, is explicit in Machiavelli's novella, *Belfagor, the Devil Who Took a Wife*. In this story the heterosexual relationship is the means by which woman controls man, with the idea that such control necessarily has evil results. The medieval symbol of woman as "the devil's gateway" is essential to the story of *Belfagor*. While these meanings are not lost on modern commentators they are oblivious of the issue of whether Machiavelli was recording, or encoding, the contexting of women. We know that Italy was the locus of Renaissance Europe and that *The Prince* "became the intellectual property of every well read European in the sixteenth and seventeenth centuries" (Bondanella and Musa 1979, 17). The other book to achieve this distinction was Castiglione's *Book of the Courtier*. First published in 1528, this work is in four parts: a discussion of the qualities of a Renaissance gentleman, the proper uses of those qualities, the qualities of a lady, and the relations of courtier and prince. The courtier and courtesan were equal members of an aristocratic and educated elite, and it is clear from a reading of Book III of Castiglione that the *donna di palazzo* was as cultured, and as influential, as her male counterpart. She is presented throughout the dialogue of this work as gracious, intelligent, and powerful. Was this an accurate representation of the lady in Urbino and in Milan, where Castiglione lived? Jacob Burckhardt maintains that in Renaissance Italy,

women stood on a footing of perfect equality with men. . . . There was no question of "woman's rights" or female emancipation, simply because the thing itself was a matter of course. The educated woman, no less than the man, strove naturally after a characteristic and complete individuality. (1961, 280–81)

Though this striking contradiction of the realism of Machiavelli's portrayal of the place of women oversimplifies a complex of men's attitudes and women's aspirations, it is useful as an addendum to the descriptive value of Castiglione's work. Philippe Ariès presents very different evidence to argue that patriarchy gained hold at the end of the Middle Ages and that before the law as well as in the household the position of women in Renaissance Europe declined markedly (1962, 355). In her review of modern discussions of this issue, Pitkin refers to the assessment of the Renaissance as "masculine in temper, through and through" (1984, 201) and shows, through a close assessment of evidence about society in Renaissance Italy, that women lost authority within the household and that the separation of the household from public life marked a contrast between medieval and Renaissance Florence (203ff). The enclosure of daughters at home and the privatization of the domain of the wife follow logically on the change from joint estate to the law of primogeniture, for the protection of a woman's chastity is then synonymous, for men, with the protection of property. The vocabulary and theorization of this slide in the economic affairs of women was a moral one, with property ownership by women attacked on religious grounds and women blamed for their own and society's economic problems (Woodbridge 1984, 132–33).

In the late fifteenth century the court of Urbino was distinguished by the prominence of women as well as by influential men and women in exile there from other parts of Italy, including the Medici from Florence. Federico Montefeltro's magnificent palace was without precedent; its architectural and artistic expressions of humanism made it famous throughout all the courts of Italy until Cesare Borgia conquered Urbino by treachery in 1502 (Rotondi 1969, 1–10, 93), the action that made him Machiavelli's hero (Bondanella and Musa 1979, 11). In celebrating the greatness of Urbino, Castiglione was concerned to depict the court as cultured and modern, and he presented the relations at the court as a new ideal, his vision of the future for the whole of Europe. He denounced "those old, malevolent ideas of the inconstancy of woman" which were reactionary, a residue of medieval thought. His courtesan is an affirmation of the qualities of strength and constancy (Whitfield 1974, xviii–xx; O'Faolain and Martines 1974, 199). Castiglione presents an idealized court, but there were there at the time both men and women who were influential, admired, and cultured. Among the figures histories record as being there were Caterina di San

Celso of Milan, Isabella Gonzaga of Urbino, Imperia di Cugnatis of Rome, the writers Cassandra Fedele and Vittoria Colonna, and the political figures Lucrezia Borgia and Caterina Sforza, said to be the first woman honored with the name *virago* (O'Faolain and Martines 1974, 192–98; de Riencourt 1974, 233–34; Burckhardt 1961, 281). Caterina Sforza exemplified the courage and forcefulness of those who opposed Cesare Borgia, and Machiavelli well knew her ability as his first and unsuccessful diplomatic mission was to her court in 1499. He recounts his story about her confounding her captors in both *The Prince* (XX) and in the *Discourses* (III.vi).

While women of powerful and noble families constituted only a small proportion of society, there were also many middle-class women whose business ability enabled the growth of family fortunes while their husbands were absent from the city for long periods on the duties of public office or attending to the management of farms. Of the women in this situation there is at least one whose skills Machiavelli was in a position to observe. While his friend Luigi Guicciardini served as governor in various provinces, his wife Isabella managed both the farm and the family's business interests in the city (Martines 1974, 16–17). Such examples indicate that the activity of women in public life continued, although apparently women were no longer recognized as valuable by men in public life, to whom it was an impediment to realizing an economic and political order in which the confinement of women within a domestic sphere followed necessarily from their role in bearing children. Keith Thomas suggests that "the very frequency with which that independence was denounced" shows that the independence Renaissance women exercised was greater than generally thought proper (Woodbridge 1984, 135). In Italy contemporary tracts on marriage were explicit on this point (King 1976), and in Florence mothers ensured the practice of codes of behavior that reinforced the different roles assigned to sons and daughters (Martines 1974, 18–24). The changed meanings of the words virago and courtesan—both of which were honorable titles in the fifteenth and sixteenth centuries—reveal the possibilities not then entirely closed to powerful women. Today, the Oxford dictionary tells us that the virago is a shrew, a scold, a "turbulent" woman ("ball-tearer" in slang usage); the courtesan is simply a prostitute (although "courtier" retains its nonsexual meaning). This degeneration of meaning is significant, especially in the way in which sexuality is the instrument through which words for powerful women are now derogatory. Similar changes have been wrought with "queen" and "mistress," the latter through reference to lovesick men as "servants" (Miller and Swift 1976, 79; Woodbridge 1984, 130), those who, despite Machiavelli's warning, were in the control of women.

The function of literary expositions on the proper role of women and on their education, plentiful in the Renaissance, is less obvious. The writing of women such as Christine de Pisan (1363–1431) and Louise Labé (1520–1566) was not concerned with setting out humanist arguments for the education of women. Their work is very different from the writings of Erasmus and of Cornelius

Agrippa, whose *On the Nobility and Excellence of Women* is an example of a genre of Renaissance literature built up around *la querelle des femmes*. This "fashionable preoccupation" with defining women's abilities failed to challenge the qualified "humanism" of Rabelaisian discourses on education, which ignored the education of women. Similarly we might question the "humanism" of Petrarch, for whom women were Eve reincarnated, if we are to accept the evidence of his *Epistle to Posterity* in which he expresses the view that "enemy of peace, source of impatience, cause of quarrels which destroy tranquility, woman is a real devil."

The formality of the exchanges within *la querelle des femmes* genre is now recognized as an indication of the formality of the controversy itself. L. Woodbridge (1984) argues that these were primarily literary exercises, so that the same writer could pen both an attack on women and then a defense. In this scholarly exchange, the subject was secondary to the art; sometimes the defense preceded the attack. In this view, the content of this writing by a host of participants in Italy, France, and England is thus of marginal value in the history of ideas. As with Machiavelli's work, this writing must always be treated in its cultural context. We are then alert to more precise evidence such as the number of editions of antiwoman tracts—these far exceeded the popularity of the works in defense of women (Wayne 1987). Woodbridge suggests that the long formal controversy created the illusion of serious debate and thus precluded a widespread questioning of new theorization about women and property and about women and political life. She sees the work of Cornelius Agrippa and Baldassare Castiglione in Italy as important exceptions to the game of literary attacks and defenses of women which served to reinforce male dominance by its very nature (1984, 134–35).

The *Malleus Maleficarum*, an influential book published in 1487, offered the argument that women were more carnal because they were less intellectual, as made manifest by their "many carnal abominations" of which menstruation was the primary one. Women were thus "contaminating to the touch" and the natural agents through which the world was made vulnerable to Satan (Thomas 1973, 520–23). The work concluded:

All witchcraft comes from carnal lust, which is in women insatiable . . . wherefore for the sake of fulfilling their lusts they consort even with devils. . . . And blessed be the Highest who has so far preserved the male sex from so great a crime: for since He was willing to be born and to suffer for us, therefore He has granted to men this privilege. (Quoted in de Riencourt 1974, 250)

Although this book was denounced by some leading churchmen, it apparently ran through sufficient editions to remain for two centuries an authority which "lay on the bench of every judge, on the desk of every magistrate. It was the ultimate, irrefutable, unarguable authority. It was implicitly accepted not only by Catholic but by Protestant legislators" (de Riencourt 1974, 250).

Despite the prominence of women religious leaders and scholars in medieval Catholicism, such work reinforced stereotypes of men as essentially spiritual and women as essentially carnal. These stereotypes promoted efforts in the fourteenth century to prevent women from teaching and underlay the condemnation of the Beguines at the council of Vienne in 1311 (Bynum 1982, 19). The Reformation merely reaffirmed that women were excluded from justification by faith because their salvation depended on "generation"—that is, through men.

A sixteenth-century theological debate centered on the fundamental question, "Are women human?" The question arose from the argument that, in procreation, man was the *causa efficiens* and woman merely the *causa instrumentalis*— woman did not qualify as human simply because man employed her as a tool to perpetuate the race. The debate was taken seriously enough to prompt a rebuttal from the faculties of theology at Wittenberg and Leipzig; regardless of this, fifty years later the controversy had "passed from the schools into the conversations of the best companies" in Holland and Germany (Fleischer 1981, 110). The popularity of the debate lasted for more than a century; again, while the arguments are interesting chiefly as an intellectual game, its popularity indicates the privileging of male attitudes to women in intellectual discourse as well as in the law courts, legislatures, and ecclesiastical councils of Renaissance Europe. There was no parallel coding of female attitudes to men, no shorthand in which an undercurrent of rules about men circulated beneath the rules of civic life.

The defenses of women certainly never became effective arguments for the admission of women to universities in this period. By the end of the sixteenth century the prominent intellectual communities were male, and the marriages of male scholars, "usually unsophisticated economic arrangements," were to wives who were seen as housekeepers rather than intellectual companions. The intellectual woman was a distraction rather than an equal in scholarship, and she was a positive obstacle to spirituality, a temptress; her intelligence was the tool of the devil (Fleischer 1981, 119). "Late humanist scholarship as a way of life which minimised women was evidently the cultural corridor through which the controversy over the humanity of women passed from study to study, amusing the learned behind closed doors" (Fleischer 1981, 115).

For the theorists of Liberalism the case was closed, and in political, intellectual, economic, and social structures women were the helpmeets of men. Writing in the seventeenth century, Hobbes and Locke, like the "classical" political economists of the eighteenth century, saw men as citizens in the world and women as instruments at home, and the cultural dominance of this practice was such as to underpin the view empirically. Machiavelli has no such excuse and must stand charged as a "vulgar" theorist who, far from being a political realist, always relating the lessons of the past to the realities of the present, ignored the evidence of autonomous women in employing a metaphorical language in which women figured not only as without autonomy, but as a threat to male autonomy as well. In this language, politics is implicitly defined as a male and a public activity.

This is not to argue that in seventeenth-century Europe there were no women who exercised authority over their own lives. Nor do I suggest that all or most women in Renaissance Europe were powerful, educated, or autonomous. I seek rather to make an appropriate acknowledgment of Machiavelli's contribution to the historical construction of the male citizen, so important to the gendered state of Liberalism. Machiavelli's sexual metaphors were part of the contextualization of gendered power in which were embedded Aristotle's gendered ethics, Aquinas' gendered soul, and an interpretation of Plato in the form of a gendered *polis*.

Machiavelli stood on a threshold where the very definition of political life was changing and new meanings were being formed, and these definitions and meanings were encoded in Machiavelli's use of imagery. The militaristic definition of the citizen depends on its contrast with an anticitizen who as female personifies all the things the effective citizen must not be—not passive, not dependent, not weak, not indecisive. The citizen has a male body, and the vocabulary of power is expressed in this metaphor, just as the female body stands for all that must be won over, used, controlled, ordered, defeated.

The role assigned to women is important to the instrumentalist view of politics—"the dominant orientation to action in the modern era" (McIntosh 1984, 196). The uncritical and un-self-conscious treatment of Machiavelli's metaphorical language in modern political analysis has tended to obscure his significant contribution to instrumentalism and to reinforce its influence, suggesting that the definitions and meanings inherent in Machiavelli's gender politics are still current. The ways in which our own cultural practices endorse this politics—in particular, the striking contemporary relevance of Machiavellian metaphor—are obvious in the language and imagery of advertising, for example. At the "higher" cultural levels the same process of cultural endorsement can be carried in vehicles even less vulnerable to challenge and regulation. The process of sensitizing ourselves to Machiavellian imagery and decoding it involves many genres; the breadth can be shown by a few examples.

The opera *The Coronation of Poppaea*, written in 1642 by the composer Claudio Monteverdi, to a text by Gian Francesco Busenello, was a major work of seventeenth-century Renaissance music and marked the birth of opera (Dunwell 1962, 111). The historical theme features the characters of Nero, his wife Octavia, his lover Poppaea, and the philosopher Seneca. The story of Nero's neglect of duty and total capitulation to Poppaea is played out at the pleasure of Amor and Fortuna, with Virtù the loser as the counsel of Seneca is ignored. The figure of Amor in the opera is true to the overweening role Machiavelli allocates to love in man's affairs, and the caprice of Fortuna also owes much to his image of a female Fate. Written more than a century after Machiavelli died, the story is so close to his concepts of the relationships of men, women, and the state that it is a signpost of the continued currency of these ideas. Monteverdi's score was in harmony with this political view, and the significance of the opera in the history of music owes much to his achievement of a music expressive of the new humanism. Poppaea is thus "Monteverdi's final embodiment of the humanist view of the passions as inexplicable, irrational forces in large part determining our thoughts and actions" (Tomlinson 1987, 236).

Composer and author have chosen to play out Machiavelli's metaphors, and the opera could be subtitled "How a State Is Ruined because of Women." A more recent musical echo is Carl Orff's *Carmina Burana*, composed in 1937 around a thirteenth-century text. Among the songs attributed to itinerant medieval singers is the hymn "Fortuna Imperatrix Mundi," addressing the all-powerful but unpredictable goddess reintroduced to a modern generation. The music brings together a simple, formal melody with primitive, evocative rhythm—a technique of composition that aptly describes the powerful undercurrent of meaning beneath Machiavelli's lessons for rulers.

The theme of the world of women as a weakening influence on men was developed in H. G. Wells's *The New Machiavelli*, published in 1911. Wells forecasts the age of the bureaucrat, the cunning official who is the modern version of Machiavelli himself. The parallel has not been lost on bureaucrats, to whom the body politic has become the body corporate. Studies of Machiavelli are replaced by studies of Machiavellianism, defined as "a sober appraisal of reality in our imperfect world," essential not only for public servants and corporation executives but also for technocrats, academics, and doctors (Haneman 1980). Wells's novel is a prophecy of Machiavelli's new relevance in a world of managers where it is not the prince but the expert—Machiavelli himself—who is powerful. *The New Machiavelli* endorses the old imagery, and its subject is "a man's statemaking dream" ruined by "the besetting of sex." The reception and teaching of this novel, one of Wells's lesser known works, treated it as a tragedy of ruined male ambition and lost political goals and ignored its most complex element, the ambiguity represented by the characters of Margaret and Isobel, the woman at home and the woman in the world.

In the medium of the cinema probably the most outstanding example of the contemporary power of Machiavelli's metaphorics is Fellini's *City of Women*. Reviews of the film that discuss "the use of the opposite sex as a symbolic embodiment of the unknown and thus as a principal agent of transformation" (Burke 1982, 145) without any sense of the irony of this reiteration of sixteenth-century political theory endorse Machiavelli's meanings. This is of course an apt interpretation of Fellini, who describes the cinema as a woman where "we make the screen assume the character . . . we expect of it, just as we do with women, upon whom we impose ourselves" (Bachman 1980–81). In *City of Women* Fellini recreates the scenario of the grotesque washerwoman exactly as Machiavelli had described it in his letter to Guicciardini, and he makes this film, and his cinema, as alien and inaccessible to women as Machiavelli was concerned to make the ruler, the state, and its citizens.

Scholarly interpretations of Machiavelli that overlook his gendered politics while teaching and discussing his work validate that politics. His definition of women as not only outside political life, but as a threat to the order and security of the state is an essential element in his contribution to modern political thought. A critical reading of metaphors in Machiavelli's writing yields a key to the paradoxical Renaissance theorization of women as inadequate or dangerous in civic life while in practice there were politically, economically, and socially influential women. The cultural recharging of the sexual metaphors Machiavelli employed is still important in keeping together the meanings embedded there and read every day—man is subject, woman is object. The political function of this implicit reiteration of Machiavelli is very effective—in this sense too, he created the myth we live by (Gramsci 1957). Machiavelli averted his gaze from the virago, and political theory has not been able to look her in the eye since. Machiavelli's work could not have had its effect without a context in which a privileged place was accorded political theory and its modern equivalent, political science. A reappraisal of his writing that explores the reinforcement of a cultural context in which gendered power is accorded the force of scientific law, or common sense, might proceed from a study of his metaphors and the contradictions they carry into the genre of political science and the discourse of Liberalism.

REFERENCES

Ariès, Philippe. 1962. *Centuries of Childhood*. Translated by Robert Baldick. New York: Random House.

Bachman, Gideon. 1980–81. "Federico Fellini: 'The Cinema Seen as a Woman...' " *Film Quarterly* 34:2.

Baron, Hans. 1955. *The Crisis of the Early Italian Renaissance*. Princeton, N.J.: Princeton University Press.

Berki, R. N. 1977. *A History of Political Thought*. London: Dent.

Bondanella, P., and M. Musa. 1979. *The Portable Machiavelli*. Harmondsworth, England: Penguin.

Burckhardt, J. 1961. *The Civilization of the Renaissance in Italy*. New York: Mentor Books.

Burke, F. 1982. "Fellini's Art of Affirmation: *The Nights of Cabiria, City of Women*, and Some Aesthetic Implications." *Canadian Journal of Political and Social Theory* 6(3):138–54.

Bynum, Caroline Walker. 1982. *Jesus as Mother: Studies in the Spirituality of the High Middle Ages*. Los Angeles: University of California Press.

Castiglione, Baldassare. 1974. *The Book of the Courtier*. Edited by J.H. Whitfield. London: Dent.

de Riencourt, A. 1974. *Sex and Power in History*. New York: Delta Books.

Dunwell, W. 1962. *Music and the European Mind*. London: Herbert Jenkins.

Eisenstein, Zillah. 1981. *The Radical Future of Liberal Feminism*. New York: Longman.

Elshtain, Jean B. 1981. *Public Man, Private Woman: Women in Social and Political Thought*. Princeton, N.J.: Princeton University Press.

Fleischer, Manfred. 1981. " 'Are Women Human?'—The Debate of 1595 between Valens Acidalius and Simon Gediccus." *Sixteenth Century Journal* 12(2):105–20.

Germino, Dante. 1966. "Second Thoughts on Leo Strauss's Machiavelli." *Journal of Politics* 28:794–817.

Gramsci, Antonio. 1957. *The Modern Prince and Other Writings*. New York: International Publishers.

Haneman, B. 1980. "In Praise of Machiavelli." *The Medical Journal of Australia* 13 (December): 652.

Jones, W. T. 1947. *Masters of Political Thought*. London: Harrap.

King, M. 1976. "Caldiera and the Barbaros on Marriage and the Family: Humanist Reflections of Venetian Reality." *Journal of Mediaeval and Renaissance Studies* 6:19–50.

Leonard, John. 1984. "Public versus Private Claims. Machiavellianism from Another Perspective." *Political Theory* 12(4):491–506.

Lucas, Angela. 1982. *Women in the Middle Ages: Religion, Marriage and Letters*. London: Harvester Press.

McDonald, L. M. 1968. *Western Political Theory*. New York: Harcourt Brace.

McIntosh, Donald. 1984. "The Modernity of Machiavelli." *Political Theory* 12(2): 184–203.

Martines, Lauro. 1974. "A Way of Looking at Women in Renaissance Florence." *Journal of Mediaeval and Renaissance Studies* 4:15–28.

Miller, Casey, and Kate Swift. 1976. *Words and Women-Language and the Sexes*. Harmondsworth, England: Penguin.

O'Faolain, Julia, and Lauro Martines, eds. 1974. *Not in God's Image—Women in History*. London: Fontana.

Okin, Susan M. 1980. *Women in Western Political Thought*. London: Virago.

Osborne, Martha, ed. 1979. *Women in Western Thought*. New York: Random House.

Pateman, Carole. 1979. *The Problem of Political Obligation*. Brisbane, Australia: Wiley.

———. 1988. *The Sexual Contract*. Stanford, Calif.: Stanford University Press.

———. 1989. *The Disorder of Women*. Stanford, Calif.: Stanford University Press.

Pitkin, Hanna. 1984. *Fortune Is a Woman. Gender and Politics in the Thought of Niccolo Machiavelli*. Berkeley: University of California Press.

Plamenatz, J. 1970. *Man and Society*. London: Longman.

Pringle, Helen. 1986. "The City v. Cradle." *The Age Monthly Review* (November): 21–3.

Rotondi, Pasquale. 1969. *The Ducal Palace of Urbino: Its Architecture and Decoration*. London: Alec Tiranti.

Saxonhouse, A. 1982. "Family Polity and Unity: Aristotle on Socrates' Community of Wives." *Polity* 15, (2):201–19.

———. 1985. *Women in the History of Political Thought: Ancient Greece to Machiavelli*. New York: Praeger.

Seltman, C. 1956. *Women in Antiquity*. London: Pan Books.

Spender, Dale. 1983. *Women of Ideas—And What Men Have Done to Them*. London: Ark.

Thomas, Keith. 1973. *Religion and the Decline of Magic*. Harmondsworth, England: Penguin.

Threadgold, Terry. 1988. "Language and Gender." *Australian Feminist Studies* 6:41–70.

Tomlinson, G. 1987. *Monteverdi and the End of the Renaissance*. Oxford: Clarendon Press.

Wayne, Valerie. 1987. "Renaissance Women." *Essays in Criticism* 37(1):62–66.

Wells, H. G. 1911. *The New Machiavelli*. London: Bodley Head.

Whitfield, J. H., ed. 1974. Introduction to *The Book of the Courtier*, by Baldassare Castiglione, i–xxiii. London: Dent.

Woodbridge, L. 1984. *Women and the English Renaissance. Literature and the Nature of Womankind, 1540–1620*. Urbana: University of Illinois Press.

9

Radical Hens and Vociferous Ladies: Representation and Class in the Mid-Nineteenth Century

Barbara Garlick _____

By inserting the word "male" in the 1832 Reform Act, the Whig majority in the House of Commons codified the exclusion of women from the suffrage that had been unofficially in effect over the previous two centuries of parliamentary government. Although much of the female political agitation contemporary with the parliamentary decision was not narrowly focused on the suffrage, this issue nevertheless motivated responses to such agitation. Implicit in these responses was the fear that acquisition of the suffrage would give women a means by which they could hasten a possible solution to the many inequities that were prompting their increasingly militant voice. Helen Blackburn, a later suffragette and historian of the earlier suffrage movement, records the comments of a politically aware woman who had lived through the period:

In my young days it was considered rude to talk politics to ladies. To introduce them at a dinner party was a hint for us to retire and leave the gentlemen to such conversation and their bottle. But the excitement that prevailed all over the country at the prospect of the Reform Bill of 1832 broke down these distinctions, while the new and, as it seemed to us, splendid idea of a "hustings at the Cross of Edinburgh" drove its inhabitants, both male and female, half frantic with delight. I caught the infection, and as soon as ever I understood the benefits expected from a ten-pound franchise I began to wish that female householders should have it too, thinking it only fair play they should. (Blackburn [1902] 1971, 14)

Through focusing political perceptions in this way, the suffrage formed a substratum of debate and argument upon which other more immediate issues of concern for both working-class and middle-class women depended. This chapter examines the way in which the responses and reactions to female political agitators were programmed through a variety of popular middle-class representations that obeyed certain class prescriptions, and in which the class demarcations were justified by fears of proletarian revolution in the middle years of the century. The initial prompting for this study came from a sense of curiosity. There was in the period no timidity or hesitation about publicly criticizing middle-class social and political female aspiration, but there appears to be a conspicuous lack of comparable material on the working-class women involved in the radical working-class movement which made the greatest impact on English bourgeois fears and habits of mind in the period leading up to the mid-century, that is, Chartism. Women had been a significant part of working-class political movements before Chartism. The *Leeds Mercury*, for instance, reporting on a strike of 1,500 female card setters, editorialized in May 1832 that "Alarmists may view these indications of female independence as more menacing to established institutions than the education of the lower orders" (Rowbotham 1973, 32). Women were particularly important in the Owenite movement, which is brilliantly documented by Barbara Taylor in *Eve and the New Jerusalem* (1983). The historical record is, however, as Taylor has pointed out (xiii–xiv), full of silences, and when we turn to the footnotes of the few excellent modern studies of Chartist women, we find evidence of a great paucity of contemporary information. The material for these historical recuperations of the Chartist women has been collected almost exclusively from Chartist newspapers such as *The Northern Star* and the *English Chartist Circular*, from a few regional newspapers, and to a limited extent from memoirs and histories by Chartist men.[1] Such reconstructive exercises clearly demonstrate how far the activities of these women were discounted and ultimately ignored. Working-class women were not, however, unsuitable subjects for certain areas of middle-class investigation; indeed, where their sexuality was concerned, they provided the subject matter for a great deal of both prurient and high-minded examination and action. This phenomenon is examined in more detail later in this chapter.

A reading of the political register within female representation of the period, its manipulation, and the desired meanings that resulted indicate a clear pattern of contrasting absence and presence along class lines. The ideological impulse implicit in any representation emanates from a desire to control and make sense of the world through the creation of cultural artifacts which reproduce a desired social ordering. The cultural politics[2] in this period dictated that meaning was constructed and represented according to certain perceived aims of the ruling classes, aims threatened by the activities of articulate working-class women.

The lack of any significant cross-class female solidarity in the middle years of the century, moreover, underscores how far the working-class, politically vocal woman remained a creature imbued with undesirable strength and strangeness, qualities that were never accommodated satisfactorily within the bourgeois worldview.[3] Honest philanthropic impulses were only too easily diverted by overt militancy. The equivocal attitude to working-class agitation is nowhere better expressed than in Frances Trollope's preface to *The Life and Adventures of Michael Armstrong the Factory Boy*: "[I]t is grievous to see misguided and unfortunate men pursuing a course which must necessarily neutralize the efforts of their true friends'' ([1840] 1968, iii–iv).

In order to establish, therefore, these gaps in the historical record, this study of these ideologically motivated representations, is, of necessity, comparative, considering not only those isolated reportings and representations produced during the most active period of Chartism, the years from 1839 to 1842, but also those representations of middle-class political women active in the 1840s and the years leading up to the mid–1860s, focusing on the 1867 Reform Act and the man/person debate, and the abortive Women's Disabilities Removal Bill drafted by Dr. Pankhurst and introduced into the Parliament by Jacob Bright in 1870.

The iconography associated with the representation of politically active women in the nineteenth century was commonly based on paradox, highlighting the disparity between what was expected of them as women—in other words, the dominant evangelical, middle-class ideology—and their actual public behavior as witnessed and interpreted by men. Walpole's description of Mary Wollstonecraft as a hyena in petticoats illustrates this type of paradox perfectly. What was never questioned was why this should even be considered a paradox, why the ideology implicit in the feminine side of the so-called paradox should disbar the type of activity being criticized.

The threat represented by working-class female political activity and its ramifications in the area of suffrage reform is made clear by the census of 1851, which set down in actual numbers the realities of the situation that had been building up throughout the 1830s and 1840s. The implications of these statistics were not lost on commentators: Harriet Martineau, for instance, had earlier complained of ignorance about the fact that "nineteen-twentieths of the women of England earn their bread,"[4] and both Martineau and J. D. Milne, the author of the 1867 *Industrial and Social Position of Women in the Middle and Lower Ranks*, clearly understood that if one-third of the working women in the census were independent working women or if three-quarters of unmarried women worked or lived on their own earnings (Basch 1974, 105), there was a large, potentially powerful group of disenfranchised people waiting to be organized into a coherent group. John Stuart Mill, in his 1869 essay *The Subjection of Women*, clarifies the danger inherent in such facts:

Under whatever conditions, and within whatever limits, men are admitted to the suffrage, there is not a shadow of justification for not admitting women under the same. The majority of the women of any class are not likely to differ in political opinion from the majority of the men of the same class, unless the question be one in which the interests of women, as such, are in some way involved; and if they are so, women require the suffrage, as their guarantee of just and equal consideration. (Mill [1869] 1974, 488)

If universal male suffrage was commonly thought to be the precursor of communism and the end of civilization, then this large body of voters, a significant number of whom would have been already politicized through their working conditions and the group commitment engendered by these conditions, was seen as a very real danger to the ruling bourgeoisie and landed aristocracy, and to the political system painstakingly built up over the previous 200 years, exacerbating the fears of class revolution which had already been fostered by the revolutionary activity on the continent. The ruling class coped with this threat, in part, through a closing of the ranks and, in part, through the careful orchestration of middle-class public opinion.

In the period when Chartism flourished, England was still newly industrialized, Queen Victoria had only just come to the throne, and Europe was simmering with revolution. The men who drafted the six points of the Charter—universal male suffrage, equal electoral districts, annual Parliaments, payment of members, secret ballot, and no property qualification for members—were a mixture of middle-class supporters and skilled artisans, known as the moral force group, and the mainly unskilled laborers of the north and Wales, known as the physical force group. In both groups, women were active from the beginning of the Chartist movement.

The 1839 Address of the Female Political Union of Newcastle upon Tyne to their Fellow Countrywomen began, "We call upon you to join us and help our fathers, husbands, and brothers, to free themselves and us from political, physical, and mental bondage, and urge the following reasons as an answer to our enemies and an inducement to our friends"; and later, "the fear of what hangs over our heads; the scorn of the rich is pointed towards us; the brand of slavery is on our kindred, and we feel the degradation. We are a despised caste; our oppressors are not content with despising our feelings, but demand the control of our thoughts and wants" (Thompson 1971, 128–29). The "despised caste" here is not just the whole of the working class, but more specifically women, women whose articulate and impassioned contributions to the movement are well documented in the Chartist newspaper *The Northern Star*. This paper, one of the few radical papers to be stamped, was owned by Feargus O'Connor, a powerful figure and one-time Irish member of Parliament who was wealthy enough to afford the newspaper tax. It therefore forms a valuable because continuous reference point for all Chartist activity. In it we see women forming their own associations, being active fund-raisers, and, most important, speaking at public meetings. Indeed, this new phenomenon of women as public political speakers both in lecture rooms and on outdoor platforms was later to be enthusiastically copied by middle-class women, who thereby fearlessly and articulately abrogated one of the most precious of male public arenas. Furthermore, one of the least known but most influential of the Chartist writers in the last throes of the movement was a woman, Helen MacFarlane, a friend of Karl Marx and Friedrich Engels, who, as Howard Morton, wrote in 1850 a series of vigorous articles putting forward concrete proposals for social improvement (Schoyen 1958, 204).

Female participation in the movement was not always welcomed by the male

Chartists; in the pages of *The Northern Star* we see a preoccupation with the dislocation caused to sexual and family relations through the substitution of woman as primary breadwinner, and Chartist propaganda continually stressed the need for a sufficient wage to keep a dependent wife and children (Taylor 1983, 268, also Chap. 4, 83 passim). Such feelings, the positive side of which can be heard in the words of the Newcastle address, were no doubt fueled negatively by the sermon preached by the Reverend Francis Close to the Female Chartists of Cheltenham: "A bad mother of a family is far more mischievous in the country than a bad father, because the infant children are entrusted to her. . . . What a curse are such women to the country! Their children must grow up revolutionists, for they have been taught revolution at home!" (Thompson 1984, 147). He goes on to castigate them for meeting in church and for appealing to the Bible to justify their cause, and ends by assuring them that if they will "become again peaceable, kind and gentle to their fellow-men and fellow-subjects, I would do all in my power to promote the removal of their grievances; and the nation would listen with attention to her loving and content sons" (256). Again, in the words of Joe Scott in Charlotte Brontë's novel *Shirley*, we hear what are probably fairly authentic workingman's opinions about any women engaging in political activity, however innocuous:

"Young ladies," continued Joe, assuming a lordly air, "ye'd better go into th' house."

"I wonder what for?" inquired Shirley, to whom the overlooker's somewhat prag-matical manners were familiar, and who was often at war with him; for Joe, holding supercilious theories about women in general, resented greatly, in his secret soul, the fact of his master and his master's mill, being, in a manner, under petticoat government, and had felt as wormwood and gall, certain business-visits of the heiress to the Hollow's counting house.

"Because there is naught agate that fits women to be consarned in."

"Indeed! There is prayer and preaching agate in that church; are we not concerned in that?"

"Ye have been present neither at the prayer nor preaching, ma'am, if I have observed aright. What I alluded to was politics: William Farren, here, was touching on that subject, if I'm not mista'en."

"Well, what then? Politics are our habitual study, Joe. Do you know I see a newspaper every day, and two of a Sunday?"

"I should think you'll read the marriages, probably, Miss, and the murders, and the accidents and such like?"

"I read the leading articles, Joe, and the foreign intelligence, and I look over the market prices: in short, I read just what gentlemen read."

Joe looked as if he thought this talk was like the chattering of a pie. He replied to it by a disdainful silence. (Brontë [1849] 1981, 326–27)

Joe's silence here is indicative of a common strategy of discounting and con-taining, which I shall examine in more detail later. Chartist fiction also, relying as it did on the melodramatic plotting and characterization of the popular fiction styles of the day, was unable to reproduce other than the stock type of heroine as passive victim (Vicinus 1982, 9–10).

It is not surprising in the light of such opinions that, in early Chartist arguments about whether universal suffrage should include women, expediency should dominate. The first draft of the Charter did in fact include the enfranchisement of women (D. Jones 1983, 2), but, while conceding the reasonableness of the proposition, many members thought its inclusion would retard universal male suffrage. In 1843 Feargus O'Connor in *The Northern Star* stated, "Not that I doubt their [female] judgment and their proper use of it [the vote]; or their honesty; but because IT WOULD LEAD TO FAMILY DISSENSIONS, while it would not advance or serve the cause of democracy one single bit" (D. Jones 1983, 2).

When we consider the number of women working in the factories—in one Stockport mill, for instance, there were 846 female hands out of 1,270, and there were 1,300 power-looms on one flat attended by 651 females and 21 males (*The Times* 22.9.1842)—the injustice of female disenfranchisement appears even more marked, and Harriet Taylor's words in her 1851 "Enfranchisement of Women" appear particularly apposite:

To declare that a voice in the government is the right of all, and demand it only for a part—the part namely, to which the claimant himself belongs—is to renounce even the appearance of principle. The chartist who denies the suffrage to women, is a chartist only because he is not a lord; he is one of those levellers who would level only down to themselves. (Taylor, 1851, 292)

While female suffrage remained a minor motivation for female participation in the movement, the threat it posed was implicit in the attacks on female activists. The main platform for female speakers and activists always remained a class one: the amelioration of conditions for the working class. Because they were closer to the economics of family life, such as the providing of food and clothing, they usually chose these subjects for their agitation, and in doing so underlined the moral basis of the Chartist struggle. Despite the economic necessity that frequently forced women into the workplace, the evangelical ideal of domesticated womanhood became as potent for women as for men, and in the later years of Chartism, in the 1840s, it was the women who fervently took up the Temperance cause and for this, and other more politically pragmatic reasons, largely dropped out of more direct agitation.

In his analysis of the rhetoric of Chartism, which he relates directly to roots in the language of eighteenth-century radicalism, Gareth Stedman Jones emphasizes the close conjunction between the centralization of the powers of the Whig government following 1832 and the rise of Chartism. The vehement opposition to Whig policies, however, most notable in Chartism but also in other radical movements, forced a change in direction: The "apparently blatant 'class legislation' of the early 1830s was now beginning to be nuanced by moves of a less obviously sinister character—towards state-provided education, for instance, and the discussion of measures to improve the health of towns" (G. S. Jones 1983, 176). To many women, such measures appeared as responses to their most immediate concerns: the betterment of conditions for their class.

In the period of the late 1830s and early 1840s, before the change in Whig policies, Chartist women who felt compelled to become politically active were distinguished by their absence from the bourgeois press. When any commentary did appear, it was brief, and the emphasis was on their willful perversion of their "natural" role, echoing the cavils of a large number of male Chartists and the fulminations of such public preachers as the Reverend Close. It was as if their strength could be contained only by a denial of femininity or by silence. For bourgeois consumption the depiction of the working-class female agitator as unnatural and unrestrained was a logical extension of the commonly held middle-class opinion of working-class female sexuality. Either as political agitator or as a creature of primitive sexuality, she was perceived as a threat, and as such she became a metaphor through which all their fears of proletarian revolution were focused.

Contemporary newspaper accounts of the 1842 Plug Riots, for instance, gave daily reports of "turn-outs" or strikes in regular columns like "The State of the Manufacturing Districts" in *The Times*. According to *The Northern Star* women were active in all of these, and it seems certain that women were politicized through such marches and "turn-outs." However, in the bourgeois press, we see women mentioned only when they are being arrested, leading the demonstrators, or harassing nonstrikers:

Three females, named Jane Walker, Elizabeth Selby, and Mary Ann Bradbury, were examined on Saturday, before the Stockport magistrates, for intimidating Amelia Boardman, a power-loom weaver at Messrs. Bradshaw's, on the evening of the 7th of September, with a view to prevent her from following her employment. The evidence was, that the defendants, and particularly Walker, pursued Boardman home, collected a mob round her, and used violence to her. (*The Times* 13.9.1842)

MANCHESTER In one instance yesterday afternoon, there was an assemblage of 500 men and women in a field near the Stretford New-road in a very few minutes . . . a knot of seven women, who abused the men for running away from the police, and who refused to quit the spot, were apprehended, and brought in a coach to the police office. . . . ASHTON-UNDER-LINE . . . Soon after the mob left Messrs. Whittaker's yesterday they held a meeting in Charlestown, when they resolved to go to Staleybridge and stop the mills there, commencing with the mill of Messrs. Bayley and Brothers. In order the better to conceal their design, they had a procession, of which some 400 women formed the head. These were followed by about 300 men and boys . . . the military, who had been kept in readiness all the morning, turned out, and the Dragoons, galloping towards Staleybridge, cut off about two-thirds of the females from the head of the procession, and forced them to return. Scores of the "ladies" scrambled over the hedges and ditches in the neighbourhood. Some were thrown down; some few crept into the gardens in the neighbourhood, and others returned home. None were hurt; but one or two fainted away from fright. The men attempted to encourage the females to go forward (knowing that the females were exposed to the greatest danger). (*The Times* 15.9.1842)

As more and more men were imprisoned, there was an obvious gap to be filled by vocal and committed women. Pamphlets such as the "Rights of Women," written in prison in 1840 by the Chartist leader R.J. Richardson and addressed specifically to Chartist women with the advice that "it is a duty imperative on woman to interfere in political affairs,"[5] and "A Plea for Women," written in 1843 by Mrs. Hugo Reid, inspired many women to demonstrate their ability to counter criticism and to speak up forcefully for their class. A Chartist woman's reply to a male critic writing in the *Halifax Express* illustrates the high level of articulateness and logical argument that was typical:

Sir,—I shall pass over the taunting language, which you made use of in reply to my letter; it proves nothing, it answers no good end; truth is my object, and if we do not elicit that, our contention will be void. In reply to my letter on the Poor Law meeting at Elland, you have misrepresented me; you wish to evade the question, which is this, that until machinery is legislated on, so as to make it go hand in hand with manual labour, that is to act as an auxiliary or helpmate, and not as a competitor, the present condition of the productive classes will never be bettered. Instead of meeting the question fairly you say that I am as fit to drag down commerce in behalf of land as the Chandos dullards. Now, sir, this is false. I set no one interest in opposition to another. I do not support the unjust monopoly of the Corn Laws; yet if the Corn Laws were repealed tomorrow, that, of itself, would not benefit the labourer. Suppose it reduced the price of his bread to one-half of its present value, the successful competition of machinery would lower his wages two thirds. At the same time the master will always have his profits so long as he has the monopoly of making the law, whether the workman has a remunerating price for his labour or not. . . . I think I have gone over the main of your foolish objections, and I conclude by telling you that there is not a deficiency of the common stock, but plenty for all, under proper arrangements. We have no occasion, therefore, to emigrate from our country. There is no over-population, as you would have us to believe; it is all fudge. Out of the eighteen millions of acres that we possess, we have only five millions of acres growing wheat. Let them cut down the forest, plough up the park and hunting ground of the nobility, and a convention be called to examine into the legality of that thing called the national debt, which produces a plunder in perpetuity on all our industry. Let those things be done, and if they do not answer, it then will be time for us to be seeking out for a fresh pasture, as you call it. Yours, Elizabeth Hanson. (*The Northern Star* 21.4.1838)

An earlier reply to the same critic by another Chartist woman exhibits a similar forcefulness and fluency and concludes, "Now, Mr. Editor, do pray in future, permit a trifling degree of latitude to my sex—do allow them to express their grievances to the world without laying your mercenary goose quill so unmercifully about them, when we oppose tyranny and oppression" (*The Northern Star* 17.3.1838). It is interesting that their replies were not printed in the *Halifax*

Express, which had originally printed the criticisms, but in *The Northern Star*. I have not been able to ascertain whether this was their choice or whether the *Halifax Express* refused them the right of reply.

We see this same unease at and finally the silencing of female fluency in the widely reported Mary Ann Walker case. There was no hesitation in the bourgeois press in reporting in full and frenzied detail working-class activism that appeared to be male or not gender specific: speeches, meetings, strikes, arrests, trials. These regular columns were justified by bourgeois values and the social responsibilities implied by them, which were summed up by the *Illustrated London News*: "This is not a country where mere riot among the lower orders can by possibility gain victorious strength or sway. The middle classes—the balancing scales of the community—must in England form the thermometer of any revolution that political fury may enact" (15 [20.8.1842], 225). Social responsibility, however, demanded a different approach to specifically female political activism.

Mary Ann Walker, a Manchester Chartist, participated in the initial meetings held to form the London Female Chartist Association in October 1842. She was obviously highly articulate and intelligent, and it is enlightening to see how the media coped with her. The first meeting of the association was reported fully by *The Times*:

Mr. Cohen would, with all humility and respect, ask the young lady what sort of office she would aspire to fill (Order, order). If she would fill one, she would fill all. He was not going to treat the question with ridicule (hear, hear), but he would ask her to suppose herself in the House of Commons, as member for a Parliamentary borough (laughter), and that a young gentleman "a lover," in that House, were to try to influence her vote through his sway over her affection, how would she act! whether, in other words, she could resist, and might not lose sight of the public interests? (Order, order.) He (Mr. Cohen) wished to be in order. He was for maintaining the "social rights" of women. "Political rights," such as he understood that meeting to aspire to, she could never, in his opinion, attain. Miss M. A. Walker was astonished at the question put by Mr. Cohen, and at the remarks made by that gentleman. (Hear, hear.) She repudiated, with indignation, the insinuation that if women were in Parliament, any man, be he husband, or be he lover, would dare be so base as to attempt to sway her from the strict line of duty. ("Hear, hear," cries of "Bravo" from the men, and much applause.) She would treat with womanly scorn, as a contemptible scoundrel, the man who would dare to influence her vote by any undue and unworthy means (cheers from the men); for if he were base enough to mislead her in one way, he would in another. ("Hear, hear," and renewed cheers.) The events which were at the moment taking place in the north, where their sisters and brothers were being cruelly and unjustly transported, or else plunged into dismal and pestiferous dungeons, for no other cause than standing up for their rights and demanding bread to appease their hunger and save themselves from dying of starvation in their native land, were unfortunately of a nature to drag woman from her retirement, and call upon her to lift up her voice against such deeds. . . . The spirited young lady, who spoke with great warmth, and suited the action to the word . . . declared herself a Chartist in name and feeling; and having appealed to her fellow-country women to "come out," in favour of the Charter, and, however ungrammatical their language, not to be dismayed by any shafts of ridicule that might be pointed against them, concluded by giving them the encouraging hope, that if it were only from the curiosity to hear "a woman" speak, the young men would come out and speak to them. (*The Times* 20.10.1842)

Five days later *The Times* reported another meeting at which she thanked *The Times* "and other portions of the press which had noticed them, had given them great popularity, and at a much safer and cheaper rate than they could hope to attain it, had they flung themselves into 'the Queen's Palace.' . . . They were much indebted to *The Times* for this notoriety." She concluded by asserting that "they might hear reason and sound political wisdom from the lips of women, and even from the daughter of a working man" (*The Times* 25.10.1842). It is ironic that it was Walker's own words that in all likelihood alerted the editors to the dangers implicit in such full reporting of her public speeches. These first two reports are distinguished by an indulgent and dismissive jocularity. Yet, only one day after the last one, a full leader attacked Walker denouncing her as "a termagant," as "a shrew," and as guilty of "an unblushing attempt to assume the masculine attire," and concluded,

We must apologise to our countrywomen in general for having given such prominence to a section, of whom all true Englishwomen are doubtless most justly ashamed . . . we would submit to them, instead of lowering themselves by claiming what would only disgrace and expose them, that they should seek true honour and power by imitating those of their sex whose silence is the most touching eloquence—whose weakness is the truest strength—and whose submission, victory. (*The Times* 26.10.1842)

This article was followed two days later by the famous "hen Chartists" article that, through the use of heavy-handed satire and the example of Aristophanes's *Ecclesiazusae*, attempted to demolish the Chartist movement as a whole. It concludes:

How the republic, so administered, contrived to proceed beyond the first four and twenty hours of its being, Aristophanes, with all his wit, humour, and invention, has not ventured to portray to us. Strange enough, absurd enough, insane enough, and disgraceful enough, were its freaks even in the four and twenty hours during which the imagination of the poet gave it a brief existence; but if we may cease to joke, and may again speak in the language of seriousness and truth, its freaks would not be more strange, more absurd, more insane, more disgraceful, more disgusting, more destructive of all the best feelings of humanity, and of all the most valuable interests of man both here and hereafter, than the proceedings which would be adopted during the first four and twenty weeks of its existence, by a Parliament elected under the auspices and upon the principles of the People's Charter, either with or without the female suffrage. (*The Times* 28.10.1842)

The Morning Chronicle, without mentioning Walker at all, chose October 27 for a long editorial on Chartism in general, which clearly encompasses the vocal termagant singled out by *The Times*: "Setting out with some show of reason and moderation, they degenerated not only into absurdity, but into violence, and without the remotest change of success, have repeatedly put in peril the peace of the kingdom.'' (*The Morning Chronicle* 27.10.1842)

Walker had one mention in the *Illustrated London News* in which the now familiar tone of comic diminishment militated against any appearance of serious news content:

A society of Female Chartists has been lately formed in the metropolis at the National Charter Hall in the Old Bailey, and at which several young ladies have been in the habit of holding forth with various degrees of *eclât* [*sic*], on the cardinal points of their political creed. A distinguished member of the body (Miss Mary Anne [*sic*] Walker) fell foul of our contemporary the *Times* during the course of one of her harangues, which has led to an interesting controversy between this patriotic maiden and the spruce gallant of Printing-house-square. The latter complains that the young lady's accomplishments smack rather spicely of Billingsgate. (*Illustrated London News* 25 [29.10.1842], 391)

Punch was not slow to see the satirical possibilities of the situation. Mary Ann formed the first—and I might add, the last—in a series ''Sketches of Female Politicians.'' The full-page article was accompanied by a sketch depicting a noticeably flat-chested, sharp-faced shrew, the stereotypical unfeminine spinster, haranguing a group of female donkeys to judge by the balloon caption ''BRAY-VO Walker'' (see Figure 9.1):

Miss Walker, the female Chartist, gave indications at a very early age of a turn for public life, and from her decidedly masculine predilections, she acquired the appellation of Tom-boy in her own immediate neighbourhood. . . . The political opinions of Miss Walker may be summed up in very few words; and it is a remarkable fact that any man with whom she has come in contact, is always fully impressed with the idea that woman may be left to herself—and that if every woman were a Miss Walker, the sex would find very little difficulty in having their right to stand alone most thoroughly acknowledged. As the female Chartists are an object just now of some interest, we have prevailed upon Miss Walker—not Mary Anne [*sic*]—but the descendant of Hookey, to give our artist a sitting. It will be seen that she is just the woman to ''keep off'' any man, and to give faith in the Chartist doctrine, that some of the sex may at least be spared from the domestic hearth, of which ladies of less pretension than the Walkers are content to be the ornament. (*Punch* 1842, 192)

To conclude the story of Walker, a report in *Lloyd's Illustrated London News-paper* on November 27 noted that ''a marriage is on the tapis between Mr. Thomas Slingsby Duncombe, M.P., and the celebrated patriotess Miss Mary Ann Walker.''[6] We should note carefully the diminishment in that ubiquitous suffix.[7] Duncombe was the Radical Member of Parliament for Finsbury, a supporter of Chartism who had introduced the 1842 Petition in the House of Commons and who had addressed a Chartist meeting on 24 October.[8] The report is, of course, a joke: another heavy-handed attempt at satire which imposes the

Figure 9.1
Sketch of Mary Ann Walker Appearing in *Punch*

Punch 3 (July–December 1842), 192.

ultimate silence on Walker, that of marriage. She is not allowed to be demystified
by becoming a familiar and therefore less dangerous public figure like later
middle-class political women.

Middle-class fiction and polemical writers were also unable to accommodate
satisfactorily a fully active working-class heroine. Once again, there is silence
or equivocation. The widely read Thomas Carlyle in his essay on *Chartism*, for
instance, makes no mention of female workers. In Chapter 4, he gives a figure
of half-a-million hand-loom weavers without ever mentioning that a very high
proportion of them would have been women. He never mentions female members
of the movement; the only female figures he alludes to are the great abstractions:

Society ([1839] 1888, 38); the Earth (6); Europe and England—the latter about to give birth to a new Man (67)—and a composite working-class figure Smart Sally, who distracts brisk Tom from higher thoughts: "Smart Sally in our alley proves all too fascinating to brisk Tom in yours: can Tom be called up to make pause, and calculate the demand for labour in the British Empire first?" (65).

In the popular middle-class Condition-of-England novels of the period, which not only actively sought to highlight the deplorable conditions of the working class, but also purported to give an accurate and sympathetic picture of Chartism, there are similar evasions and stranger solutions to the problem of the articulate working-class woman. Mrs. Gaskell's *Mary Barton*, for instance, depicts a fairly unconvincing working-class heroine with a singular lack of knowledge about or indeed interest in her Chartist father's political activities:

With all this, Mary had not her father's confidence in the matters which now began to occupy him, heart and soul; she was aware that he had joined clubs, and become an active member of the trades' union, but it was hardly likely that a girl of Mary's age (even when two or three years had elapsed since her mother's death) should care much for the differences between the employers and the employed,—an eternal subject for agitation in the manufacturing district, which, however it may be lulled for a time, is sure to break forth again with fresh violence at any depression of trade, showing that in its apparent quiet the ashes had still smouldered in the breasts of a few. (Gaskell [1848] 1967, 20–21)

Mary's friend Margaret, who is handicapped by being almost blind and who is therefore unable to fulfill any romantic heroine role, does sing a mildly revolutionary song, "The Oldham Weaver" (33), but the real thrust of the novel is romantic. Mary's decisiveness emerges only when she has to make a hazardous journey to catch the only man who can prove her lover's innocence of murder. Dion Boucicault's successful 1866 stage version of *Mary Barton*, *The Long Strike*, emphasized the romantic plot at the expense of the political, and King Mob was present only to provide the large crowd scenes that were the delight of Victorian theatergoers.

Benjamin Disraeli's Sybil is one of the few supposedly lower-class politically active women found in these novels. She is a daughter of the Chartist leader, and most of the men in the novel offer her their elevated thoughts on the class struggle, the political situation, and the future of England at some point in the novel. Throughout it all though, she remains a melodramatic cipher. This child of the People, with a capital P, as she is constantly called, and indeed calls herself, is always "shrinking." Her political assertions are so mixed in with idealism and angelic purity—she is first discovered emblematically framed in the ruins of the old abbey—that she appears to be extolling the virtues of some heavenly utopia rather than an imminently possible amelioration of the living and working conditions of what is presumed to be her own class. When she does act, it is to avoid the rampaging mob of the People who are now "hellcats." Like Thomas Hardy's Tess, she is of an ancient family and acts like an aristocrat manqué, but unlike Tess she is elevated in the end to her rightful place as lady of the manor. Surely a rapid transmigration to the aristocracy is as effective a weapon as any others we have encountered—of defeminization, of ridicule, of marriage, and finally of silence.

Raymond Williams calls *Sybil* a "political fantasy" and views the movement upward through society as a movement of solidarity between working class and aristocracy against the industrial bourgeoisie (n.d. [1983], 164). There is, however, no indication in the novel that those who move out of the working class are reluctant to do so, and the movement seems to be rather toward a consolidation of the bourgeoisie at the expense of the working class, and a recognition that class solidarity depends purely on common economic interests. Some women in the novel do talk politics in a much more down to earth way than Sybil:

"Life's a tumble-about thing of ups and downs," said Widow Carey, stirring her tea, "but I have been down this time longer than I can ever remember."

"Nor ever will get up, widow," said Julia, at whose lodgings herself and several of Julia's friends had met, "unless we have the Five Points."

"I will never marry any man who is not for the Five Points," said Caroline.

"I should be ashamed to marry any one who had not the suffrage," said Harriet.

"He is no better than a slave," said Julia. The widow shook her head. "I don't like these politics," said the good woman, "they bayn't in a manner of business for our sex."

"And I should like to know why?" said Julia. "Ayn't we as much concerned in the cause of good government as the men? And don't we understand as much about it? I am sure the Dandy never does anything without consulting me."

"It's fine news for a summer's day," said Caroline, "to say we can't understand politics, with a Queen on the throne."

"She has got her ministers to tell her what to do," said Mrs. Carey, taking a pinch of snuff. "Poor innocent young creature, it often makes my heart ache to think how she is beset."

"Over the left," said Julia. "If the ministers try to come into her bedchamber, she knows how to turn them to the right about."

"And as for that," said Harriet, "why are we not to interfere with politics as much as the swell ladies in London?" (Disraeli [1845] 1981, 380)

Two of these women marry their working-class lovers and move up into the middle classes immediately with Sybil's aid, and the third remains a spinster: "Though pretty and clever, she is selfish and a screw" (420).

In Charles Kingsley's *Alton Locke* (1850), there are not even these occasional politicized voices of the working-class women. The only articulate women are Alton's mother, who is strongly Christian and turns her son out of the house when he becomes a freethinker for fear he will corrupt his own sister; and the aristocratic Eleanor, who converts both Alton and the Chartist organizer Crossthwaite to her vision of Christian repentance in an example of cross-class sympathy that would not have been possible with a different class/gender pattern.

Clearly then the politicized working-class woman was a creature who was difficult to accommodate within a middle-class worldview. She was articulate when she should have been mute and suffering, and she was active when she should have been submissive. Dorothy Thompson has characterized Chartism as "the response of a literate and sophisticated working class." She continues, "Much of the Chartist propaganda took the form of argument, a dialogue with the middle classes" (1971, 13). In the case of women Chartists, it was as often as not a monologue, to which the middle classes found themselves unable to respond. Working-class women were, for the philanthropic, objects of pity, and for many men, objects of sexuality. The attraction of their short skirts, boots, and trousers and their direct challenging gazes, seen in Arthur Munby's photographs[9] or in the line drawings in Henry Mayhew's *London Labour and the London Poor* [1862], is obvious. Arthur Clough in his long poem *The Bothie* is quite explicit that their sexual attraction lies in the freedom of their bodily movements as they are engaged in what he sees as natural labor:

> Never I properly felt the relation of man to woman,
> Though to the dancing-master I went, perforce, for a quarter,
> Where, in dismal quadrille, were good-looking girls in plenty,
> Though, too, school-girl cousins were mine—a bevy of beauties,
> —Never (of course you will laugh, but of course all the same I shall
>   say it,)
> Never, believe me, revealed itself to me the sexual glory,
> Till in some village fields in holidays now getting stupid,
> One day sauntering 'long and listless,' as Tennyson has it,
> Long and listless strolling, ungainly in hobbadiboyhood,
> Chanced it my eye fell aside on a capless, bonnetless maiden,
> Bending with three-pronged fork in a garden uprooting potatoes,
> Was it the air? who can say? or herself, or the charm of the labour?
> But a new thing was in me; and longing delicious possessed me,
> Longing to take her and lift her, and put her away from her slaving:
> Was it to clasp her in lifting, or was it to lift her by clasping,
> Was it embracing or aiding was most in my mind; hard question!
> But a new thing was in me, I too was a youth among maidens;
> Was it the air, who can say? but in part 'twas the charm of the
>   labour.[10]

The reverse side of this is found in the degradation so often involved in such labor, and illustrations such as those of girl miners or factory workers provided much of the spur to the philanthropic endeavors of the middle-class women agitators who were active from the late 1840s onward. The contrast between bourgeois representations of working-class female activists and of those within their own class is striking: Both written and visual representations of middle-class activists in the mid-century are frequent, the ideologies are firmly entrenched, and the controlled absence seen in the first part of this chapter is here balanced by an overwhelmingly pervasive presence.

Middle-class audiences for such representations were able to accommodate the female mavericks in their midst quite easily simply because the subjects remained anchored within their class. In the later histories of this period of the suffrage movement by the new generation of suffragettes, such as Sylvia Pankhurst and Helen Blackburn, this is stated quite clearly. The suffrage proposals were always based on property, and the reasons for acquiring the vote always included those moral ones of woman as the spiritual presence within the home and the maintaining of domestic harmony and therefore of national harmony: precisely those reasons offered to Chartist women as reasons for not fighting for female enfranchisement.

During the period leading up to the late 1860s there was a wide variety of middle-class female political agitation—for the suffrage; for educational, property, and marriage rights; and for the remedying of many different social ills such as the Contagious Diseases Acts. Agitation for the repeal of the Contagious Diseases Acts, for instance, was immediate upon the passing of the first act in 1864. It was a period of intense public activity for women, during which their public image was very rapidly tamed and channeled into recognizable and acceptable forms in a way that had never been successfully achieved with working-class political women.

The taming process took many forms: the creation of a female vocabulary containing many flower metaphors, the association of women with allegorical figures of peace and plenty,[11] gentle ridicule of many types (Queen Victoria for instance labelled them "The Sex," an appellation that was used widely), and most immediately via the male illustrators for weekly papers, for novels, and for collections such as Cruikshank's annual editions of *The Comic Almanack*. Illustrations of the strong-minded woman, invariably depicting her in the midst of domestic turmoil, are characterized by a tone of affectionate ridicule by which the threat posed by such women is contained. The caption to one such illustration in the *Punch Book of Women's Rights*, entitled "The Parliamentary Female," reads:

Father of the Family: "Come, dear: we so seldom go out together now—can't you take us all to the play tonight?"

Mistress of the House, and M.P.: "How you talk, Charles! Don't you see that I am too busy. I have a committee tomorrow morning, and I have my speech on the great crochet question to prepare for the evening." (Basch 1974, 57)

Similarly, in "My wife is a woman of mind," an early example in Cruikshank's 1847 *Almanack*, the harassed husband attempts to control several crying children while the wife, with severely drawn back hair and dark glasses, grapples with an intellectual problem, chewing on her pen and seated before an overflowing desk (Vogler 1979, 78). Another caption to a cartoon entitled "Success in Life," in *Punch's Almanack for 1867*, reads, "Dr. Elizabeth Squills has barely time to snatch a hurried meal and hasty peep at the periodicals of the day in her husband's boudoir."

The indulgence is less in evidence than the distaste, however, in Dickens's 1852 novel *Bleak House*, which has two such women, Mrs. Jellyby and Mrs. Pardiggle, both of whom neglect their children in the interests of their causes:

The room, which was strewn with papers and nearly filled by a great writing-table covered with similar litter, was, I must say, not only very untidy, but very dirty. We were obliged to take notice of that with our sense of sight, even while, with our sense of hearing, we followed the poor child who had tumbled down-stairs: I think into the back kitchen, where somebody seemed to stifle him. . . .

"You find me, my dears," said Mrs. Jellyby, snuffing the two great office candles in tin candlesticks which made the room taste strongly of hot tallow (the fire had gone out, and there was nothing in the grate but ashes, a bundle of wood, and a poker), "you find me, my dears, as usual, very busy; but that you will excuse. The African project at present employs my whole time. It involves me in correspondence with public bodies, and with private individuals anxious for the welfare of their species all over the country. I am happy to say it is advancing. We hope by this time next year to have from a hundred and fifty to two hundred healthy families cultivating coffee and educating the natives of Borrioboola-Gha, on the left bank of the Niger."[12]

At the end of the novel Mrs. Jellyby is able to move on to another cause without a more caustic authorial treatment only because her children are now being satisfactorily watched over by the female avatar of the novel, Esther Summerson:

I have heard that Mrs. Jellyby was understood to suffer great mortification, from her daughter's ignoble marriage and pursuits; but I hope she got over it in time. She has been disappointed in Borrioboola-Gha, which turned out a failure in consequence of the King of Borrioboola wanting to sell everybody—who survived the climate—for Rum; but she has taken up with the rights of women to sit in Parliament, and Caddy tells me it is a mission involving more correspondence than the old one. (990)

When we come to the agitation for the vote in the mid–1860s prior to the 1867 Reform Bill, we see the same gentle and familiar ridicule:

The ladies, not in the least troubled by all Bovill and Byles had been saying of them, displayed their usual beautiful colours, and seemed a little disappointed at the Returning Officer not appearing in uniform, nor could they make out to what regiment he belonged. Perhaps they thought more of the Candidates' looks than their views, and although not generally partial to statistics, they were delighted with many of their figures. In one or two cases of uncompromising wigs, the state of the poll was not considered satisfactory. When the speakers treated (thereby breaking the law) the electors to equalisation of the poor-rates, county financial boards, Regium Donum, &c., the ladies exercised the franchise, despite the Court of Common Pleas, and voted them a bore; but on the whole they received the addresses of their favourite Candidates with marked approval and pocket-handkerchiefs. The gentlemen who proposed were in high favour, and perhaps to the ladies the most interesting event of all was—the Declaration. A great many votes were split, and a few heads. Special Trains ran, and so did Special Constables. (*Punch* 21.11.1868, 211)

Many of the figures ridiculed in this way were recognizable people, such as Lydia Becker,[13] who became household names, and I would recall here the way in which the possibility of this happening in the Mary Ann Walker case was so abruptly terminated. Poems like "The Enfranchised Washerwoman"; articles like "Female Self-Emancipation" ("Emancipate yourself from the tyranny of fashion, and then you shall enjoy the rights of free women"), a series in *Punch* of Mrs Punch's Letters to her Daughter; the creation of characters like Hannah Claxon, Governess, Single Woman who has Mill's photograph on her wall and initiates Parliamentary petitions—all these and more supported the view that an enfranchised woman was somehow slightly ridiculous.

It was the actual Mill amendment to the act, though, which provoked the most mirth, rather than the substance of his campaign. The amendment was to replace "man" by "person," thereby reversing the exclusivity enacted in 1832. The ensuing verbal battle focused, as might be expected, on the generic argument, occasioning such ridicule as the following:

Woman and Her Mr.

Miss Becker—for so we must call her, although she is probably ashamed of being obliged to be a woman—the lady who read a paper before the British Association, which bore on the Two Sexes of Man, is doubtlessly highly gratified at the superior rank to which the Times has promoted her. That paper in its account of what passed before the Revising Barrister at Manchester, with excellent irony stated that "Mr. Becker, who, with several other ladies, had been present since the opening of the Court, applied, on behalf of the women claimants in Chorlton-upon-Medlock, for a case of appeal." (*Punch* 3.10.1868)

With the amendment lost and "man" still exclusively male, Dr. Pankhurst, arguing for the 1870 Women's Disabilities Removal Bill, had no option but to make as good a case as possible for generic "man":

In arguing that the Act of 1867 had enfranchised women by the use of the word man, he submitted that man was equivalent in good law with homo. In good Latin homo did not mean man as contradistinguished from woman, it meant human being. He could not cite a greater historical case, he said, than the one referred to by St. Augustine, Homo sum: humani nihil a me alienum puto [I am a man:I regard nothing that concerns man as foreign to my interests]. When that line from Terence's "Self-Tormenter" was spoken in the Roman theatre, the whole vast audience, composed of representatives from almost every nation in the world, rose with one consent and applauded, attesting thereby their acceptance of the doctrine that everything human had a distinct relation to every man.

Homo was obviouly intended there to mean human being. In Roman law the word man meant human being. (Pankhurst [1931] 1977, 39)

In most contemporary male eyes, the strongest threat to the patriarchy was posed not by English suffragists but by American women who were exporting their radical ideas: Harriet Martineau had very early shown English women what American women were achieving in her 1837 *Society in America* written after her extensive travels, eleven years before the Seneca Falls Convention in 1848. When Mrs. Bloomer came to London in 1851, showing off a more relaxed fashion than had been seen in England for many years, a fashion that would give women greater freedom of movement than was thought seemly, she and her followers were still greeted with a benign good humor, and they formed the subject of countless cartoons and satirical articles for most of the second half of the year. By the end of the 1860s, however, the danger filtering over the Atlantic was perceived as more real, and the American feminist whom we see in Anthony Trollope's novel *He Knew He Was Right* is the only thoroughly devalued character in a novel full of strong-minded women:

Miss Petrie was honest, clever, and in earnest. We in England are not usually favourably disposed to women who take a pride in a certain antagonism to men in general, and who are anxious to show the world that they can get on very well without male assistance; but there are many such in America who have noble aspirations, good intellects, much energy, and who are by no means unworthy of friendship. The hope in regard to all such women—the hope entertained not by themselves, but by those who are solicitous for them—is that they will be cured at last by a husband and half-a-dozen children. In regard to Wallachia Petrie there was not, perhaps, much ground for such hope. She was so positively wedded to women's rights in general, and to her own rights in particular, that it was improbable that she should ever succumb to any man; and where would be the man brave enough to make the effort?[14]

Gentle satire and indulgence, though a feature of male reactions, were not replicated in the majority of female reactions at the time. On the contrary, these were frequently characterized by a virulence that paradoxically served to keep female activism at the center stage of public awareness for much of the period. Mill's comment about literary women ("The greater part of what women write about women is mere sycophancy to men," Mill [1869] 1974, 456) illustrates why bourgeois men were able to maintain their lofty patriarchal stance as long as the harshest criticism came from women themselves. It is ironic that this sound and fury resulted in the maintaining of public knowledge about female activism even when the more immediate issue of suffrage was lying fallow in the 1870s and 1880s.

Often these indictments of female striving were subtle and were insidiously acceptable, such as in the popular novelist Charlotte M. Yonge's *The Daisy Chain*, in which a strong-minded young woman complains throughout the novel that she needs space to breathe and find herself but finally opts for a conventional role without fulfillment as the unmarried daughter who performs her duty precisely along the lines advocated by Mrs. Ellis and Mrs. Craik. Other popular fictions of the period also depict this ultimate diminishment or role fixing. In Elizabeth Barrett Browning's *Aurora Leigh* and in Charlotte Brontë's *Shirley*, *Jane Eyre*, and *Villette*, for instance, there is the same pattern of articulateness, desire for freedom, and tentative action followed by submission—however much it is qualified and structured according to the woman's rules—a pattern that is built up and incorporated into the ideology. It is acceptable for a woman to have such yearnings and even to achieve something through them, but her ultimate well-being rests in an accommodation with the principles of her class.

The female antifeminist campaign predictably increased at the time of the controversy over the vote, which was fanned by an anonymous essay called "The Girl of the Period" in *The Saturday Review* (14.3.1868) and the heated responses that the essay provoked. It was only later in the year that its author, a woman, Eliza Lynn Linton, was identified when the essay was republished as a pamphlet. It is indicative of the slow rate of change that an 1883 collection of Lynn Linton's essays, containing "The Girl of the Period," "The Shrieking Sisterhood," "The Modern Mother," and "Ideal Woman," was equally popular nearly twenty years after the 1868 sensation. In her preface to that edition, she stated,

In re-reading these papers I am more than ever convinced that I have struck the right chord of condemnation, and advocated the best virtues and most valuable characteristics of women. I neither soften nor retract a line of what I have said. One of the modern phases of womanhood—hard, unloving, mercenary, ambitious, without domestic faculty and devoid of healthy natural instincts—is still to me a pitiable mistake and a grave national disaster. And I think now, as I thought when I wrote these papers, that a public and professional life for women is incompatible with the discharge of their highest duties or the cultivation of their noblest qualities. (Linton 1883, viii)

A short quotation from "The Modern Mother" sums up some of the issues raised elsewhere in this chapter:

Society has put maternity out of fashion. With some of the more intellectual and less instinctive sort, maternity is looked on as a kind of degradation; and women of this stamp, sensible enough in everything else, talk impatiently among themselves of the base necessities laid on them by men and nature, and how hateful to them is everything connected with their characteristic duties. This wild revolt against nature, and especially this abhorrence of maternity, is carried to a still greater extent by American women. (10–11)

Lynn Linton herself epitomizes a common strain of ambivalence and doubt characteristic of the period. A radical in her youth, sympathetic to Chartism, she married a much older man, William Linton, also a radical, in a spirit of idealism to look after his motherless children, but she always kept herself by her writing. She was helpful and kind to many women friends, recommending them to publishers and helping them to work their way through a university, and yet she produced, not once but many times over a long period, articles that blatantly pandered to the most reactionary public opinion.

Middle-class women were moreover successfully contained within their class and gender boundaries by constant metaphoric association with the great abstractions we saw in Carlyle, in which the angel in the house also presided over the wider domain of country and empire. The great age of the Empire could not continue into a glorious future unless the home and hearth were stable, harmonious, and hierarchically sound. This state of good health was maintained through a careful, usually gentle, colonization of the moral domain presided over by women, allowing freedom within a class-oriented and well-defined sphere. When this demarcation of boundaries had been threatened as the Chartist women had done, fighting and speaking beside their men, the bourgeois response ultimately crystallized into a tactic that we are now quite familiar with—the news blackout.

NOTES

1. See, for instance, Thompson 1976, 112–38; Thomis and Grimmett 1982; Jones 1983, 1–21; Taylor 1983, chap. 6; Thompson 1984. Dorothy Thompson has also indicated how far historians of the movement, both working-class men involved in it and middle-class observers, have consistently ignored or underplayed the role of women because "the presence of women in a movement, or at any occasion, was seen as somehow lessening the seriousness of the event" (1984, 121).

2. I use the term "cultural politics" as defined by Barrett 1982, 37–58. Barrett begins her definition by referring to Raymond Williams's use of the term "culture," which he sees as giving evidence of a "contemporary convergence" between the anthropological/sociological senses of culture, the more common popular use of the term, and a "distinctive 'signifying system' . . . essentially involved in *all* forms of social activity" (Williams 1981, 10–13).

3. This is in contrast to the suffragette movement from the 1880s onward, in which a large number of working-class women were involved.

4. "In the autumn of 1849, my misgivings [about contributing to *Household Words*] first became serious. Mr. Wills proposed my doing some articles on the Employments of Women . . . and was quite unable to see that every contribution of the kind was necessarily excluded by Mr. Dickens's prior articles on behalf of his view of Woman's position; articles in which he ignored the fact that nineteen-twentieths of the women of England earn their bread, and in which he prescribes the function of Women; viz., to dress well and look pretty, as an adornment to the homes of men" (Martineau [1855] 1983, 2:419).

5. The pamphlet is reproduced in full in Thompson 1971, 115–27.

6. Quoted in Thompson 1984, 378. It is interesting to note that *Lloyds Illustrated London Newspaper* was aimed at a working-class market. It relied on purveying satirical, often inaccurate information to its audience and not on nurturing radical opinion. See Berridge 1978, 247–64.

7. Regardless of the survival of the "-ess" female suffix into the twentieth century, it was certainly regarded as belittling by many people in the mid-nineteenth century. See, for instance, the discussion in the preface to Rowton n.d. [1848].

8. The *Illustrated London News* of 29.10.1842 in its report of this meeting placed heavy emphasis on its supposedly lighthearted spirit resulting from the presence of a majority of female Chartists in the audience: "two other toasts were given, one recommending union, and the other expressing a hope for the removal of all legal trammels, for the freedom of the press, and for the displacing of despotic judges and arbitrary magistrates. A vote of thanks having been unanimously awarded to the chair, for which the gallant gentleman [Duncombe] returned thanks, the meeting separated at half-past eleven o'clock." It is possible that *Lloyds Illustrated London Newspaper* seized on this mention of political union for its satirical comment on the Walker-Duncombe "marriage."

9. Leonore Davidoff deals at length with Munby's relationship with his working-class mistress Hannah Cullwick (1983, 16–71). The article also contains reproductions of photographs Munby took of Hannah in various role-playing poses, such as the black slave, the middle-class lady, the angel, the young man.

10. Clough [1848] 1976: Book 2, lines 36–53. See also, for example, lines 110–26. Carlylean overtones of the moral worth and hence the beauty of labor are pervasive through *The Bothie*. Labor is here seen mainly in class terms: The sexual desirability of working women is directly contrasted by Clough with the passive quality of idle middle-class women who are likened to "unhappy statuettes . . . miserable trinkets" (2:38). The sensual confusion of gender identity is as marked in Clough's portrayals of working-class women as it is in Munby's.

11. See Warner 1985 for a wide-ranging discussion of the pervasive allegorizing of woman in patriarchal societies.

12. Dickens, *Bleak House* [1852] n.d., 56–58. The depiction of Mrs. Pardiggle is even harsher, see 128ff. It is enlightening to weigh Dickens's portrayal of Mrs. Jellyby against the positive achievements of Caroline Chisholm on whom she is based.

13. Lydia Becker is the major figure in Blackburn's history of the suffrage movement ([1902] 1971), Part II of which is devoted to "Biographical notes and reminiscences of Miss Becker."

14. A. Trollope [1869] 1974, 2:208. A similar treatment is given to the American Dr. Olivia Q. Fleabody in Trollope's *Is He Popenjoy?* [1878] who scores a victory over the equally unpleasant German feminist Baroness Banmann.

REFERENCES

Barrett, Michèle. 1982. "Feminism and the Definition of Cultural Politics." In *Feminism, Culture and Politics*, edited by Rosalind Brunt and Caroline Rowan, 37–58. London: Lawrence & Wishart.

Basch, Françoise. 1974. *Relative Creatures: Victorian Women in Society and the Novel 1837–1867*. London: Allen Lane.

Berridge, Virginia. 1978. "Popular Sunday Papers and Mid-Victorian Society." In *Newspaper History from the Seventeenth Century to the Present Day*, edited by G. Boyce, J. Curran, and P. Wingate, 247–64. London: Constable.

Blackburn, Helen. [1902] 1971. *Women's Suffrage: A Record of the Women's Suffrage Movement in the British Isles*. New York: Kraus Reprint.

Brontë, Charlotte. [1849] 1981. *Shirley*. London: OUP World's Classics.

Carlyle, Thomas. [1839] 1888. *Chartism*. London: Chapman & Hall.

Clough, Arthur Hugh. [1848] 1976. *The Bothie: The Text of 1848*. Edited by Patrick Scott. Brisbane, Australia: University of Queensland Press.

Davidoff, Leonore. 1983. "Class and Gender in Victorian England." In *Sex and Class in Women's History*, edited by Judith L. Newton, Mary P. Ryan, and Judith R. Walkowitz, 16–71. London: Routledge and Kegan Paul.

Dickens, Charles. [1852] n.d. *Bleak House*. London: Oxford. (The Oxford "Illustrated" Dickens)

Disraeli, Benjamin. [1845] 1981. *Sybil*. London: OUP World's Classics.

Gaskell, Elizabeth. [1848] 1967. *Mary Barton*. London: Everyman.

Jones, David. 1983. "Woman and Chartism." *History* 68:1–21.

Jones, Gareth Stedman. 1983. *Languages of Class: Studies in English Working Class History 1832–1982*. Cambridge: Cambridge University Press.

Linton, Eliza Lynn. 1883. *The Girl of the Period and Other Social Essays*. London: Richard Bentley.

Martineau, Harriet. [1855] 1983. *Autobiography*. 2 vols. London: Virago.

Mill, John Stuart. [1869] 1974. *On Liberty, Representative Government, The Subjection of Women: Three Essays by John Stuart Mill*. London: OUP World's Classics.

Pankhurst, E. Sylvia. [1931] 1977. *The Suffragette Movement*. London: Virago.

Rowbotham, Sheila. 1973. *Hidden from History: 300 Years of Women's Oppression and the Fight against It*. London: Pluto.

Rowton, Frederic. [1848] n.d. *The Female Poets of Great Britain, Containing the Choicest Poems of our Female Poets*. London: Longman, Brown, Green & Longman.

Schoyen, A. R. 1958. *The Chartist Challenge: A Portrait of George Julian Harney*. London: Heinemann.

Taylor, Barbara. 1983. *Eve and the New Jerusalem: Socialism and Feminism in the Nineteenth Century*. London: Virago.

Taylor, Harriet. 1851. "Enfranchisement of Women." *The Westminster and Foreign Quarterly Review* 55, 2 (April-July): 289–311.

Thomis, Malcolm I., and Jennifer Grimmett. 1982. *Women in Protest 1800–1850*. London: Croom Helm.

Thompson, Dorothy. 1971. *The Early Chartists*. London: Macmillan & Co.

———. 1976. "Women and Nineteenth-Century Politics: A Lost Dimension." In *The Rights and Wrongs of Women*, edited by Juliet Mitchell and Ann Oakley, 112–38. Harmondsworth, England: Penguin.

———. 1984. *The Chartists*. London: Temple Smith.

Toynbee, Mrs., ed. 1905. *Letters of Horace Walpole*, vol. 15. Oxford: Oxford University Press. Letter no. 2956.

Trollope, Anthony. [1869] 1974. *He Knew He Was Right*. Edited by P. D. Edwards. Brisbane, Australia: University of Queensland Press.

Trollope, Frances. [1840] 1968. *The Life and Adventures of Michael Armstrong the Factory Boy*. London: Frank Cass.

Vicinus, Martha. 1982. "Chartist Fiction and the Development of a Class-based Literature." In *The Socialist Novel in Britain: Towards the Recovery of a Tradition*, edited by H. Gustav Klaus, 7–25. Brighton, England: Harvester.

Vogler, Richard A., sel. and intro. 1979. *Graphic Works of George Cruikshank*. New York: Dover.

Warner, Marina. 1985. *Monuments and Maidens: The Allegory of the Female Form.*
    London: Weidenfeld and Nicolson.
Williams, Raymond. 1981. *Culture.* London: Fontana.
————. [1983] n.d. *Writing and Politics.* London: Verso.

10

Schemers, Dragons, and Witches: Criminal "Justice" and the Fair Sex

Jocelynne A. Scutt

Question VI
...Why it is that Women are chiefly addicted to Evil Superstitions.

...All wickedness is but little to the wickedness of a woman. Wherefore S. John Chrysostom says on the text, It is not good to marry (S. Matthew, xix): What else is woman but a foe to friendship, an unescapable punishment, a necessary evil, a natural temptation, a desirable calamity, a domestic danger, a delectable detriment, an evil of nature, painted with fair colours! Therefore if it be a sin to divorce her when she ought to be kept, it is indeed a necessary torture; for either we commit adultery by divorcing her, or we must endure daily strife. Cicero in his second book of *The Rhetorics* says: The many lusts of men lead them into one sin, but the one lust of women leads them into all sins; for the root of all women's vices is avarice. And Seneca says in his *Tragedies* : A woman either loves or hates; there is no third grade. And the tears of a woman are a deception, for they may spring from true grief, or they may be a snare. When a woman thinks alone, she thinks evil.

(Kramer and Sprenger |1487| 1971, 40, 43)

On the evening of Sunday 17 August 1980, some little time before 8:00 P.M., Alice Lynne Chamberlain nursed her baby daughter, Azaria, nine-and-a-half weeks old, at a barbeque near Ayers Rock in the center of Australia. Michael Chamberlain, husband and father, stood nearby, together with the couple's elder son, Aiden. A second couple was present, and the Chamberlains' younger son, Reagan, was asleep in the tent. Shortly after, the child Azaria disappeared. Following that disappearance, two inquests, a trial, and an appeal to the Federal Court of Australia, the conviction and sentence of life imprisonment of Alice

Chamberlain, and the conviction as accessory after the fact of her husband, the matter went on appeal to the High Court of Australia. There, counsel for the Chamberlains described the Crown case:

[At the barbeque], the child was alive. . . . That much is not in dispute. . . . [But] the Crown alleges that, although Mrs. Chamberlain said that she was going to the tent to put Azaria down, and although there is evidence from one of the persons at the barbeque that Mrs. Chamberlain did go to the tent, the Crown case is that Mrs. Chamberlain did not go—or, if she did go to the tent, she immediately went to the front seat of the Chamberlains' motor vehicle, which was parked alongside the tent. The car faced the direction of the barbeque. It was alongside the tent and both were something like about 20 metres away from the barbeque. There was light from the barbeque which was described as good. The Crown alleges that, in the front of the car, Mrs. Chamberlain sat in the passenger side front seat and that she held the child in an upright position and cut the child's throat. (Transcript, *Chamberlain* v. *The Queen* 1983, 1–2)

In 1979 Emily Gertrude Perry was charged and prosecuted in South Australia allegedly having attempted to murder her husband, Kenneth Perry, by arsenic poisoning. Kenneth Perry had been seriously ill as a result of poisoning by lead and arsenic. His evidence was that he had been poisoned as a result of his work, which was restoring pianolas and organs. He protested his wife's innocence, but the prosecution failed to accept his version of events. Rather, the Crown put into evidence matters concerning the deaths of three other men with whom Emily Perry had had a close relationship in the past: a former husband, Constable Haag; her brother, Montgomerie; and a de facto husband, Duncan. Constable Haag died in 1960 of arsenic poisoning, in circumstances where, according to the South Australian prosecution thesis, it could openly be surmised that his then wife, now Emily Perry, had administered the arsenic to him. Brother Monty died in 1961 of a minute amount of arsenic. Again, the prosecution position was that Emily Perry could well be responsible for that death, by (it was alleged) placing the arsenic in a wine bottle from which he drank immediately before his death. Duncan, Emily Perry's former de facto husband, died of barbiturate poisoning while living with her. The Crown alleged that the barbiturates were thrust down Duncan's throat by his de facto wife Emily; it was alleged, too, that she had been feeding him arsenic but that the delay in bringing about his death led her to act precipitately with barbiturates to hasten the end.

CRIME AND SEXUAL POLITICS

None of the crimes alleged to have been committed by Emily Perry, nor that by Alice Lynne Chamberlain, would ordinarily be termed "political." Unlike Leila Khalid, charged during the 1970s with hijacking a plane with terrorist or secular political motives; unlike Diane Oughton, who died on 6 March 1968 in a townhouse on 11th Street in New York City when, together with members of the Weathermen, she was reputedly manufacturing bombs; and unlike Jiang

Q'ing, imprisoned in China following Mao's death for crimes against the Communist state, Perry and Chamberlain were charged with domestic crimes. Their alleged targets were not the impersonal victims of purported terrorist activity, nor were they victims singled out for their standing in the eyes of the establishment and community. Yet the responses of the legal system, the media, and the public had political dimensions which are part of a long history of legalized control of women.

It is not insignificant that both the Chamberlain case and the Perry case involved women defendants in trials alleging unlawful killing and attempted murder in circumstances seen in folklore as particularly "female." Tales of women secretly using poison to relieve themselves of the tedium of husbands or other unwanted relatives, or similarly surreptitiously transgressing, fill criminological textbooks which resort to myth and illogic in "explaining" women as (alleged) criminals. The picture of woman as infanticide, infamous killer of little children, takes pride of place in criminological treatises, so easily is it suggested that the maternal instinct and bottomless mother love can be turned into wickedness and hate. "Rarely is a woman wicked," wrote Cesare Lombroso, renowned nineteenth-century criminologist quoting an old Italian proverb as fact, "But when she is, she surpasses the male."

Lombroso, billed as author of the first treatise on women and crime, *The Female Criminal*, published in the late nineteenth century, classified women offenders as either "mannish" criminals or "feminine" instigators of their husband's or lover's crimes. A third category fell into the role of passive collaborator, easily led astray by the "born criminal," the woman of masculine disposition. These stereotypes were not manufactured out of Lombroso's uninformed imagination. The view of the woman as compliant and conformist, and in criminality less vigorously appealing than the male criminal, was replicated in treatises theorizing about madness. According to Elaine Showalter in *The Female Malady—Women, Madness and English Culture 1830—1980*, the Victorian psychiatrist Henry Maudsley "maintained that even in violent dementia women were limited and bounded by the qualities of femininity; they did not 'evince such lively exultation and energy as men, and they had quieter and less assertive delusions of grandeur conformable with their gentler natures and the quieter currents and conditions of their lives' " (1987, 8).

Lombroso's work linked women's crimes to women's biology. The mad woman was similarly affected. Theories of female insanity in the Victorian era were "specifically and confidently linked to the biological crises of the female life cycle—puberty, pregnancy, childbirth, menopause—during which the mind would be weakened and the symptoms of insanity might emerge" (Showalter 1987, 55). Even the penchant of criminologists for measuring the physiognomy of criminals extended to the insane, and the characteristics seen as typical of the "born" female offender were viewed by the psychiatric profession as typical of mad women (Winslow 1912, 287, 288–89; Pollak 1950, 10–11, 29; Thomas 1907; Thomas 1923; Lombroso 1895).

But it is ahistorical to assert that this way of looking at women arose out of the criminological or psychiatric movements of the nineteenth century, as has too often been accepted (Klein 1973; Smart 1976; Leonard 1982). The criminal justice system has long relied upon the notion of woman as "other" to explain female deviance and to justify the treatment of women within the system as the perfidious sex. As early as 1541—by the Statute of 33 Henry VIII, c. 8— witchcraft and sorcery were punished in England by death (Riddell 1926–1927, 5–12; Riddell 1927–1928, 11–16; Riddell 1930–1931, 257–60). Matthew Hale, a judge (and sometime Chief Justice of England) much venerated by generations of establishment lawyers and academics, particularly in the field of criminal law, played a central role in seventeenth- and early eighteenth-century classification of women as witches. Rather than being applauded for his contribution to the development of the British system of criminal justice, he ought rightly to be seen as an embarrassment, but his performance in witchcraft trials is (mostly) conveniently forgotten. At the last recorded trial and conviction for witchcraft in England, when Jane Wenham of Walkerene was condemned to death at Hereford on 4 March 1712 (although the sentence was not, finally, executed), Hale's traditional view of witchcraft as real was called upon to support Wenham's prosecution and condemnation.[1]

In 1664 Chief Justice Hale had condemned to the stake at St. Edmondsbury two women, Amy Duny and Rose Cullender, upon "Evidence most Ridiculous."[2] These two elderly women, whose conventional ugliness led villagers to believe they were witches, went to a local shop to purchase herrings. When they were refused service, they were loud in their abuse at the indignity and went away "discontented and grumbling." As was reported at the trial, at this very "Instant of time, the child [Deborah Pacy] was taken with terrible Fits, complaining of a Pain in her Stomach as if she was pricked with Pins, shrieking out with the Voice of a Whelp and thus continued till the 30th of the Month." The doctor who was called in to treat the child found no accountable medical reason. Between fits Deborah Pacy said that Amy Duny had appeared to her and [had] frightened her; she said that the woman was "the cause of her disorder." Duny and Cullender were also indicted for bewitching Elizabeth, Anne, and William Durent, Jane Bocking, and Susan Chandler, as well as Deborah Pacy and her sister Elizabeth.

At the conclusion of the presentation of the evidence, Sir Matthew Hale addressed the jury, saying that he would waive repeating the evidence to prevent any errors arising from the repetition, and he told the jury that there were two things into which they must inquire: first, whether or not these children were bewitched and second, whether these women bewitched them. Hale added he did not in the least doubt that these women were witches:

First, Because the Scripture affirmed it; *Secondly*, because the Wisdom of all Nations, particularly our own, has provided Laws against witchcraft; which implies their Belief of such a Crime. He desir'd [the jury] strictly to observe the Evidence and begg'd of

God to direct their Hearts in the Weighty Concern they had in Hand since to condemn the Innocent and let the Guilty go free are both an abomination to the Lord.

There were thirteen counts. Half an hour later, the jury brought in a verdict of guilty on all counts. The verdict was given on Thursday 13 March 1665, and the two women were executed on Monday 17 March, just four days later.

Hale was a judge and lawmaker whose antifemale values were based on a mixture of prejudice and romanticism. His misogyny is revealed in his works and judgments not only on witchcraft, but also in relation to sexual offenses against women. Three centuries later his misogyny, though better concealed, continues to find expression.

PERRY, CHAMBERLAIN, AND WITCHCRAFT

Alice Lynne Chamberlain was a Seventh Day Adventist as was her husband Michael, who was a Seventh Day Adventist minister at the time of the events at Uluru (Ayers Rock) in the Northern Territory that eventually led to their trial for the alleged death of their child Azaria (no body was ever found). They had, they said, set off for a holiday at the Rock, together with their three children. Much was made of a visit to the "fertility cave," an Aboriginal landmark. Later, rumors (picked up by the media) began to circulate—rumors apparently designed to indicate that the Chamberlains were "oddly" religious and that this was in some way linked with the disappearance of Azaria. It was said that "Lindy" Chamberlain had dressed the child in black on at least one occasion, that the name Azaria meant sacrifice in the desert, and that, when police searched the Chamberlain household, they found a miniature coffin.

Despite the absurdity of the Crown case against Lindy Chamberlain, a dominant view prevailed in the press and the community that the mother had in fact killed her daughter, and that the story that a dingo had taken the child from the tent where she was sleeping was no more than that—a story designed to conceal the truth, an unlawful killing. When an inquiry was begun into the affair on 9 June 1987, following Lindy Chamberlain's release from prison upon the discovery of fresh evidence, it became public knowledge that police had originally expected an early confession to the murder of Azaria Chamberlain. A witness at the hearing, Melbourne school teacher Max Whittaker, said Northern Territory police told him during an interview in September 1981 that they were conducting a "murder enquiry" and were "not interested in dingo stories":

"One of the things they said was that they had been told by their superiors to disregard any mention of dingoes," Mr. Whittaker said. "It was a murder enquiry."

"I was told it would be out in the evening papers that they did not expect it to get to a trial. There would be a confession; an early confession."

"That was the climate in which my interview was conducted and, I suppose, the climate leading up to the second inquest and the trial." (Murphy 1986)

Whittaker was one of the campers at Uluru who had joined the search the night Azaria Chamberlain disappeared. He said the police "had not been interested" in his statement. He was interviewed seven months after the Alice Springs coroner, Dennis Barritt, Stipendiary Magistrate, found that a dingo or wild dog had taken Azaria and three months before the second inquest (in Darwin) committed Alice Lynne Chamberlain and Michael Chamberlain to trial.

The prosecution's case was recounted by Justice Lionel Murphy in his written decision in *Chamberlain* v. *The Queen*, when the case went on appeal to the High Court in 1982 and 1983:

The Crown charged a murder committed in a most gruesome manner, within an extremely limited time and in difficult circumstances where the chances of discovery were high. During a period of between five and ten minutes Mrs. Chamberlain is alleged to have gone with Azaria and her son Aiden from the barbeque area to their tent some 20–30 metres away; donned tracksuit pants over her dress; taken Azaria from the tent to the family car which was parked alongside; slit Azaria's throat with a sharp instrument (possibly scissors) while sitting in the front passenger seat of the car; returned to the tent with blood on her hands and the tracksuit pants; removed the tracksuit pants and washed her hands in an ice-cream container; and returned, quite composed, to the barbeque area with Aiden.

In view of the Crown's claim that a great deal of blood was shed in the car during the killing, Mrs. Chamberlain must also have managed to clean up at least the obvious signs of blood in the car during this period. The registered nurse who travelled in the car later in the evening did not notice any blood. Mrs. Chamberlain also found time during these few minutes to put Aiden to bed in his sleeping-bag, hear him complain he was still hungry and to collect a can of baked beans from the car. (Transcript, *Chamberlain* v. *The Queen* 1983, 570–71)

Against this, there was ample evidence of dingoes being around and about the camping grounds. Frequently they intruded into tents, took foodstuffs and other items from camps, and attacked campers. At the trial there was sufficient information of this sort to lead the Acting Chief Justice of the Supreme Court of the Northern Territory in his summing up and directions to the jury to say,

I merely suggest . . . that the evidence merits a finding that on the night of 17 August dingoes did prowl in that area. That they were properly regarded by those, such as [the witness] Derrick Roff [the Senior Ranger], who had responsibility, as a potential danger, and that they had the strength and capacity to take and carry or drag away, a nine-week-old baby. (Quoted, *Chamberlain* v. *The Queen* 1983, 573)

One of many reports available to the 1987 inquiry was carried in the *Daily Telegraph* in Sydney on 11 August that year:

Tourist tells of dingo tent raid

An Ayers Rock camper has called for more adequate warnings about dingoes, claiming a dingo ripped his tent open and made off with a travel bag containing about 8 kg of provisions.

The tourist, Barry Eaton, may now be called to give evidence at the special inquiry into the conviction of Lindy and Michael Chamberlain, which resumes in Darwin this morning.

Mr. Eaton, a New Zealander on a year's holiday in Australia, said in Darwin a neighbouring camper had chased the dingo and returned the bag to the tent.

Paw marks

But the dog had made another visit to the unattended tent the following day and left the bag in shreds on the ground.

The incidents had happened in broad daylight. . . .

Mr. Eaton said he had been camped at Yulara—a few kilometres from where the Chamberlains were camped—on July 13. He had returned to his tent to find two slits bitten into the side and saw paw marks where the dingo had drawn the canvas tight enough to slit it.

Another camper had chased the dingo across the scrub to recover the damaged bag.

The following day Mr. Eaton returned to his tent to find the bag in shreds, with food everywhere. The dog had, on the second occasion, made off with a 1 kg pack of cheese.

One camper recounted how his daughter had been attacked by a dingo and dragged by the arm until rescued by another person at the campsite. Similar stories reached the inquiry.

Why, then, was credence given for so long to the prosecution's version of events? For some who had sympathy for Alice Lynne Chamberlain, the disappearance (and acceptance of death) of Azaria Chantal Loren Chamberlain was attributable to the "raging hormones" theory, which gained currency after the medicalizing of criminality in the nineteenth century:

. . . the most terrible act of the puerperal maniac was child murder. It was during the nineteenth century that the infanticidal woman first became the subject of psychiatric as well as legal discourse. Her crime was the worst that could be imagined by a society that exalted maternity; medical theory struggled to account for it in a way that maintained the mythology of motherhood and the maternal instinct. The psychiatric explanation of puerperal insanity was that after childbirth a woman's mind was abnormally weak, her constitution depleted, and her control over her behavior diminished. (Showalter 1987, 58–59)

This was a convenient way to deal with the events of 1980 at Ayers Rock, despite the difficulty of rationalizing the timing put forward in the prosecution's version (and the lack of any evidence of mental disturbance or postnatal depression on the part of Chamberlain; *Chamberlain* v. *The Queen* 1983, 572). But for the less charitable, Alice Lynne Chamberlain's attitude and actions throughout the time following the disappearance of the child pointed inexorably to her guilt, and her failure to confess made her, in their eyes, the more wicked.

Chamberlain did not act, according to this latter assessment, as a mother, who has lost her child to a dingo, should act. She was rarely observed in tears. During an interview five days after the disappearance, Lindy Chamberlain told a journalist that the dingo that took the child "had a beautiful gold color and was probably a female with puppies" and that she "had tried to calm her sons, Aiden and Reagan, by telling them that Jesus Christ had told dingoes not to steal babies but that the puppies would have been hungry." Michael Chamberlain was observed taking photographs and posing for photographs for the media, telling the story, and cooperating without demur with the press. This was held against Alice Lynne Chamberlain, adding to the "peculiarity" of *her* behavior, even though *she* took no photographs. She did appear on a television program where she described "how a dingo might unpeel the body of a dead baby, gobbling up the exposed bits of flesh as it progressed" (Brown 1986, 15). To many, this seemed inhuman, as did the stoic expression she maintained throughout the trial when photographs appeared emphasizing her dark hair and complexion, her stony face and heavy features, and a body which the photographs and television cameras contrived to depict as "ungainly" (she was heavily pregnant at the time).

Yet however Chamberlain had acted, she could not have overcome the fundamental problem. She was perceived to have killed her child, or at least to have placed her child in a position of danger. What "good" mother would "allow" her child to be taken away by a marauding animal? How could any "good" mother be implicated in the disappearance of her child? What was she doing with a young baby in the middle of the Australian desert, anyway? These questions conveniently ignore the role of the "good" wife—to go wherever her husband goes, to be by her husband's side wherever that side may be. There was no suggestion that it had been Lindy Chamberlain's idea to go to Uluru with a nine-week-old infant, but every example was presented of Michael Chamberlain's being unmindful of the needs and care associated with a very young child.[3]

The maternal role generally demands of women superhuman effort. Twenty-four-hour-a-day responsibility falls mainly upon an infant's mother; feeding, whether with bottle or breast, is a nursing mother's duty; changing diapers, bathing, remaining alert to a cry at any time of the day or night, soothing the child through the rigors of teething—all these and more fall to the mother. At the same time there is a belief, based strongly in the realm of myth, that this superhuman being, the mother, maintains the role while remaining calm, peaceful, loving, eternally gentle, warm, soft, and even tempered. Any suspicion that a woman does not fulfill this role can result in an overreaction to the most minor "falling down on the job." In analyzing witchcraft myths, Philip Mayer points to the "unnaturalness" of the women who engage in witchery and its connection with (among other matters) antimaternalism:

First, the myth defines a category of persons who may be witches, and states how they can be recognized by particular signs. Witches are practically always adults, very often women, and apt to spring from witch families. They may bear physical stigmata . . .

Secondly, the myth tells what sorts of misfortune can be caused by witches. Often these include natural calamities such as death, sickness, drought or plague. However, the context of the misfortune is usually more significant than its intrinsic nature. Witches typically send particular and unaccountable blows that seem somehow out of the common run.

Thirdly, the myth states that witches turn against their own neighbours and kinsmen; they do not harm strangers or people from far away . . .

. . . *witches reverse all normal standards. They particularly delight in "unnatural" practices* such as incest or bestiality; *they eat their own children*, they dig up corpses. (1982, 56; emphasis added)

The German monks Kramer and Sprenger in their primer *Malleus Maleficarum* similarly affix crimes against children as peculiarly within the realm of women:

Here is set forth the truth concerning four horrible crimes which devils commit against infants, both in the mother's womb and afterwards. And since the devils do these things through the medium of women, and not men, this form of homicide is associated rather with women than with men . . .

. . . certain witches, against the instinct of human nature, and indeed against the nature of all beasts, with the possible exception of wolves, are in the habit of devouring and eating infant children. And concerning this, the Inquisitor of Como . . . has told us the following: that he was summoned by the inhabitants of the County of Barby to hold an inquisition, because a certain man had missed his child from its cradle, and finding a congress of women in the night-time, swore that he saw them kill his child and drink its blood and devour it. (Kramer and Sprenger [1487] 1971, 66)[4]

Linked with Chamberlain's religious background, it seems that the disappearance or death of the child Azaria drew subconsciously upon the historical roots of witchcraft. As Nancy van Vuuren points out in *The Subversion of Women as Practised by Churches, Witch-Hunters, and Other Sexists*:

Religion must include magic/witchcraft and sex, especially since it deals with supernatural powers, fertility, and creation. The sex roles are tinged with religious beliefs and attitudes and with magical beliefs. Magic/witchcraft cannot be separated from religion or from sex, for the purpose of magic/witchcraft is to control the supernatural and natural forces, and sex is always a part of this since sex can determine life, and death. (1973, 14)

Throughout the second inquest into the disappearance of Azaria Chamberlain, continuing reports appeared about Alice Lynne Chamberlain's clothes. The impression gained from media coverage was that she wore a different dress every day. This offended the sensibilities of those who thought that a woman in mourning for her child should pay no mind to secular things, particularly the triviality of fashion geegaws, sensibilities unconsciously nourished by the centuries-old religious demand for modesty in women's dress, as exemplified in Paul's letter to Timothy:

with shamefacedness and sobriety; not with braided hair, or gold, or pearls, or costly array but (which becometh women professing godliness) with good works. Let the woman learn in silence with all subjection. But I suffer not a woman to teach, nor to usurp authority over the man, but to be in silence. (I Tim. 2: 9–12)

As van Vuuren notes, in the Middle Ages:

The aristocratic abbesses and nuns were frequently the subject of complaints and reprimands, mostly for wearing fine clothes and dressing in a manner "unbecoming nuns." In 1141 . . . the prioress Clemence Medford at Ankerwyke, in Buckingham, England, was complained of for wearing gold rings and silk veils. The bishop criticized the nuns at Elstow, in Bedfordshire, England, for wearing too colorful and too revealing clothes. A prioress was accused of wearing expensive furs and silk. (1973, 35–36)

With Lindy Chamberlain, no allowance was made for the heat and humidity of Darwin and the recycling of her clothes, except where the press latched on to a repeat wearing of a dress as a point of importance to be made in what was being turned into a media circus.

Chamberlain's failure to betray emotion was seen as "proving" her guilt during the trial. Yet, had she cried, that too could have been used against her, as evidence of her manufacturing emotion for the benefit of outside onlookers and the courtroom audience. This attitude, too, has its origins in the cult of witchcraft. Keith Thomas, writing about the perceived characteristics of witches, says,

The English witch . . . was . . . sometimes believed to have physical peculiarities, in addition to the witch's mark. In 1599, for example, a judge, Sir Richard Martin, said that he had heard that the hair of a witch could not be cut off. Others asserted that a witch sitting in bright sunshine would leave no shadow and that *witches could shed no tears*. (1971, 464; emphasis added)

Question XV of the *Malleus Maleficarum* related to the "Devices and Signs by which the Judge can Recognize a Witch":

If he wishes to find out whether she is endowed with a witch's power of preserving silence, let him take note whether she is able to shed tears when standing in his presence, or when being tortured. For we are taught both by the words of worthy men of old and by our own experience that this is a most certain sign, and it has been found that even if she be urged and exhorted by solemn conjurations to shed tears, if she be a witch she will not be able to weep: although she will assume a tearful aspect and smear her cheeks and eyes with spittle to make it appear that she is weeping; wherefore she must be closely watched by the attendants. (Kramer and Sprenger [1487] 1971, 227)

And later:

And it is found by experience that the more [witches] are conjured the less are they able to weep, however hard they may try to do so, or smear their cheeks with spittle. Nevertheless it is possible that afterwards, in the absence of the Judge and not at the time or in the place of torture, they may be able to weep in the presence of their gaolers.

And as for the reason for the witch's inability to weep, it can be said that the grace of tears is one of the chief gifts allowed to the penitent; for S. Bernard tells us that the tears of the humble can penetrate to heaven and conquer the unconquerable. Therefore there can be no doubt that they are displeasing to the devil, and that he uses all his endeavour to restrain them, to prevent a witch from finally attaining to penitence. (1971, 227–28)

In passing sentence after a woman had been found guilty of witchcraft, it remained for the judge to test her further, lest there be an error in the finding. But Kramer and Sprenger saw that the devil might benefit from false tears, so that even if, after judgment, a woman was able to cry and did so, she would nonetheless be forced to renounce the heresy of witchcraft:

But it may be objected that it might suit with the devil's cunning, with God's permission, to allow even a witch to weep; since tearful grieving, weaving and deceiving are said to be proper to women. We may answer that in this case, since the judgments of God are a mystery, if there is no other way of convicting the accused, by legitimate witnesses or the evidence of the fact, and if she is not under a strong or grave suspicion, she is to be discharged; but because she rests under a slight suspicion by reason of her reputation to which the witnesses have testified, she must be required to abjure the heresy of witchcraft. (1971, 228)

Emily Perry, too, fitted the traditional view of woman-as-witch in the popular mind. Although she could rightly be described as a handsome woman, Perry's age was against her as well as her sex and the crime with which she was charged. Traditionally, poison has been seen as the weapon of women, although there is every reason why today, with their dominance in medicine and in controlling roles in laboratory work, men arguably have greater access to the means. But a knowledge of herbs and potions fits with woman's original role of herbalist and midwife. Dominant views of their activity have been negative; the herbalist is depicted as one addicted to old wives' tales that are of no avail to the sick, who are represented as "lost" without the help of modern medicine—that is, without professionally trained male practitioners, in a field where women were deliberately kept out (Ehrenreich and English 1973; Ehrenreich and English 1978; Shorter 1982).[5] The midwife was frequently seen as an incompetent old woman, much given to incantation, her involvement in births resulting more often in death than life, or at least in injury to child or mother (Ehrenreich and English 1978; Oakley 1976).

The witch was also seen as an old woman who was at the center of mysterious happenings—particularly where others were suffering from pains, becoming ill, having fits, and were the subject of mysterious illnesses and maladies. The implication was that particular women went about their business leaving a trail of inexplicable misfortune behind them, the misfortune often happening to other people and frequently resulting in their death. If a series of deaths or other such instances occurred, medieval society looked for an explanation. The explanation came increasingly to be found in the crone who muttered spells over potions and lotions.

When Constable Haag, Emily Perry's second husband, died in 1960 she was twice questioned, for long periods, at the police station by investigating police.[6] On the second occasion Emily Perry was told that her son, then about sixteen or seventeen years of age, had confessed to murdering Constable Haag (his stepfather) and had implicated her in the death. (This untrue statement was a tactic apparently used in certain police inquiries.) Emily Gertrude Perry (then Emily Haag) stood firm in protesting her innocence of any wrongdoing. An inquest was held, and there was no finding of any suspicious circumstances that in any way implicated her or anyone else. The arsenic found in Constable Haag's body was not evenly distributed in his nails and hair, although it should have been had he ingested the poison over an extended period. Rather, Constable Haag was a keen gardener who utilized weed killer extensively in the garden. He had been using weed killer on the day he died, and he may also have eaten some corncobs directly from the garden without washing them.

It is a common law rule (and indeed a principle based upon common sense) that dated facts should not be determined against standards of a more modern age; that where scientific and other developments have significantly altered present reality, these developments should not be transposed back into the past to locate a happening in a reality that has no relationship to it. In the 1960s there were no general safety regulations in Australia that required the listing of ingredients of household insecticides, sprays, and cleaners. The increased safety consciousness about consumer goods was absent from the 1960s, and it is highly likely that the arsenic content of weed killer was far higher then than it is today. Yet, when the trial against Emily Perry commenced in Adelaide twenty years after Constable Haag's death, no credence was given to the notion of accidental ingestion of the poison.

When Montgomerie, Emily Perry's brother, died one year later, this second death of someone closely related to her undoubtedly would have sparked a vigorous investigation—particularly since it followed the death of a police officer, her second husband, Constable Haag. It is hardly likely that the Victoria Police at the time would have acted other than diligently when one of their own had so recently died in Emily Perry's household. Yet there was no finding against Perry in relation to her brother; no charges were laid against her; no prosecution took place. Obviously there was no feasible evidence that she had brought about her brother's death by poisoning or any other means; nor were there any feasible grounds for launching an action against her through the criminal justice system.

Montgomerie was an alcoholic. He went on drunken binges and had done so for some considerable time before his death. He had fought in World War II and suffered continuing ill health as a result. He had spent two periods in Callan Park, a mental institution in New South Wales, some years before, as a consequence of his having been found to be sexually molesting his daughter who was about eight years old at the time. On the evening before he died, his de facto wife Marge left him. She had threatened on a number of previous occasions to leave him, and he had consistently met these threats with tearfulness, anxiety, emotional distress, and statements that he "would die" if Marge left him. The next morning he was found dead, lying in bed with an almost empty bottle of fortified wine beside him. Also beside him was a note signed "Marge," which stated that she was leaving him.

Duncan, de facto husband of Emily Perry when he died, had been through the war too, with consequent continuing poor health. He also was an alcoholic. He spent long periods in the hospital, sometimes suffering from diarrhea, sometimes from constipation. He had been hospitalized for these complaints long before he met Emily Perry. In the Perry case, expert evidence was given for the prosecution that diarrhea is a sign of arsenic poisoning—and that so, too, is constipation. Indeed the idea appeared to be, on the part of the prosecution, that all Duncan's health problems were attributable to arsenic poisoning (apart from his actual death, by barbiturates) with Perry as the obvious culprit. (When arsenic poisoning failed to work, or to work sufficiently quickly, ran the Crown case, Perry resorted to thrusting an alternative down her de facto's throat.) The prosecution conveniently omitted to recognize that Duncan had suffered from such health problems for years before Emily Perry came into his life; indeed, well before she was even living in Adelaide. And in the year before he died, Duncan suffered a serious car accident. He was driving. His best friend, a passenger in the vehicle, died as a consequence. Shortly before Duncan's death, his dog, to which he was closely attached, died. Duncan died not from arsenic poisoning but from an overdose of barbiturates that he had on prescription because he was sleeping badly at nights.

Kenneth Perry was found by the prosecution to have been suffering from lead and arsenic poisoning. He worked closely with lead in his repair business. At the time he was hospitalized, he had been working extensively on an old pianola he had found at a farmhouse. The farmhouse was infested with rats, as was the pianola immediately before he bought it and took it away. Ratsak was layered extensively throughout the house in which the pianola had stood. There was a large, jagged hole in the base of the pianola, through the hessian backing, and a packet of rat poison had been thrust into the hole, right up into the body of the pianola. Kenneth Perry found it during his restoration work.

Although the law has restricting rules, to be strictly applied, in relation to previous offenses or events in which an accused is implicated or said to have been involved, in Emily Perry's case all these events were put into evidence by the prosecution and allowed by the court. When the appeal went to the High Court, Chief Justice Gibbs and Justices Murphy, Wilson, and Brennan ruled that evidence relating to the death of the de facto husband, Duncan, was inadmissible, because, to make it admissible, it was necessary to assume Emily Perry's guilt of the very offense with which she was charged, namely, the attempted poisoning of Kenneth Perry. Chief Justice Gibbs and Justice Murphy decided that the evidence concerning the death of her brother Montgomerie was inadmissible as being unacceptably circumstantial. Furthermore, if viewed alone, it would hardly even raise a suspicion; there was no striking similarity between it and the case before the court.

In holding that the evidence relating to Duncan and that relating to Montgomerie had been wrongly admitted because it was circumstantial, of highly dubious value, and not classifiable as "similar fact," Justice Murphy said:

In the present case, the prosecution alleges that the accused is an arsenic poisoner, that she has poisoned three other persons with arsenic, and that in these circumstances the arsenic poisoning of her husband is explicable rationally only by her poisoning him. Although if his poisoning is considered alone there is an obvious explanation consistent with her innocence—the abundance of arsenic in his work environment and his evidence that he unwittingly exposed himself to arsenic in the course of his work—the prosecution claim is that his evidence should be disbelieved, and that even though the poisoning could have occurred without her participation, the earlier events make this an affront to commonsense. (*Perry* v. *The Queen* 1982, 465)

Justice Murphy alone determined that the evidence relating to Constable Haag was inadmissible:

There was ample evidence providing a rational explanation of Constable Haag's death consistent with Mrs. Perry's innocence. He used arsenic weed killer in gardening on the week-end of his death. There was some tenuous evidence suggesting earlier arsenic poisoning, but this was explicable as resulting from many other causes than poisoning. The trial judge observed: "It is clear that the arsenic concentrations in [Haag's] hair were low, indeed they were within normal limits for random members of the public." After his death there was a thorough police investigation of all the circumstances, including extensive interrogation of the accused [Perry]. An inquest was held, resulting in a finding of accidental death. It was not then suggested that Mrs. Perry was responsible for the death of Constable Haag. (1982, 466)

But, despite the High Court's finding, which was that justice demanded Emily Perry's conviction be overturned, with her entitlement to a new trial without the inadmissible evidence being allowed in, the perception of the public was negative to Perry's position. Indeed, it was not only the perception of the public that was based on stereotyping and medievality. Not long after the High Court decision and the consequent determination by the South Australian authorities that they would not proceed with a retrial but (at least on the surface) leave Perry alone, the Victorian authorities commenced extradition proceedings to have Emily Perry stand trial in Melbourne on charges relating to the death of Constable Haag. How it could be considered that legitimate evidence existed sufficient to warrant charges being laid against Perry more than twenty years after the death of Constable Haag, when at the time of his death there had been no evidence at all to substantiate any such charges, beggars belief. Indeed, some might be led to believe that in some sense the adverse publicity attaching to Emily Perry's arrest and trial on the charges relating to Kenneth Perry might have played some part. Eventually, the Victorian authorities dropped the charges against Emily Perry.

In discussing the introduction into the Perry case of the evidence related to the other deaths, Justice Murphy alluded specifically to the part that notions of witchcraft had played in the legal system in the past and the part they were playing for Emily Perry. He pointed out that there is no universal formula for proof of guilt by circumstantial evidence and that the process of reasoning relied upon by the Crown in the case against Perry, "proof of guilt by association with circumstances," is theoretically acceptable, but dangerous to the interests of justice:

If there is a sufficient accumulation of events which, according to human experience, would not occur unless the accused were guilty, the tribunal is entitled to act on this material in arriving at a guilty verdict even though each event standing alone would not of itself justify an adverse finding. The other events need not be strikingly similar, but no doubt the conclusion that their occurrence is inconsistent with the accused's innocence will more usually be reached when they are. However, this is an extremely dangerous method of determining criminal guilt. For centuries it was regularly used in England, other parts of Europe and the American colonies to convict millions of persons of the impossible crime of witchcraft. (1982, 467)

DRAGONS AND SCHEMING WOMEN

Chamberlain and Perry suffered simultaneously from being depicted, and seen, as domineering, dragons even, and scheming women. The view that Lindy Chamberlain was the dominant force in her marriage gained currency in Darwin and was repeated by word of mouth and through the media around Australia. Although Michael Chamberlain appeared often in media pictures, where he presented himself as a virile type bouncing about the tennis court and although it was recorded that he had spent a great deal of his time prior to the disappearance of Azaria in climbing Ayers Rock, a feat requiring some strength and staying power, rumor had it that "she" was "really the brains" not only behind the events but behind the marriage and family itself. She was the strength of the couple, ran the accepted wisdom. This portrayal was necessary for any credence to be given to the prosecution case that Michael Chamberlain was an accessory after the fact and must have played some (possibly not inconsiderable) part in the jury's finding of guilt against both parties.

For Michael Chamberlain to be an accessory after the fact, in law, Alice Lynne Chamberlain must at some stage have informed him of "the truth" (that is, what the prosecution saw as the truth—her killing of the child) and must have persuaded him not to reveal it to the authorities or, indeed, to anyone. She must indeed have been a dominant person if this were true. When the child disappeared, there were moments when the two were left together, although not for long periods, while the search party conducted its tracking. Did she work on him swiftly then? Did she tell him of the killing of the child, of her part in it, and did she emphasize that he should remain silent and stick to the dingo story? Almost from the time of Azaria's disappearance, the police took the view that Alice Lynne Chamberlain had somehow killed the child. They kept the couple under continual surveillance, and the Chamberlains were subjected to frequent questioning, individually and together.

When the Crown case is dissected, Michael Chamberlain must have been told, for that case to be true, of the death of the child almost immediately after it occurred. He must immediately have acquiesced in Lindy Chamberlain's "demand" that he assist her in concealing the truth, because (the prosecution story ran) he stuffed the dead child's body into a camera bag he had in the front seat of their car and knowingly drove a nursing sister in that car while the camera bag, bodily contents intact, lay between his feet. Sister Downs, the nurse, stated at the trial that she did not see or smell blood despite the proximity of the camera bag with its apparently bloodied contents.

Similarly with Emily and Kenneth Perry, although the husband was reputably a fighter pilot in the Royal Air Force during World War II and was apparently a normal, dominant male, the view depicted during the trial was that he was dominated by his wife. Why else would he protest her innocence? Why else would he attribute his illness, which the Crown saw so clearly as a result of perfidious planning on Emily Perry's part, to his own working conditions unrelated to any malign activity of his wife? Here, the contrast of police action in the Perry case in ignoring Kenneth Perry's protestations of Emily's innocence, and the police inaction in cases where a woman, although clearly having been a victim at her husband's hands, says she does not want criminal charges laid against him, is stark. Evidence is readily available of women suffering severe and obvious injuries when struck, bashed, beaten, and otherwise abused by their husbands. The police response when confronted with their own failure to take action against these husbands is frequently that the woman "did not want them to take action" or that she "refused to give evidence" against the husband. Yet despite a perfectly reasonable explanation for Kenneth Perry's condition, one unrelated to any criminality on the part of Emily Perry, the police pursued their investigation vigorously and ignored the fact that Kenneth Perry did not believe that he had been poisoned by his wife; did not want any action to be taken against her; and was not a witness for the Crown. On the contrary he was a witness for the defense. Medical evidence in cases of wife bashing is often indisputable, yet police usually take the matter no farther. In the Perry case, the medical evidence said to substantiate a claim that Emily Perry had been feeding her husband arsenic and lead did not in fact support such a supposition; all it could show was that Kenneth Perry was apparently suffering from a medical condition that could be attributed to arsenic and lead poisoning. Reasonably, this illness could have come from the pianolas and organs about the Perry household and workshop. When a woman is bruised, broken limbed, bloody nosed—unless there is some other party to whom the injuries can reasonably be attributed—the case against the husband is right there for police to pursue legitimately and in accordance with their duty.[7]

For the Crown case to stand against Emily Perry, the jury had to be persuaded she was a dragon, a domineering woman. Duncan, the de facto, was portrayed as a poor specimen of a man, dominated by Emily Perry and thus unlikely to protest or resist when she shovelled capsule after capsule of barbiturates into his mouth (according to the prosecution). With her brother Montgomerie, she was apparently the dominant figure in her wider family, in the Crown's version of events. Because Montgomerie was such a hopeless layabout, a man who spent most of his time drunk, who could keep neither his marriage nor his de facto relationship together, Emily Perry put him—and her wider family—out of his misery, so the story ran. With Constable Haag, it was more difficult. How to depict a police officer, a member of an acknowledged dominant profession, daily being confronted with situations where "manhood" is called for, as at the mercy of a domineering dragon of a wife? Dealing with two problems simultaneously, it was said that Emily Perry (as Emily Haag) had helped her husband through his professional training, by tutoring him in the poisons part of his course. Therefore, the jury was to accept, Constable Haag was not the dominant one in the Haag marriage; rather, it was Emily, his wife, who had, like a schoolmarmish "mother," to teach him his lessons in poison. This also conveniently provided the necessary intelligence about Emily Perry's alleged proficiency in the successful utilization of poison.

Both Perry and Chamberlain fell into the scheming woman category too. No one but a schemer could have manipulated evidence in the way Lindy Chamberlain was alleged to have done: the attempt (according to the Crown) to make the jagged cuts in the baby's jumpsuit, discovered later in the area, look like dingo's teeth. The prosecution said that she (or Michael under her command) used scissors to make the garment look as if a dingo had indeed taken the child in it and had cut the cloth with its teeth while dragging the baby's body out of it. The entire tale of a dingo was that of a schemer, according to the Crown. Lindy Chamberlain, ran the prosecution case, had (for whatever motive—none was ever put forward) killed the child, then created a complicated tale of a dingo attack, leading many campers and others to participate in a search for Azaria that went on for some considerable time. She had dissimulated and lied when talking with police, campers, and others at the scene. From the time of the child's death and right through the trial, as well as when she was in prison serving out her life sentence, on this rationale, Lindy Chamberlain continued her scheming. She continued to protest her innocence although she was, in the Crown's eyes, guilty; she had continued to enmesh her husband Michael in the deception; she had inveigled others into her scheming, which led to thousands of ordinary citizens around Australia being "duped": They joined "Release Lindy Chamberlain'' groups, gave talks from platforms about what they said "really" happened at Uluru that night, and generally agitated for Chamberlain's release, despite "justice" properly having been done.

Was there any supposed motive for Emily Perry's alleged career as poisoner? There is no duty on the prosecution's part to show any motive in putting forward its case. However, a number of issues were raised that justified, in the Crown's view, the admission into evidence of the deaths of the three men that preceded the alleged attempt on Kenneth Perry's life, which purportedly supported a notion of motive. In the case of Constable Haag, it was said that Emily Perry had a reason for bringing about his death: money. An insurance policy had been taken out on Haag's life, with his then wife, Emily, as the beneficiary. Instead of Constable Haag's having signed the policy, Emily had forged his signature. Her explanation was that she had asked her husband time and again to sign the policy, but he had failed to do so. In despair at not completing the requirements of the policy, she had signed his name for him. There was also a policy on the life of Duncan, the de facto; Emily again was the beneficiary on this policy. Again, the Crown latched onto this as a motive. Yet both actions must be seen in the then existing sociocultural context. In the 1950s and early 1960s, women living at home, as housewives, were constantly prevailed upon by visiting insurance salesmen to take out all manner of insurance policies—life policies, term policies, policies for each of their children to mature when they reached twenty-one years, and so on. A whole cultural attitude grew up around insurance policies where housewives and mothers were concerned. Emily Haag (as she then was) was confronted by this cultural need, as were thousands of women in a similar position around Australia in those years. Fortunately for other women, relatively rarely does a husband die in circumstances that might raise suspicions about the means and mode of death. Unfortunately for Emily Haag, her husband Constable Haag, died in circumstances that led to an inquest, and where his workmates had a definite interest in viewing the circumstances of his death as suspicious. The fact that there was a life insurance policy on Constable Haag does not in itself show that his wife harbored ill will toward him and made effective that ill will by bringing about his untimely death. Although forging a signature is an illegal act and is inexcusable, it is nevertheless explicable in the then existing sociocultural attitudes surrounding insurance and the relative lack of independent means for women who were widowed by natural misfortune at that time. And it is notable that, although it was found that she had forged the signature (which she acknowledged), no charges were laid against Emily in respect of Constable Haag's death despite this evidence, and the finding from the inquest harbored no suspicion about her role: The finding was of accidental death. As for the policy on Duncan, it was specifically taken out because Emily Perry wished to purchase a house in Adelaide when she moved there to live. She was unable to raise money on a loan *without a male guarantor*. Even today many women continue to find themselves in this invidious position—being required to produce a male guarantor when desirous of taking out a loan, for whatever purpose (New

South Wales Anti Discrimination Board, *Report* 1983). In the 1960s and 1970s this requirement was even more stringently applied.

Emily Perry's "scheming" (in the eyes of the Crown) extended to her giving a "false" name to police when they arrived at the scene of her brother Montgomerie's death. That she did not give her name as "Haag" was seen as evidence of a guilty mind, of her wishing to conceal from the police her earlier connection with a death by poisoning. Yet, rather than as evidence of any clever scheming, this can be seen either as sheer stupidity—it would hardly be calculated to keep her "true" identity from the police in any but the very shortest of terms—or as a very normal human reaction. In the year after her husband's death, telephone calls were made continually to Emily Haag's employers, Myer Melbourne, a department store, charging that they had a "murderess on the staff." She had gone through rigorous questioning when it was obvious that the police thought she had killed her husband. She had been through an inquest into the death of Constable Haag. Little wonder she was upset when her brother died in circumstances where it seemed he had ingested poison—both because of her loss of him and because of the possible implications for her. Of course, there is another explanation with which other women will find much in common: She could simply have reverted to the use of her former name, with the added incentive of wishing to escape notoriety for which she was not to blame.

CONCLUSIONS

The legal system individualizes offenses and offending. It individualizes accused persons. Crimes are seen as individual aberrations rather than as responses to social, political, and economic realities. The crime of infanticide well illustrates this. During the nineteenth century, as Showalter has shown, an "enlightened" attitude was taken toward the killing of infants by their mothers (1987, 58–59). In the 1980s, many of those professing sympathy for Alice Lynne Chamberlain questioned why she did not simply acknowledge killing the child Azaria and plead guilty to infanticide. Those taking this stand were unaware that, under Northern Territory law, there was in 1980 no crime of infanticide; that is, had she pleaded guilty, Lindy Chamberlain would have been obliged to plead guilty to murder. The crime of infanticide is a special statutory offense, introduced into most Australian jurisdictions (and many other jurisdictions in the common law world), whereby a woman who kills her child shortly after the birth can plead guilty to (or be found guilty of) manslaughter rather than murder. Where there is a mandatory penalty of life imprisonment for murder, a conviction for manslaughter is attractive: The penalty can vary from imprisonment for a set term to a noncustodial sentence, such as a bond, at the discretion of the judge.

But this was not the only problem. The offense of infanticide depoliticizes the crime of child killing. The creation of a special offense is a token response, a band-aid measure on the part of the criminal law, to extreme cases where a woman is unable to cope with the mammoth task of caring for her child. As

Showalter notes, in the nineteenth century, infanticide did not appear randomly in the population:

in middle-class households, where there were nurses and servants to help with child care, puerperal insanity rarely ended in infanticide. . . . [C]hild murder was much more likely to occur in conjunction with illegitimacy, poverty, and brutality. . . . [T]he psychiatric definition of puerperal violence . . . ignored both the social problems of unmarried, abused, and destitute mothers and the shocks, adjustments, and psychological traumas of the maternal role. Rather than looking at the social meaning of infanticide and its contexts, doctors, lawyers, and judges categorized it as an isolated and biologically determined phenomenon, an unfortunate product of woman's "nature." (1987, 59)

If the view of those in favor of an infanticide verdict in the Chamberlain case had been true, and Lindy Chamberlain had indeed killed her child, would the proper "solution" have been to bring in that verdict (had it been available) or to have heaved a sigh of relief if she had volunteered her willingness to accept the label of infanticide by pleading guilty?

On the face of it, the infanticide provision may appear to be an easy way out for women. Showalter accepts that this was so during the Victorian era:

[The factors of illegitimacy, poverty, and brutality] whether or not they were considered by medical specialists, were certainly taken into account by Victorian judges and juries, who were reluctant to sentence infanticidal women to death, and who responded compassionately to the insanity defense generally used in their behalf. Infacticidal women who were committed for life to Bethlem or Broadmoor were also more likely to be released by order of the home secretary than any other group of the criminally insane. (1987, 59)

Alternatively, the infanticide "loophole" may be a simple recognition of a medically accepted fact.

But neither of these approaches is acceptable, for both ignore the reality of women's situation, and that of the individual woman. To be classified as suffering from puerperal insanity and confined to a mental institution may seem "easier" than being sentenced to imprisonment for life. However, review procedures exist in the prison system which are less likely to exist, or to be effected, within the mental institution (Report of the Royal Commission into the NSW Prison System [the "Nagle Report"] 1981). A person serving a life imprisonment will more than likely be released having served, at maximum, about ten years. Release is on parole, but it is release. Those in mental institutions, having pleaded guilty to criminal charges, may be confined for life. There is no assurance that a woman who has been convicted of manslaughter on the ground of a postnatal medical condition will be released in any less time than a person sentenced to life imprisonment. Indeed, getting out may well be much more difficult (Nagle Report 1981). Even if it is a medically accepted fact that, following the birth of a child, some women suffer postnatal depression, it remains to be asked why this is so.

Is it simply due to woman's biology, or is there a far less glib, and more realistic, explanation? And if it were a medically accepted fact that postnatal depression, in some women, leads them to kill their children, it should be instructive to look behind that medically accepted fact and at who makes the assessment.

For a long time, our society has adhered to a model of woman: the mother, as the perfect carer of children, particularly of those she has borne. The maternal instinct is regarded as inevitably ensuring that women are destined to be "good" mothers. Only a few transgress—and they are aberrations, runs the accepted litany. Although some efforts are made to provide child care as a government and community responsibility, society continues to be framed upon a base of women-as-mothers providing the major care for children, alone, in the home. Although there may be some changes of attitude, parts of the community continue to deplore "working mothers" (meaning those in paid employment outside the home, failing to recognize the work involved in being a full-time child carer in the home, albeit an unpaid one). The community still enthuses about the maternal instinct (now fashionably called bonding), and the agonies of the "latch key child" remain relevant to many agendas. Locked into a situation where she is responsible for the full-time care of a child, it is little wonder that, for some women, the responsibility is too much; the effort is impossible, and the result is child killing.

When a woman becomes pregnant, there is generally a positive response. Women are led to believe that the culmination of the pregnancy will result in happiness all around; and that a gurgling, glowing baby will add to the joys of home and family life. Yet, after the birth, the woman is often left alone, with total responsibility for taking care of the infant's every need. Even with a husband, she often lives the life of a single parent owing to his working hours, his job, and other commitments, which he continues, in the main, without reorganizing his life-style to accommodate the new member of the household (Russell 1983). A mother has few means of escaping depression, yet she is required to feel perpetually pleased with her offspring.

Alice Lynne Chamberlain traveled with her husband Michael and her three children—Aiden, six years old; Reagan, four years old; and Azaria, nine-and-a-half weeks old—from Broken Hill, where the family was living, to Uluru in the middle of the Australian desert. It was hot. The journey was long. The children no doubt were fractious through heat and traveling, growing tired. What effect such a journey would have upon the equanimity of a nine-week-old baby is worthy of speculation. Michael Chamberlain was mostly away from the camp, it seems, taking photographs and climbing the Rock. If Alice Lynne Chamberlain had indeed succumbed to the pressure of being a full-time carer of three young children (one a very young baby) out in the desert in the heat, dust, and flies; if she had been responsible for the child's death (though she could not possibly have done so in the manner put forward by the Crown—the timing was ludicrously short; the cries were heard from the child when, according to the Crown, she was already dead; and other flaws can be found in the case), the legal system would have dealt with the problem in an individualized way. The economic and social position of a woman in her position would not have been relevant in any way that could have led to a real change in the lives of women similarly placed, nor in her own (at least with regard to child care, support services for young mothers, raising fathers' consciousness so that their activities focus on the real needs of their children and on the needs of the children's mother). Even had she done the act, and even if she had pleaded guilty, there would have remained many, no doubt, who continued to think of her as a "wicked" mother, one disentitled by her very act from being allowed to remain in the traditional motherhood category. Had she indeed ended the child's life, in the eyes of others, she may, by their sympathy, have escaped classification as witch, dragon, domineering wife, or scheming woman. But she would have taken upon herself that other role so often the lot of women, that of victim.

For Emily Gertrude Perry there appeared to be little sympathy. She was not a figure who could easily attract such feelings: Age no doubt was against her; the crime she was alleged to have committed and the other acts attributed to her did not readily led themselves to ordinary feminist support. Had she, for example, been a battered wife who had retaliated in a physical way against Kenneth Perry, Duncan, and Constable Haag perhaps by using an axe or a hammer or even a gun, there certainly would have been women's groups ready to come to her aid. Examples abound: the Georgia Hill case in New South Wales (Scutt 1983; Scutt 1990,185–88, 190–96); the case of Beryl Birch in Queensland (Rathus 1985); the renowned axe murder case, *R. v. R.*, in South Australia (Scutt 1983; Scutt 1990, 188–96); and the case of Violet and Bruce Roberts in New South Wales (Scutt 1983; Scutt 1990, 192–96). Although it is far more difficult for a woman to retaliate against a man by physical means, and poisoning may be the only way out that a woman locked into an exploitative and oppressively violent situation can see, the element of planning that is presumed to precede such a killing operates more readily to eliminate any feelings of empathy or compassion. Yet, although any form of unlawful killing is inexcusable, it should still be understood that the economic, social, and political underpinnings of women's lives may be such as to result in their eliminating what they see as the source of their oppression and exploitation and of intense cruelty toward them, with apparently no way out, by less instant means than axe or gun. The very powerlessness that a woman experiences in a home filled with the brutality of an abusive husband may lead her to adopt a relatively passive means of ending the abuse. That she has the ability to get to a shop to buy arsenic or cyanide does not mean that she is in control of her life; it does not mean that she is any less in terror than the woman who uses more direct means. Even had Emily Perry been in this situation, could she have expected any useful response from the legal system?[8]

In both the Perry case and the Chamberlain case, forensic evidence played a key role in the convictions. The forensic evidence is generally seen as the key to the conviction of Lindy Chamberlain and, ultimately, to her release and the setting up of an inquiry into the convictions of her and her husband, with the resultant conclusion that neither should have been convicted (Commission of Enquiry into *Chamberlain* v. *The Queen* [the "Morling Report"] 1987). Although it was the method of proof—placing in evidence material that was inadmissible—that led to the determination by the High Court that Emily Perry's trial verdict should be overturned and a retrial without the extraneous evidence take place, rather than the nature of the forensic evidence itself, evidence purporting to show that Duncan, the de facto, had been suffering from arsenic poisoning despite his death from barbiturate poisoning was a crucial part of the Crown case. For Chamberlain, evidence of fetal blood in the front seat of the car turned out to be no good evidence at all: It was a substance known as Dufix HN1081, a sound-deadening emulsion sprayed on all cars during their construction. For Perry, all the symptoms suffered by Duncan were viewed by the major forensic witness for the Crown as evidences of arsenic poisoning, although this witness had no training in the arsenic poisoning area and, when questioned about this lack of expertise, said derisively that it was a very old-fashioned field. (The major forensic witness for the defense had extensive training in the field of arsenic poisoning, having studied and written in the area for a significant period of time and therefore being specifically competent in giving evidence about the symptoms attributed to Duncan and those experienced by Kenneth Perry.)

But, in the ultimate analysis, forensic evidence would not have carried the day (just as it did not in the final analysis with decisions favoring Lindy Chamberlain [by the Morling Enquiry] and Emily Perry [by the High Court]) had there not been the underlying reality with which both women had to contend. That is, the reality of a society that has a subconscious allegiance to an angry and misogynist past, the ideology of woman-as-witch, and a subconscious resort to the stereotypes of domineering and scheming women.

NOTES

1. The *Witchcraft Act* remained on the statute books in Britain until 1951, when it was repealed. As M. J. Kephart points out (1982, 326–42), the persecution of witchcraft and witches was directed by those in the upper reaches of society and gained support from the general community:

before the Elizabethan period [in England], no compact or sabbath was believed in by the peasant villagers; but the whole point of the satanic-witch craze, in Britain as in Europe, was the heavy involvement of the nobility and the gentry, education persons in university, Church, government and the judicial system. The satanic-witch ideology, including the notion that all magic was done by an implicit or explicit pact with Satan, had been invented and elaborated in the highest circles in Europe and when the ideology got to Britain, in the usual way, it was taken up by the highest in the land, from the reading gentry, up to and including the monarch. Whether or not the Marian exiles had a critical role in importing Continental notions, it was certainly educated people who did it, not peasants. Educated people formed opinions, imported and wrote books on satanism. . . . Of the Elizabethan [witchcraft] law of 1563, Robbins notes: "Witchcraft was not merely the vulgar prejudice of uneducated people. This bill was framed by some of the ablest and most learned men in England." . . . Notestein mentions that Henry More, for example, in the next century, believed that he had absolute proof of the "nocturnal conventicle of witches" in his book, *Antidote to Atheisme*. . . . As the upper classes spread beliefs in satanism, the peasantry came to hear of it. Finally, the highest personage in the land took active notice. . . . James Stuart, while still James VI of Scotland, developed an interest in satanism. He wrote a book on the topic called *Demonology*, first published in Edinburgh in 1597. Before writing his book James had involved himself in a famous "witch" trial in North Berwick, 1590–1592. Judicial torture was not permitted for this crime in England, but North Berwick is in Scotland and the peasant suspects were questioned under torture and a lot of "evidence" of satanism was gathered. James played the role of the Continental demonologist. . . . He was convinced that the trial provided the existence of Continental-style compact and sabbath in Britain. Upon becoming king of both Scotland and England, James I (as he was then styled) had *Demonology* reprinted in London, and personally supervised the passing of the new, harsher "Witchcraft Statute" in 1604. This new law was critical for English prosecutions . . . because it "changed the emphasis from *maleficium* to the pact with the Devil, in line with Continental thinking, and certainly heightened the attack against witches." . . . Now peasant women could be executed for nothing more than "entertaining evil spirits" or compact. Most often the charge was still for harm allegedly done, for *maleficium*, by [there were] convictions for compact alone. . . . For example, "at Chelmsford in 1645 seven women were hanged for the sole charge of entertaining spirits." (Kephart 1982, 332–33)

2. For an overview of this case, see Riddell 1926–1927. Quotations are taken from Riddell's article.

3. In later interviews with Michael Chamberlain, after Alice Lynne Chamberlain had given birth to Kahlia, the daughter born after the trial and convictions of the Chamberlains, he acknowledged an awareness of the time and care necessary in looking after a young baby. This acknowledgment came after he had had a major responsibility for the care of Kahlia Chamberlain during her mother's incarceration in Berrima Gaol in Darwin, in the Northern Territory. The child was taken from Mrs. Chamberlain after the birth and placed in Mr. Chamberlain's full-time care.

4. The first English edition of *Malleus Maleficarum* was published in 1928 by John Rodker, London. It is uncertain when the first edition of the book was published, but Montague Summers, translator of the English edition, puts the likeliest year at 1486. Fourteen editions were published between 1487 and 1520, with at least sixteen editions more between 1574 and 1669. All were issued by leading German, French, and Italian presses. See Summers [1928] 1971, vii–viii. It is worth quoting in full from his 1928 introduction Summers's view of the *Malleus Maleficarum* as it stands in relation to women:

Possibly what will seem . . . more amazing to modern readers is the misogynic trend of various passages, and these not of the briefest nor least pointed. However, exaggerated as these may be, I am not altogether certain that they will not prove a wholesome and needful antidote in this feministic age, when the sexes seem confounded, and it appears to be the chief object of many females to ape the man, an indecorum by which they not only divest themselves of such charm as they might boast, but lay themselves open to the sternest reprobation in the name of sanity and common-sense. For the Apostle S. Peter says:

"Let wives be subject to their husbands: that if any believe not the word, by the conversation of the wives, considering your chaste conversation with fear. Whose adorning let it not be the outward plaiting of the hair, or the wearing of gold, or the putting on of apparel; but the hidden man of the heart is the incorruptibility of a quiet and meek spirit, which is rich in the sight of God. For after the manner heretofore the holy women also, who trusted in God, adorned themselves, being in subjection to their own husbands: as Sara obeyed Abraham, calling him lord: whose daughters you are, doing well, and not fearing any disturbance."

With regard to the sentences pronounced upon witches and the curse of their trials, we may say that these things must be considered in reference and in proportion to the legal code of the age. Modern justice knows sentences of the most ferocious savagery, punishments which can only be dealt out by brutal vindictiveness, and these are often meted out to offences concerning which we may sometimes ask ourselves whether they are offences at all; they certainly do no harm to society, and no harm to the person. Witches were the bane of all social order; they injured not only persons but property. They were, in fact, . . . the active members of a vast revolutionary body, a conspiracy against civilization. Any other save the most thorough measures must have been unavailing; worse, they must have but fanned the flame. . . . We must approach this great work—admirable in spite of its trifling blemishes [faults in etymology]—with open minds and grave intent; if we duly consider the world of confusion, of Bolshevism, of anarchy and licentiousness all around to-day, it should be an easy task for us to picture the difficulties, the hideous dangers with which Henry Kramer and James Sprenger were called to combat and to cope; we must be prepared to discount certain plain faults, certain awkwardnesses, certain roughnesses and even severities; and then shall we be in a position dispassionately and calmly to pronounce opinion upon the value and the merit of this famous treatise. . . .

As for myself, I do not hesitate to record my judgement. . . . The interest . . . lies in the subject-matter. And from this point of view the *Malleus Maleficarum* is one of the most pregnant and most interesting books I know in the library of its kind—a kind which, as it deals with eternal things, the eternal conflict of good and evil, must eternally capture the attention of all men who think, all who see, or are endeavouring to see, reality beyond the accidents of matter, time, and space. (Summers, [1928] 1971, xxxix–xl)

Summer's briefer introduction to the 1946 Pushkin Press, London, edition of the *Malleus Maleficarum* omits the strident antiwoman and antifeminist dimensions of the 1928 edition, but it is, if anything, more laudatory in its peroration:

Certain it is that the *Malleus Maleficarum* is the most solid, the most important work in the whole vast library of witchcraft. One turns to it again and again with edification and interest. From the point of psychology, from the point of jurisprudence, from the point of history, it is supreme. It is hardly too much to say that later writers, great as they are, have done little more than draw from the seemingly inexhaustible wells of wisdom which the two Dominicans, Heinrich Kramer and James Sprenger, have given us in the *Malleus Maleficarum*.

What is most surprising is the modernity of the book. There is hardly a problem, a complex, a difficulty which they have not foreseen, and discussed, and resolved.

Here are cases which occur in the law-courts to-day, set out with the greatest clarity, argued with unflinching logic, and judged with scrupulous impartiality.

It is a work which must irresistibly capture the attention of all men who think, all who see, or are endeavouring to see, the ultimate reality beyond the accidents of matter, time and space. The *Malleus Maleficarum* is one of the world's few books written *sub specie aeternitatis*. (xv–xvi)

5. Women were deliberately kept out of medicine. In the 1840s Elizabeth Blackwell qualified in the United States in medicine and was admitted to the British Medical Register in 1859. Women were able to qualify in medicine on the Continent (although they certainly did not do so in the numbers of their male counterparts). Elizabeth Blackwell's registration raised the awareness of the British medical fraternity that women could join their ranks, so that from then onward a conscious campaign was waged to keep women out. In the 1860s Sophia Jex-Blake gained entry to Edinburgh University in Scotland to study medicine, but this, together with the efforts of six other women to enter, raised the anger of male students and led the university to deny entry to all women. Sophia Jex-Blake and the six other women brought a lawsuit against the university, basing their argument on the ground that the university regulations stated that "any person" with particular qual-

ifications was entitled to enter and study in the faculties. The court held that the women were not "persons." The same argument was used—that women were not persons— against women seeking to gain entry to various professions, including law, in the United Kingdom, Canada, and Australia. See Sachs and Hoff-Wilson 1978, 197; Scutt 1984. All quotations come from Scutt.

6. Information relating to the Perry case comes directly from the Appeal Books lodged in relation to the matter when heard by the High Court of Australia in 1982 and the reported judgments of the High Court in *Perry* v. *The Queen* (1982), 44 *Australian Law Reports* 449. All quotations come from the latter source.

7. On the lack of police prosecution of woman-bashing in these circumstances see McCulloch 1984; Western Women's Refuge Group 1978; O'Donnell and Craney 1982; Scutt 1980; Scutt 1986; Scutt 1983; Scutt 1990, 216–41.

8. Women receive little constructive help from the police, or from the legal system generally, owing to inbuilt bias and structural prejudices. See, for example, Edwards 1985b; Edwards 1986; Bacon and Lansdowne 1982a; Bacon and Lansdowne 1982b; Lovejoy and Steel 1978.

REFERENCES

Bacon, Wendy, and Robyn Lansdowne. 1982a. "Women Homicide Offenders and Police Interrogation." In *The Criminal Injustice System*, edited by John Basten, Mark Richardson, Chris Ronalds, and George Zdenkowski, 4–16. Melbourne, Australia: Legal Service Bulletin/Legal Workers Group.

———. 1982b. "Women Who Kill Husbands: The Battered Wife on Trial." In *Family Violence in Australia*, edited by Carol O'Donnell and Jan Craney, 67–81. Melbourne, Australia: Longman Cheshire.

Basten, John, Mark Richardson, Chris Ronalds, and George Zdenkowski, eds. 1982. *The Criminal Injustice System*. Melbourne, Australia: Legal Service Bulletin/Legal Workers Group.

Blandford, G. Fielding. 1871. *Insanity and Its Treatment*. Philadelphia: Henry C. Lea.

Brown, Malcolm. 1986. "The Chamberlains' 'Calm' Becomes an Issue at Hearing." *Sydney Morning Herald*, 23 August 1986, 15.

Bucknill, J. C., and Daniel Hack Tuke. 1858. Reprint 1968. *A Manual of Psychological Medicine*. London: Hafner.

Chamberlain v. *The Queen*, No. 2. 1983. 153 *Commonwealth Law Reports* (CLR), 521.

Commission of Enquiry into *Chamberlain* v. *The Queen* (The "Morling Report.") 1987. Darwin, Australia: Government Printer.

Dwyer, Nan. 1986. "Jail Doors Will Open Tomorrow for Beryl Birch." *The Sunday Mail*, 31 August 1986.

Edwards, Susan S. M., ed. 1985a. *Gender, Sex and the Law*. London: Croom Helm.

———. 1985b. "Male Violence against Women: Excusatory and Explanatory Ideologies in Law and Society." In *Gender, Sex and the Law*, edited by Susan S. M. Edwards, 183–216. London: Croom Helm.

———. 1986. "Neither Bad nor Mad: The Female Violent Offender Reassessed." *Women's Studies International Forum* 9 (1): 79–88.

Ehrenreich, Barbara, and Deidre English. 1973. *Complaints and Disorders: The Sexual Politics of Sickness*. New York: Feminist Press.

————. 1978. *For Her Own Good: 150 Years of Experts' Advice to Women*. New York: Anchor Press/Doubleday.

Kephart, M. J. 1982. "Rationalists vs Romantics among Scholars of Witchcraft." In *Witchcraft and Sorcery*, edited by Max Marwick, 326–42. Harmondsworth, England: Penguin.

Klein, Dorie. 1973. "The Etiology of Female Crime: A Review of the Literature." *Crime and Social Justice: Issues in Crime* (Fall): 3–30.

Krafft-Ebing, Richard von. 1882. *Psychosis Menstrualis*. Cited in Otto Pollak. 1950. *The Criminality of Women*. Philadelphia: University of Pennsylvania Press.

Kramer, Heinrich, and James Sprenger. [1487], *Malleus Maleficarum*. First English edition 1928, London: John Rodker. Reprint 1971, New York: Dover. 1946 edition, London: Pushkin Press.

Leonard, Eileen B. 1982. *Women, Crime and Society—A Critique of Criminology Theory*. New York: Longman.

Lombroso, Cesare. 1895. *The Female Offender*. New York: Appleton.

Lovejoy, Francis, and Emily Steel. 1978. "Sex Object as Corpse." *Legal Service Bulletin* 3:251–53.

McCulloch, Jude, and St. Kilda Community Legal Centre. 1984. *Submission to the Commissioner for Equal Opportunity in Relation to Discrimination against Women on the Ground of Sex and Marital Status in Failure of Police to Prosecute Domestic Crimes*. Melbourne, Australia: St. Kilda Community Legal Service.

Marwick, Max, ed. [1970]. *Witchcraft and Sorcery*. 2d ed., rev. and enl. 1982. Harmondsworth, England: Penguin.

Maudsley, Henry. 1895. *The Pathology of Mind—A Study of Its Distempers, Deformities and Disorders*. London: Macmillan & Co.

Mayer, Philip. 1982. "Witches." In *Witchcraft and Sorcery*, edited by Max Marwick, 54–70. Harmondsworth, England: Penguin.

Mitchell, Juliet, and Ann Oakley, eds. 1976. *The Rights and Wrongs of Women*. Harmondsworth, England: Penguin.

Mukherjee, S. K., and Jocelynne A. Scutt, eds. 1981. *Women and Crime*. Sydney, Australia: George Allen and Unwin.

Murphy, Damien. 1986. "Police Told to Ignore Dingo Claim, Inquiry Told." *The Age*, 9 August 1986, 6.

New South Wales Anti-Discrimination Board. 1983. *Report into Financial Discrimination against Women*. Sydney, Australia: Government Printer.

Oakley, Ann. 1976. "Wise Woman and Medicine Man: Changes in the Management of Childbirth." In *The Rights and Wrongs of Women*, edited by Juliet Mitchell and Ann Oakley, 45–47. Harmondsworth, England: Penguin.

O'Donnell, Carol, and Jan Craney, eds. 1982. *Family Violence in Australia*. Melbourne, Australia: Longman Cheshire.

Perry v. *The Queen*. 1982. 44 *Australian Law Reports* (ALR), 449.

Pollak, Otto. 1950. *The Criminality of Women*. Philadelphia: University of Pennsylvania Press.

Rathus, Zoe. 1985. "The Case of Beryl Birch." In *National Conference on Domestic Violence: Proceedings*, edited by Suzanne E. Hatty, 359–68. Canberra, Australia: Australian Institute of Criminology.

Report of the Royal Commission into the NSW Prison System [Nagle Report]. 1981. 5 vols. Sydney, Australia: Government Printer.

Riddell, William Renwick. 1926–1927. "Sir Matthew Hale and Witchcraft." *Journal of Criminal Law, Criminology and Police Science* 17:5–12.

————. 1927–1928. "William Penn and Witchcraft." *Journal of Criminal Law, Criminology and Police Science* 18:11–16.

————. 1930–1931. "The Trial of Witches." *Journal of Criminal Law, Criminology and Police Science* 21:257–60.

Russell, Graeme. 1983. *The Changing Role of Fatherhood*. Brisbane, Australia: University of Queensland Press.

Sachs, Albie, and Joan Hoff-Wilson. 1978. *Sexism in Law*. London: Martin Robinson.

Scutt, Jocelynne A. 1981. "Sexism in Criminal Law." In *Women and Crime*, edited by S. K. Mukherjee and Jocelynne A. Scutt, 1–21. Sydney, Australia: George Allen and Unwin.

————. 1983. *Even in the Best of Homes—Violence in the Family*. Ringwood, Australia: Penguin Australia.

————. 1984. "Sexism in Legal Language." *Australian Law Journal* 5:163–73.

————. 1986. "Going Backwards: Law 'Reform' and Woman Bashing." *Women's Studies International Forum* 9 (1):49–56.

————. 1990. *Women and the Law*. Sydney, Australia: Law Book Co.

Scutt, Jocelynne A., ed. 1980. *Violence in the Family*. Canberra, Australia: Australian Institute of Criminology.

Shorter, Edward. 1982. *A History of Women's Bodies*. Harmondsworth, England: Penguin.

Showalter, Elaine. 1987. *The Female Malady: Women, Madness, and English Culture, 1830–1980*. London: Virago.

Smart, Carol. 1976. *Women, Crime and Criminology: A Feminist Critique*. London: Routledge & Kegan Paul.

Summers, Montague. [1928] 1971. Introduction to *Malleus Maleficarum*. London: John Rodker.

Thomas, Keith. 1971. *Religion and the Decline of Magic*. London: Weidenfeld and Nicolson.

Thomas, W. I. 1907. *Sex and Society*. Boston: Little Brown.

————. 1923. *The Unadjusted Girl*. New York: Harper & Row.

van Vuuren, Nancy. 1973. *The Subversion of Women as Practised by Churches, Witch-Hunters, and Other Sexists*. Philadelphia: Westminster Press.

Western Women's Refuge Group. 1978. *Report on Police Responses to Domestic Violence*. Victoria, Australia: Western Women's Refuge Group.

Winslow, L. Forbes. 1912. *The Insanity of Passion and Crime*. London: John Ousley.

11

Conclusion—The Enduring Theme: Domineering Dowagers and Scheming Concubines

Suzanne Dixon _____

In 1984 M. Sawer and M. Simms noted the dearth of works by political scientists on women in politics. This seems odd at first sight. There is a substantial bibliography on women and politics but it falls into specific categories. There was a time when women and politics were perceived as mutually exclusive categories, and the legacy of that long tradition is very much with us. But the rise of the latest women's movement and the revolution in ''history from below'' and in social scholarship generally made it inevitable that women-and-politics should come in for a new academic treatment. A number of works now exist which discuss the place (or absence) of women in Western political theory (Okin 1979; Saxonhouse 1983, 1985; Elshtain 1981; Coltheart in this volume; Kennedy and Mendus 1987). There is also a growing literature on distinguished individual women, past and present—women who have clearly gained a place in the public, masculine world of power in spite of the theory. General and academic interest in women such as Catherine the Great, Queen Elizabeth I, Cleopatra, or Imelda Marcos is high at present, and current publication reflects and responds to this. People have always known that such women existed, but from time to time it has been deemed important to pull together examples of famous women simply to make the point that women can be powerful. This was the impulse behind much of Christine de Pisan's *Trésor de la Cité des Dames* and now of Rosalind Miles's *Women's History of the World* (Yarde 1988, 14). Such compensatory history is important, but it does not automatically change or explain ideas about power. It is perhaps more significant that there has been a serious attempt to redefine radically the notion of power and politics and to see ways in which the history of resistance reveals female power in a number of areas (cf. Collier 1974; Newton 1981 esp. xv; Dauphin, Farge, and Fraisse 1986: 280) so that women generally appear as agents rather than objects on the historical spectrum. This revised notion of political activity has obvious relevance for assessing the historical role of women and other subordinate groups and in reprocessing the traditional imagery of power relations.

The concern of this chapter—as of the others—is not with the better served subject of what women "really" did, but with the relationship between perceived female roles and the exercise of power in the public sphere. Why should representations of "political women" continually hark back to notions of femininity when masculinity is typically an incidental or nonexistent element of hostile propaganda involving political men? One tentative answer involves drawing together more general ideas about the feminine and about male fears and fantasies insofar as they bear on the perception of women and power. This entails ranging across material that is normally put into separate disciplinary pigeonholes—but this whole volume represents an attempt to transcend such distinctions in the interests of uncovering the raison d'être of the remarkably persistent imagery invoked against women suspected of reaching for power. For with all the apparent wealth of material on the subjects of political women and of the place of women in political theory, it is difficult to find modern writings that address specifically the way in which women powerful (or seeking power) in the public sphere are perceived and represented by the image makers of their own and subsequent ages. We are all familiar with the attempt—sometimes conscious,[1] sometimes not (Ralston 1987, 119)—to obliterate the memory of such women, and it is in response to this that many historians are now eagerly demonstrating how many such women there have been. In the process, they often show that the particular women have been maligned and trivialized, but this still fails to analyze why so many women in so many different public arenas should have been cast in such limited roles. After all, hierarchical societies are used to women in positions of authority, revolutionary socialist governments are committed to equality of the sexes, modern parliamentary democracies subscribe to an ideology of egalitarianism. Why do such different systems react with uniform repugnance to the notion of a woman in power? Why do they all scream "unnatural!", "uncontrolled!" (meaning cruel, oversexed, emotional), "devious!"? It is, after all, not difficult to demonstrate that such women are typically no more emotional, devious, or highly sexed than many males in equivalent positions who get a rather different treatment from chroniclers, even when the chroniclers are equally ill-disposed to them. Many of the chapters in this volume make this abundantly clear. Consider the doubts expressed by historians about the "real" position of the vizier Nebet, discussed by Callender, or the attack on Mary Ann Walker, described by Garlick.

WOMEN AND THE CONCEPT OF LEGITIMATE POLITICAL PROCESS

Male reaction to female power seems to contain an element of sincere horror as well as a conscious attempt to control and diminish that power by defining it as illegitimate and unnatural and by making it sound ridiculous or offensive. Specific manipulation of media is ready to hand: Octavian (later Augustus) used Cleopatra's femaleness and foreignness as key weapons in a propaganda war against Mark Antony; the *Times* and *Punch* attacked the Chartist Mary Ann Walker as an unnatural lower-class hoyden (Garlick); Mao's widow Jiang Q'ing was denounced in Beijing wall posters as a "dowager empress." Where traditional femininity is grudgingly acknowledged, it becomes part of the paradox—as in describing Imelda Marcos as an "iron butterfly" or in saying of Mrs. Bandaranaika, "Nobody tangles with Granny" (Owen 1980). Femininity actually becomes a liability when there is a frank imputation of sexually based influence on a legitimate ruler or politician, or insinuations that this is the real basis of a woman's political position.

Of course, some male rulers or men close to them are also represented as illegitimate in certain situations. In some societies, "low" birth is seen as incongruous with power: Roman senators strongly resented the freed slaves who advised the emperor Claudius, and eunuchs at the Byzantine and Chinese courts (the "Inner Court" of the Ming dynasty mentioned by Soullière) were seen as anomalous and devious in ways that bear some resemblance to the perception of powerful women. In modern democracies, nonelective advisers are subject to criticism: Both President Kennedy and Prime Minister Whitlam aroused particular resentment for their reliance on the advice of "bright young men" whose perceived flaw was not so much that they were not elected as that they had not come through the seniority testing of the party process. Henry Kissinger was not only a political outsider, being an academic by profession, but one who spoke with a foreign accent. The three men in the "Gang of Four" were, like Jiang Q'ing, represented as using illegitimate channels to conspire with each other and control events.

In any political system, there is likely to be an overt and an understood, second, mode of political behavior. The king has his council but also his courtiers, kin, and more diverse consultants; modern democracies have Parliaments and Houses of Representatives but also party machines, personal advisers to ministers, and a wide range of pressure groups, all subject to a tacit hierarchy of legitimacy. Political opponents can draw deliberately on the distinction between proper and shadowy channels to rally public disapproval. It then becomes politic to make much of the secrecy, deviousness, and unaccountability of the group or individual under attack even when such groups are known to be part of the usual political process. The palace is inevitably a center of intrigue in a monarchic system, but secret trials and palace politics are represented as particularly sinister when a royal or imperial woman or retainer is being set up for disgrace.

It is also useful in a propaganda war to deflect the full fury from a male leader to his illegitimate advisers, who kept the truth from him, misled him, or blocked access to him. This is a stock style of political rhetoric, a *topos* which has been invoked in relation to many male rulers—Pericles, the Roman emperor Claudius, Kwame Nkrumah, and U.S. President Kennedy, to name only a few. Implicating a woman in this process adds to the force of the attack. The implicit assumption that women close to power must be exerting undue and inappropriate influence arises from the view that political woman is a paradox. Her desire for such power is unnatural, her means dubious—probably behavior that has a place in male-female relations in the private world (sexuality, maternal ambition) but not in the Boys' Own world of public power and prestige. This becomes clear in the accusations that Chinese concubines or Roman mistresses sap the powers of male political figures with their distracting sexuality as well as their improper political demands. The personal secretary of Australian Prime Minister Gorton came under media attack in the 1960s for carrying out her assigned task with efficiency in spite of her youth and inexperience in the party training ground. Predictably, she was accused of blocking access to the prime minister.[2]

Certain general features emerge from this image of the political woman. They reflect a wider stereotype of the feminine personality, characterized by a personal view of the universe, favoritism, lack of control, and selfishness (Ortner 1974; Lloyd 1984; Elshtain 1981) as well as *techniques* seen as characteristically female—insidious, indirect, and therefore doubly illegitimate. It is common now for many historians and political scientists to reassess individual portraits that fall into these categories. This is an important reconstructive task. The arguments put forward by traditional chroniclers and recent historians can and should be scrutinized and refuted point by point—a relatively straightforward, if demanding process. It is, after all, not difficult to match examples of female favoritism with male patronage and to show that many women represented as behaving aberrantly or dishonorably are actually quite as sensible as their male counterparts, but the point of an idealizing stereotype is that it has a nonrational power almost independent of individual supporting examples. Demolishing the elements of an argument does not, therefore, automatically reduce its overall force. Nancy Mitford's statement (of Madame de Pompadour) "To her, as to most women, politics were a question of personalities" (Mitford 1954, 169) can be countered in its specifics, since Mitford's own evidence shows de Pompadour to have been neither more nor less given to favoritism than the king's other advisers or the king himself. Further, one can argue that such autocracies were entirely based on personalities and did not even pretend to anything resembling our modern meritocratic ideology. Yet the generalization will stand, bolstered by Mitford's modern parallel of "those ladies who adorn today the *Chambre des Députés*" and the picture of a charming but frivolous courtesan dabbling in men's business to please her lover and help her family. The power of the image readily transcends the refutation of the particular case.

FEAR OF WOMEN

The reprocessing of women's behavior and its re-presentation in terms sometimes patently inconsistent with the facts related with it include several elements: a checklist of super-female characteristics, which are seen as flaws, unnatural, unfeminine characteristics such as the wish to exert power over men. Behind the reprocessing lurks a genuine male dislike of women in a position of power over men—perhaps the usual fear a dominant class retains of the suppressed group (totalitarian and monarchic governments usually block freedom of assembly; slave owners live in dread of uprisings; South Africans constantly fantasize about black revolution) reinforced by more fundamental feelings. Most men are supervised in early childhood by women, especially their mothers, and perhaps they retain for life an infantile resentment of having been governed by people they later learn are inferior to their own group. P. E. Slater (1974) attempts to explain the towering female protagonists of Greek myth and drama in this way. T. Africa (1978) discerned a "Coriolanus complex" among Roman politicians who seemed to him ludicrously deferential to their mothers. P. Walcot (1987) has collected examples of dominant mothers and nagging wives—"terrible women," he calls them—in the ancient world and tries to systematize them. These analyses are open to criticism on a number of fronts, not least their tendency to assume that powerful mothers and men who listen to women are by definition deviant even in cultures that did not seem to find them so. Scholars have identified a masculine revolt at the turn of this century against the moral supremacy of the bourgeois mother within the home, expressed partly in supervirile literature, either excluding or denouncing the feminine principle.[3] The readings of psychohistory typified by such authors do not seem to me to be helpful as historical explanations, but they are interesting in themselves for their ready identification of female (especially maternal) strength within the family as a destructive force damaging to individual men and to society as a whole. Psychoanalysis arose historically within specific modern cultures and until recently reinforced bourgeois fin-de-siècle Euro-American notions of gender relations that might not be applicable to cultures with quite different ideals and behaviors. It could, however, be argued that the suspicion and fear of women evident in so many diverse societies demand some general explanation, such as the argument that the young male learns to define himself by separation from females, a process which is often accompanied by great aggression toward women and all things deemed womanly (Chodorow 1974, 50). Masculine identity is thus threatened by a resurfacing of the powerful female figure of the male's relatively helpless childhood.

Another reading, which I favor, would emphasize the interstitial status of women, who are seen as falling between male descent groups and thus symbolize disorder unless they are kept under strict control.[4] Tension is heightened by the knowledge that women are crucial to the continuation of social structures which are seen as essentially male. Thus in patrilineal succession systems, the woman is a vital reproductive element and her chastity is an important guarantee of the purity of the male line of descent. This gives her particular power to disrupt the system with her sexuality. An autonomous mother or sexual partner is a woman to be feared. Yet a woman is intended to be a mother and a sexual partner, so in their right places these are seen as essentially female roles, in a sense in which fatherhood and male sexuality are not universally seen as going to the essence of masculinity.

Many systems set up institutional checks on female power within the succession networks. Official empresses and concubines are thus potentially powerful as mothers, and to an extent the Chinese system acknowledged the power of a dowager empress but tried to check it by guaranteeing that the empress should come from an inferior social group or foreign country so that her influence would not be bolstered by an important family.

The hatred and fear that can be exploited by invoking traditional images was made very clear in the case of the unseating of Jiang Q'ing after the death of Chairman Mao. Even before Mao's death, as early as April 1976, she was referred to as a "dowager empress," and the people were exhorted to remember Mao's third wife, whom he had divorced in 1939 to marry Jiang. So, while she was called a dowager empress, she was also associated with the unfavorable image of the "usurping concubine" who schemed, nagged, and cajoled her way from her more subordinate position to gain the respectable status of dowager empress, now discredited in modern China, particularly by the memory of Empress Tzu Hsi (Bonavia 1976; Stevens, Liu, and Jensen 1976). After Mao's death and the arrest of the Gang of Four, all four were publicly ridiculed, but Jiang was singled out. She was accused of being a nagging wife who tormented Mao's last days and distorted or invented his orders to suit her own aims. The Western media quickly took up this style of criticism, adding to it their own stereotypes of female motivation. The Australian Broadcasting Commission evening news telecast of 23 November 1976 stressed Jiang's usurping role: "She seduced Mao . . . away from his third wife; [she] snatched the apparently enthusiastic Mao from her." This was clearly building on the traditional Chinese image of the usurping concubine, but a more creative contribution followed in the intimation that Jiang had "insidiously sidled into the political arena" through her cultural projects. This and other media also suggested that she had used her position to pay back old scores of a personal character and overlooked or played down the political issues involved, especially during the Cultural Revolution. The particular example on which the media focused was that of the downfall of Wang Guangmei who had been publicly humiliated during the Cultural Revolution, which was represented as an exercise in feminine jealousy.[5]

Interestingly, a similar charge was made against the Roman empress Messalina of bringing about the murder of two women in the imperial family, one because of her beauty and the other because of "feminine jealousy," although both women were part of the dynastic politics of the time and there would have been ample political reasons for their elimination.[6] It would seem that Roman chroniclers, Australian journalists, and Nancy Mitford all agree on the essentially personal character of women's interest in politics. In all of these cases there were plausible alternative explanations for the actions by political women. In all of these cases the media chose to draw on a stereotype of personal feminine jealousy, particularly jealousy of appearance and social priority. History suggests rather that, within dynastic and closed systems, the jealousy is more likely to be of other mothers, where power for women commonly means power exercised through sons.

Female power seeking, even at a fairly high level of political callousness, is thus trivialized and put down to petty motives. Female cruelty is portrayed as wilder and more personal than male cruelty. This in turn draws on the more elaborated, philosophical characterization of women as less rational than men and less capable of perceiving the wider perspective (Ortner 1974; Lloyd 1984; cf. Dixon 1984; Coltheart in this volume). At a more popular, less rationalized level women are also viewed as chaotic and closer to nature, in strong need of male discipline to keep them under control. This seems to lie behind such recurrent social phenomena as the strict segregation of the sexes and the ritual taboos that are applied to women (Ortner 1974).

An ugly side of this phenomenon is described in Chapter 10 of this volume. Here, we see the fear of women and their power in more everyday spheres and the particular fear of women who seem not to be fitting into a proper feminine stereotype. Thus the older woman, doubly interstitial within an interstitial gender, is particularly suspect. Older women are subject to special stereotypes. Sometimes these are relatively favorable: The older widow can be seen as a wise woman, free from the foibles of her sex and therefore to be put into a symbolically male category for certain purposes. Often, though, this status is dangerous, and the power associated with such women is feared. This is the case with magic— often seen as a particularly female skill—and is evident in the legal tradition surrounding the witchcraft trials. These trials and, as Jocelynne Scutt has shown, the media coverage of modern trials, uncover deep-seated fears of women and their power through poison or magic and their access to male food. The trial of Alice Lynne Chamberlain similarly disclosed innumerable deep-seated emotions. The stereotype of the mother is the archetypal "good woman" stereotype. Transgressing this in any way—by appearing to neglect a child, by appearing not to show appropriate emotions, by belonging to a religious group out of the mainstream—compromises maternity and shows a woman to be entirely unreliable and dangerous.

In all of these cases, long-standing male stereotypes and fears of women can be invoked easily. The modern world does not appear to believe in witches. There are few empresses. Concubines are hardly in a position to foster the interests of their progeny. Yet the images of domineering dowagers, scheming concubines, powerful poisonous witches, and murdering mothers are there to be called up in a peculiar necromancy by the modern media. The stereotypes persist even when their specific origins seem quite anachronistic.

Sometimes these images are deliberately used to gain a political response. This was the case with the Beijing demonstrations and the wall posters directed against Jiang Q'ing. It is also the case with many political cartoons, for example those depicting Margaret Thatcher as domineering, particularly within her own marriage. At other times, however, historians and the media alike *unconsciously* fall into these forms of reasoning. This seems to be the case with the Western media's use of the Chinese stereotypes and their Western adaptations. While accusing women close to power of being unfeminine or monsters, men are also drawing on a fear of Woman and her "real" nature.

THE "FIRST LADY" ICON: THE ACCEPTABLE PUBLIC WOMAN

Yet the picture has another side. Women are rewarded for conforming to the proper image. This extends to women in the public sphere as long as they forswear real power or disguise it very carefully. Women in caste or highly stratified societies have often been able to perform a public role which identified them as benefactresses. Amy Richlin's delineation of what she calls the "first lady" icon makes this clear. Before Julia's disgrace, she was held up as an example of imperial femininity, as an ideal mother and ruling-class woman. The Empress Ma in China and, more surprisingly, the Empress Theodora of the Byzantine empire were both seen as first ladies in this mode. The model typically extends the super-mother role of a woman in the ruling group. She distributes bounty to the lower orders, particularly the women and children of the subject group. In the Roman Empire, the empresses who won praise were associated with programs to aid the children of the poor.[7] According to the tradition, Empress Ma countered her husband's criticism of her "interference" in public affairs by stating firmly that she and the emperor fulfilled the role of parents of their subjects, and she was simply fulfilling this role in guiding him in certain areas. This was apparently the acceptable way of casting her political role, for it could be invoked by subsequent empresses who wished to justify their own political actions.

In some ways, the first lady icon can be seen as one of the compensations of the female condition, the acceptable face of femininity which many women have found to be an adequate recompense for the lack of real power in most spheres of life (i.e., according to Dauphin, Farge, and Fraisse 1986, 283–84). This concept seems to me rather illusory. It is clear, for example, that in the modern world "good" wives and mothers are as likely to be abandoned by husband and children as those who do not conform to the image. The definitions, moreover, are couched in ideal terms which are virtually unattainable by all but a very small number of women. This is particularly the case when they are tied to absolute ideals of beauty (which often imply youth) and virtues such as unending patience, or they are bolstered by models such as the Virgin Mary, where the ideal of parthenogenesis disqualifies normal motherhood itself from an absolute standard of purity.

In fact, the so-called compensatory ideal offered to women is simply a means of social control. Such compensatory ideologies are offered to all subject groups. We have not only "good women," but "good children," "good servants," "good subjects." All of these categories are defined by the ruling group in their own interests and not intended to be of any real benefit to the subject. They can be invoked to prevent insurrection, and a certain proportion of the subject group will always be lulled by this ideology. But it could hardly be seen as a genuine compensation for lack of autonomy.

Of course, the first lady of the icon is in a privileged position. Her compensations are greater than those of, for example, a "good peasant." At least she has wealth and a certain prestige. There is a hidden bargain behind the occupation of this position. It is that the first lady should have no real power and that if she dares to attempt such power, she must exert it in a very limited way and for restricted purposes, disguising even that exercise of power with reference to the feminine ideal, as Empress Ma did. Today this first lady icon is best illustrated by the British royal family, who are entirely removed from any real power but act out a public spectacle of young, comely motherliness for the masses by careful judgment of the audience's requirements. The role of women linked to public/political men, such as the wife of the president of the United States, or of women in a public/political role, such as Golda Meier or Margaret Thatcher, is more difficult. A Nancy Reagan or Eleanor Roosevelt inspires admiration insofar as she maintains the role of gracious Lady Bountiful, but she arouses aggression if she becomes seen as a genuine political influence. Issues which are not seen as political, such as drug abuse, are acceptable and ladylike. When Anita Bryant launched a successful campaign against gay rights, her image, of a lovely, concerned, moral lady, was built on her beauty and her feminine qualities. She was, however, eventually brought down by frankly sexist propaganda that trivialized her and therefore her cause. It is ironic that the success of the liberal opposition was based on such illiberal tactics, when countering her own methods with rationality had not been successful.

The first lady icon presents a great problem for women who seek real power and its open acknowledgment. It still involves some attempt to prove that political women are not unnatural. It becomes a tightrope. Empress Ma and perhaps Margaret Thatcher have been among the few successful walkers, and political women today tread very carefully. Women in these positions are aware of a hidden agenda. In seeking power they must not only master [sic] traditional skills in a world that was not set up for them and from which to a great extent they are still excluded (i.e., the world of male bonding, politicking, and patronage), but they must second-guess the image makers and maintain a public face that makes it look as if power is not really their business. Even Mrs. Thatcher, who was identified with a firm economic line and was seen as a political person who disavowed "women's issues,"[8] was filmed shopping in supermarkets (Sawer and Simms 1984, 21) and took obvious care with her personal appearance. This is something virtually all female politicians feel obliged to do, no matter what the demands on their time. In the nineteenth century, cartoons made clear the assumption that women with an interest in public/political life were unfeminine and a threat to the family. This idea is clearly still present. Women who did enter parliament in countries where that was possible in the early part of this century took great pains to ensure that they were not seen as aggressive or unfeminine, and they tended to promote issues concerning the welfare of women and children—issues often perceived as not political.[9] The depiction of women in their roles as mothers, grandmothers, and housewives is seen as allaying public fears that they are neglecting their proper duties in entering public life and that they are unnatural women.[10]

Of course, politics is notoriously a bitter and dirty business. Anyone who enters the public sphere—including royalty, actors, and other celebrities—is open to all sorts of innuendo and to the invasion of private life. This is particularly the case in politics. Public requirements extend in many countries to private morality, and transgressions can help bring down political figures—witness Gary Hart and Papandreou. Yet women are open to a greater range of insults and attacks, and a woman who is attacked on her feminine credentials is likely to be seriously hurt at the personal level. It is shattering to the strongest woman to read that she is domineering, ugly, unwomanly, a bad mother, a bitch, a witch, a trollop, a joke. The female stereotype is deeply embedded, and it is difficult for women to shrug off the pain caused by being told publicly that they flout it. Male politicians can be called ugly or unmanly or be assailed as bad fathers and husbands, but men are conditioned to see these features as a lesser part of their total self-image. Attacks of this kind on women are typically particularly vicious and call on common stereotypes that seem to have greater general force and a wider application. Thus sexual gossip about women is potentially more damaging than sexual gossip about men.

The paradox is that women become particularly prone to such attacks once they are taken seriously; the aim of the attack is, after all, to ridicule and thereby ensure that nobody *will* take them seriously again. This was the case, for example, with Anita Bryant in the recent past and with Mary Ann Walker in the nineteenth century. The press reaction to Walker was initially mild, but it became very vigorous and personally insulting as soon as she was taken seriously as a political figure. The image of such women as ugly and domineering has also been a constant in cartoons from the nineteenth and twentieth centuries. The main change that has occurred is that the political women of the nineteenth century were invariably shown as emaciated and unattractive. The modern depiction tends to show them as overweight and unattractive. The other features—spectacles, long noses, straggly hair, and pointed chins—endure. None of these features seems to be authenticated by photographs of the women concerned. They all appeal to current notions of ugly viragos. In the case of Jiang, the traditional animosity to unsurping concubines, who misuse their sexual position, and domineering dowagers, who misuse their official position as imperial women, was conjured up skillfully to promote an image of a power-crazed, dangerous woman. This gained particular force in the revolutionary context in being used against a woman who had associated herself with specifically proletarian and popularizing values and was now identified with earlier, decadent, imperial traditions with the specific aim of discrediting her politically.

We thus have a mixture of conscious manipulation of imagery with the specific intention of denigrating individual women and an apparently genuine fear of powerful women which draws on deep-seated prejudices and suspicions. One reputable southeast Asian expert makes this combination clear in his own question: "If writers down the centuries have noticed and picked up this common female trait, does it not suggest there is more than a grain of truth in it?" He questioned my "desire to expel human passion (in this case, the passion of men for women) from the shaping of history" and asked, "Does it not impoverish the image of women to suggest that their sex appeal is necessarily subordinate to their other qualities?"[11]

It is clear from this and other statements that he felt that women's access to political power through sex and their tendency to trivialize and personalize political issues were intrinsic traits rather than manufactured stereotypes. He also argued that Jiang was unlikely to have had any influence on the views that male political leaders held on the important questions of policy. All this suggests that the image makers themselves might believe the stereotypes and regard them as truth.

The chapters of this volume contain many examples of conscious manipulation of images. Thus the writers in *Punch* did not actually believe the statements they made about the female Chartists in detail, but in some sense they did see the women as unnatural and unattractive, irrespective of each individual woman's appearance and marital state. The presumption of modern politicians is still that the populace at large needs to be reassured of the essential femininity of female political figures. This involves a transference of the individual woman's private life, suitably transformed and homogenized, to the public sphere as her "image" or "profile"—a variant of the notion of separate spheres which still acknowledges the spheres as such (Elshtain 1981; Sawer and Simms 1984).

CONCLUSIONS

The key issues which emerge from this debate are the ideological construction of the feminine and the equivocal status of women vis-à-vis power. These are related in their turn to issues of legitimacy and authority. Most societies do have a legitimate public role for women, but it is usually one without the most prestigious kind of power and tends to be an extension of the society's private construction of the feminine—such as a benevolent super-mother, bestowing largesse and concern on subjects; a pious wife or daughter performing a sacral function; the lady of impeccable virtue, producing perfectly pedigreed heirs. These acceptable images, all of which fall within Richlin's first lady icon, carry great rewards for the women involved. But the image is fragile and the first lady who tries to assume real power beyond the prescribed sphere is immediately subject to virulent attack that turns the acceptable icon upside down; ungovernable selfishness, impurity, and whorishness are the inverse of feminine generosity, piety, and chastity. There is no midway status. This phenomenon extends even to women who have never aspired to a public role. In Chapter 10 Scutt gives us an impressive demonstration of what happens when a woman's maternal credentials have been called into question: A woman is either a perfect mother or an unnatural monster, capable of infanticide. The weight of historical legal opinion and the modern media and their audience apparently accept this either-or reasoning.

Some things vary between political systems and historical periods. In many modern states, even a successful attack is more likely to mean political than physical extinction for the woman in question—but most political women have suffered from contemporary and later media, which have imposed a kind of publicity death or at least severe mutilation of the historiographic corpse. The fact that so many political systems are set up for male rulers has meant that women have inevitably been judged as *influences on* men, and the hostile imagery has played on male fear of female domination and on male contempt for men who have fallen victim to it. Thus, even in the Chinese context, where private life in the imperial palace was systematically concealed from outsiders, it was possible to damage an emperor by suggesting that he was distracted by female sexuality, just as it was possible to denigrate a Roman Republican officeholder or modern Greek prime minister by the same charge. In modern China, Mao himself was represented posthumously as nagged and misled by his wife, whose early alleged sexual behavior was dredged up to discredit his and her political views of some forty years later!

The traditional wisdom has been that women are supposed to serve men as wives, sisters, mothers, and mistresses, but the traditional fear has also been that women in these positions might exert undue power. This fear is reinforced by the dual roles women invariably play in their lives—one man's wife is another man's sister, and she might be promoting his interests instead. This suspicion is institutionalized in many cultures[12] and recurs in the philosophical construction of woman as other—*ir*rational, *un*trustworthy, and so on—so the stereotype and the fear are ready to hand whenever a woman appears to be gaining power and entering the public male arena.

Modern female politicians have chosen different strategies to deal with these problems. Deprived of access to many male political networks, women who climb the visible political ladder are likely to be fairly tough. They must by that time have worked out some way of dealing with the disruption that the demands of modern political life impose on their domestic circumstances—this is generally true of "successful" women in other spheres. Yet they know that this very competence can count against them; unlike men, they cannot legitimately call upon their partners to shoulder all domestic responsibility even for the relatively brief duration of an election campaign. They therefore take pains to be seen as "ordinary" women—even Golda Meier was photographed bathing her grandchild. Projecting this acceptable image is a way of anticipating the old criticism that she is unnatural and dangerous because she has crossed the gender barrier. Yes, the woman is saying, I am really a grandmother or a housewife, a nice lady with a nice hairstyle and a handbag, even if I presume to govern a country.

Sometimes it works. These chapters have concentrated on the power of hostile images, but the process can operate in favor of women who cultivate their image carefully. As in other areas of politics, a combination of skill and luck determines success from one moment to the next. Margaret Thatcher's husband came in for repetitive ridicule from satirists and, like the hypothetical parliamentary husbands of *Punch* cartoons in the nineteenth century, he has been represented as a foolish, henpecked ditherer who defers to his powerful, mannish wife. This depiction made no appreciable difference to Mrs. Thatcher's prolonged political success.

In spite of the nearly universal uniformity of the negative images of powerful women, there are great differences among societies, differences that might influence the general readiness to accept female rule. Perhaps it is no coincidence that those women who have gained the top political position (excluding figurehead titles) have often done so in countries with relatively hierarchical structures in which women of the top class or caste have traditionally exercised authority of some kind over the men and women of the lower social groups. The chiefly women of Polynesia continued to play a political role in the post-contact modern period, in spite of attempts by white administrators to exclude them from this sphere (Ralston 1987, 117–19). Modern Scandinavia, the United States, and Australia have until recently interpreted their notionally egalitarian ideology to mean "all men are brothers." Margaret Thatcher does not herself come from the traditional governing class, but she ruled a country accustomed to forceful county "first ladies" who speak publicly with a similar voice. Of course, the reasons why any one politician or ruler succeeds over another are always complex—the province of the expert in the particular society rather than of this work—which argues only that imagery and general expectations play some part in the process.

There has always been some general acknowledgment of a relationship between imagery and practical politics. The most secure of dynastic rulers have always had advisers who expended great energy on promoting particular images and slogans ("son of heaven," "father of the country," "the sun king") through the media available in their own ages. Modern media, market research, and the increasing use of popular election have developed this ancient art into a near science, and male politicians, too, are advised about their dress and hairstyle and are even shown on occasion with their families or in some other role that identifies them as "ordinary." But male heads of governments are *not* commonly depicted bathing their grandchildren or doing the shopping.

Hostile propaganda is also an ancient art, one that can be even more revealing about the implicit assumptions of political life. Women seen as exercising or attempting power are subject to the same criticisms as men in their position, but they are likely in addition to be attacked for compromising their essential femininity. This recurrent style of denigration seems to emanate still from the presumption of separate spheres which a "political woman" has offended. Posterity, even when not overtly hostile to the memory of a female ruler or other influential historical figure, tends to depoliticize her role by reinterpreting her actions in

feminine terms, as motivated by sexuality, maternity, or "feminine jealousy."
A. Fraser's sympathetic biography of Mary Stuart is replete with expressions
reflecting this line of reasoning, one that has been illustrated in this chapter as
a style of criticism employed by ancient chroniclers and modern political journalists alike. It is, sadly, to be found all too often in academic treatments. Some
changes have been brought about by feminist scholarship and a new level of
consciousness among journalists, but in the media today economic and editorial
power tends still to rest with men trained in a particularly conservative style of
"masculine" leadership, which bodes ill.

In this volume we have examined different theories to explain the prevalence
and consistency of hostile stereotypes concerning women and power (and even
women, such as presidents' wives or kings' mistresses, who are perceived as
being close to power). We have also seen the successful political exploitation
of positive imagery which typically stresses the essential femininity of women
in the public eye. The actual impact of such imagery is not always clear, but
modern politicians continue to treat it seriously and take no chances. Many of
the shibboleths of politics—that women will not vote for other women—have
been overturned by hard research and demonstration in recent years. Women
might still not have full access to male power sources, but modern developments,
not least the women's movement, have provided them with alternative support
groups and with a different atmosphere within electoral systems and even among
the power brokers. Perhaps the imagery will slowly yield to changing conditions.
Or is this just a pious hope? In any case, we need to become more alert to its
use and its unsuitability to many of the cases in which it is unthinkingly applied.

This book has covered a unique range of societies and historical periods to
reveal a dauntingly homogeneous bank of imagery to be drawn on whenever
women look like they are stepping into the political arena. It is very important
that this collection has deconstructed so many elements of the process by which
female relations to public power have been represented by contemporary and
later media. Exposing the elements and laying them out for analysis and consideration are important steps toward combating their use or being caught off
guard by them. The conscious and unconscious manipulation of the image of
the powerful woman needs to be teased out again and again, in academic and
public media. It is important to question what have become stock readings of
past and present actions and to scrutinize the evidence. A closer look at the
nature of power and access to it is also vital, but study of the imagery itself is
a prime example of theory which should and must affect practice.

NOTES

1. Miles is quoted as saying "On a political level, men have deliberately and consciously kept [women] out of the history books and kept them out of the processes of
writing history." Yarde 1988, 14, on Miles's new book, *The Women's History of the
World*.

2. Aitchison 1970. The assistant was Ainslie Gotto. There was never any overt suggestion of sexual impropriety about her relationship. In analyzing the sudden burst of media interest in Gotto, Aitchison himself goes into some detail about her appearance and personal style and the way in which she suddenly came to public notice: "Although she was not an actor on the stage, she was always in the wings and one wondered how much prompting she did" (146). I am grateful to Tom Hillard for drawing this treatment to my attention and kindly allowing me to consult his discussion of it, which he originally composed as an appendix to his own chapter.

3. Dauphin, Farge, and Fraisse (1986, 285) refer to "Magazines dont la Mère est absente," and antifeminist theory. See also note 40: "Femmes ambitieuses et acariâtres, maris diminués et anxieux sont, selon [Sennett], la rançon des familles étroites, repliées sur elles-mêmes et 'féminisées' " (293). This refers to the work of R. Sennett 1978, *Les tyrannies de l'intimité* (Paris: Seuil) and 1980 *La famille contre la ville: Les classes moyennes de Chicago à l'ère industrielle* (Paris: Recherches). Dauphin, Farge, and Fraisse also cite the thesis by A. L. Maugue 1983 *La littérature antiféministe en France de 1871 à 1914* (Paris: University of Paris III) and J. Le Rider 1982 *Le cas Otto Weininger. Racines de l'antiféminisme et de l'anti-sémitisme* (Paris: PUF). I have not been able thus far to consult these works directly.

4. Ortner 1978, 24: "Insofar as women are moved around in marriage, in a social exchange system controlled by, and culturally seen as composed of, structured groups of men, women appear interstitial within the fundamental kinship architecture of society."

5. ABC broadcast as above and Melbourne *Age*, 5 December 1980, p. 1, an article headlined "Hatred and Revenge for Queens of Communism," where the journalist emphasized the social rivalry between the women rather than the political and ideological issues at stake (notably, foreign trade).

6. The women involved were both called Julia, a mark of their relationship to the ruling imperial family. One, the niece of Messalina, was banished for adultery in A.D. 41 (Dio 60.8.5); the other, the granddaughter of the emperor Tiberius, was killed in A.D. 43 (Dio 60.18.4).

7. For example, the Faustinian girls (*puellae Faustinianae*), a foundation set up for poor girls under the aegis of the Roman imperial family by the emperor Pius in his wife's memory (*SHA* Pius. 8.1; *RIC* Pius 398 a & b). Coin issues also celebrated the association of the women of the second century A.D. imperial families with programs to help the poor children of Italy, e.g., *RIC* Hadrian 1030, associating the emperor's childless wife Sabina with *pietas*, a symbolic female figure shown with a small boy and girl.

8. In a conference paper delivered in 1985, Sawer quotes an interview in the *Australian*, 19 April 1981, 10 in which Mrs. Thatcher says, "You come to a point where you have to look at the personalities available and their policies and you forget whether they're men or women. And really that's how women have got on."

9. Consider, for example, Irene Longman, a member of Parliament in the Australian state of Queensland, 1929–1932. She was complimented on having "nothing aggressive about her" and went out of her way in her maiden speech to assure the men of the Parliament that she had been driven to enter politics from a sense of duty. Sawer and Simms 1984, 66–67.

10. See especially the examples given by Sawer and Simms 1984, 100–2.

11. David Bonavia, editor of the *Far Eastern Economic Review*, in private correspondence with me, 22 February 1981, rejecting an article I had written on the Western media's treatment of the trial of Jiang Q'ing.

12. Consider Sacks 1982; Lévi-Strauss, esp. 1967; Ortner 1978, 24; Douglas 1966; and Klapisch-Zuber 1983, 1097, on the women of the noble houses of Florence as "transient guests" or Ralston 1987, 119, on the reaction of a nineteenth-century missionary to the tendency of the Tongan Tupoumohefeo to pursue the political interests of her natal kin over those of her husband.

REFERENCES

Classical References

Dio = Cassius Dio, *Roman History*—any edition.
SHA = *Scriptores Historiae Augustae*—Leipzig, Germany: Teubner.
RIC = *The Roman Imperial Coinage*, H. Mattingly et al. London: Spink, 1923–1981
     in 12 vol. Entries are arranged under the names of the issuing emperors.

Secondary Sources

Africa, T. 1978. "The Mask of an Assassin: A Psycho-Historical Study of M. Iunius Brutus." *Journal of Interdisciplinary History* 8:599–626.
Aitchison, R. 1970. *From Bob to Bungles. People in Politics 1966–1970*. Melbourne, Australia: Sun.
Bonavia, D. 1976. "Chiang's Most Infamous Role?" *Far Eastern Economic Review*, 5 November, 17–18.
Chodorow, N. 1974. "Family Structure and Feminine Personality." In *Women, Culture and Society*, edited by M. Z. Rosaldo and L. Lamphere, 43–66. Palo Alto, Calif.: Stanford University Press.
Collier, J. 1974. "Women in Politics." In *Women, Culture and Society*, edited by M. Z. Rosaldo and L. Lamphere, 89–96. Palo Alto, Calif.: Stanford University Press.
Dauphin, C., A. Farge, and G. Fraisse. 1986. "Culture et pouvoir des femmes: Essai d'historiographie." *Annales ESC* 41:271–93.
Dixon, S. 1984. "*Infirmitas Sexus*: Womanly Weakness in Roman Law." *Tijdschrift voor Rechtsgeschiedenis* 52: 343–71.
Douglas, M. 1966. *Purity and Danger*. London: Routledge and Kegan Paul.
Elshtain, Jean B. 1981. *Public Man, Private Woman: Women in Social and Political Thought*. Princeton, N.J.: Princeton University Press.
Fraser, A. [1969] 1985. *Mary Queen of Scots*. London: Methuen.
Kennedy, E., and S. Mendus, eds. 1987. *Women in Western Political Philosophy*. Brighton, England: Wheatsheaf.
Klapisch-Zuber, C. 1983. "La 'Mère cruelle'. Maternité, veuvage et dot dans la Florence des xiv–xve siècles." *Annales ESC* 38:1097–109.
Lévi-Strauss, C. 1967. *Structural Anthropology*. Garden City, N.Y.: Doubleday.
Lloyd, G. 1984. *The Man of Reason: "Male" and "Female" in Western Philosophy*. London: Methuen.
Mitford, N. 1954. *Madame de Pompadour*. Rev. ed. 1968, reprint 1970. London: Sphere.
Newton, J. L. 1981. *Women, Power and Subversion. Social Strategies in British Fiction, 1778–1860*. Athens: University of Georgia Press. Reprint. London: Methuen, 1985. (Especially preface, xi–xxi)

Okin, S. 1979. *Women in Western Political Thought*. Princeton, N.J.: Princeton University Press.

Ortner, S. B. 1974. "Is Female to Male as Nature Is to Culture?" In *Women, Culture and Society*, edited by M. Z. Rosaldo and L. Lamphere, 67–85. Palo Alto, Calif.: Stanford University Press.

————. 1978. "The Virgin and the State." *Feminist Studies* 4: 19–35.

Owen, L. 1980. "The Myth of the Iron Lady." *Observer* 9 March, 45.

Ralston, C. 1987. Introduction to special issue of *The Journal of Pacific History* on "Sanctity and Power; Gender in Polynesian History," 22 (3–4): 115–22.

Rosaldo, M. Z., and L. Lamphere, eds. 1974. *Woman, Culture, and Society*. Palo Alto, Calif.: Stanford University Press. (Especially Rosaldo, "Women, Culture, and Society: A Theoretical Overview," pp. 17–42.)

Sacks, K. 1982. *Sisters and Wives*. Westport, Conn.: Greenwood Press.

Sawer, M. 1985. "From Motherhood to Sisterhood. Attitudes of Australian Women Members of Parliament to Their Roles." Paper presented at the annual conference of the Australian Political Science Association, Adelaide, Australia, August.

Sawer, M., and M. Simms. 1984. *A Woman's Place: Women and Politics in Australia*. Sydney: George Allen and Unwin.

Saxonhouse, A. 1983. "Classical Greek Conceptions of the Public and Private." In *Conceptions of Public and Private in Social Life*, edited by S. I. Benn and G. R. Gaus. New York: St. Martin's Press.

————. 1985. *Women in the History of Political Thought: Ancient Greece through Machiavelli*. New York: Praeger.

Slater, P. E. 1974. "The Greek Family in History and Myth." *Arethusa* 7:9–44.

Stevens, M., S. Liu, and H. Jensen. 1976. "The Dowager Empress." *Newsweek*, 25 October, 13.

Walcot, P. 1987. "Plato's Mother and Other Terrible Women." *Greece & Rome* 34:12–31.

Yarde, R. 1988. "Dismembering Masculine Myths." *The Times Higher Education Supplement*, 22 July, 14.

Index

About the Editors and Contributors

PAULINE ALLEN has taught in Australia, England, Germany, Belgium, and Holland and is now an Associate Professor at the Australian Catholic University in Brisbane. She has published several editions of Greek patristic texts and articles on ecclesiastical historiography and Byzantine literature and art. She is currently engaged on a large research project concerning early Christian homilies as a source for social history.

V. G. CALLENDER is head history teacher at a large Sydney high school. She is the author of several textbooks on ancient history and has published articles on Egyptian, Greek, and Roman historiography. Currently she is finishing her PhD. dissertation on the wives of Egyptian kings, Dynasties I–XVII.

MARGARET CLUNIES ROSS holds the McCaughey Chair of English Language and Early English Literature at the University of Sydney. She has written extensively on Old Icelandic and Anglo-Saxon literature, social custom and mythology, and Aboriginal oral literature.

LENORE COLTHEART is a lecturer in Politics at the University of Adelaide. She has written on social and political theory and Australian history, and on Aboriginal land claims. She coedited *The Violet Pages*, the Australian women's studies research directory, and was founder of the Women's Academy in Sydney.

SUZANNE DIXON is senior lecturer in Classics and Ancient History at the University of Queensland and is the author of *The Roman Mother* (1987), *The Roman Family* (1991), and *Wealth and the Roman Woman* (in progress), and she is coeditor of *Pre-Industrial Women: Interdisciplinary Perspectives* (1984).

She has also written a number of articles on the political and economic role of Roman women and on the history of marriage, kinship, and inheritance. She is currently compiling a data base of women with an attested economic role in the Roman Empire (*An Economic Catalogue of Roman Women*). She has held visiting fellowships at Stanford University and Corpus Christi, Cambridge.

BARBARA GARLICK teaches English and is the present coordinator of Women's Studies at the University of Queensland. She has published on French Renaissance poetry and nineteenth- and twentieth-century British and Australian feminism, literature, and art.

TOM HILLARD teaches Ancient History at Macquarie University in Sydney. He has written a number of articles on Roman republican politics and has participated for eight years in the underwater excavations at Caesarea Maritima.

AMY RICHLIN is Associate Professor of Classics at the University of Southern California and is the author of *The Garden of Priapus: Sexuality and Aggression in Roman Humor* (1983, 1991). Her new work on gender in Roman society includes the edited volume *Pornography and Representation in Greece and Rome* (1991).

ARLENE W. SAXONHOUSE is Professor of Political Science at the University of Michigan and the author of *Women in the History of Political Thought: Ancient Greece through Machiavelli* (1985). Her publications range widely over classical political theory and early modern thought.

JOCELYNNE A. SCUTT is a lawyer in private practice in Melbourne, Australia. She was Commissioner and Deputy Chairperson of the Law Reform Commission, Victoria, and has written several books on the women's movement and on the family, violence, crime, and marriage. Her latest book, *Women and the Law*, appeared in 1990.

ELLEN SOULLIÈRE received her doctorate from Princeton University in 1987, and she is a lecturer in Chinese at Wellington Polytech. She has published several articles on women in the Ming dynasty.